ETYMON

WISDOM IN YOUR POSSESSION

ALEIUS SOFAR

Subconscious in Man

Contents

Contents

Contents

Contents

Contents

Contents

Contents

Foreword

Silence of mind is the presence of goodness in you
And the thought outside your technical work and knowledge is
Satan

"And ye shall know the truth, and the truth shall make you
free."
"There is nothing called faith if you are faith yourself.
Faith is not just a term but action, power and hence power of
action is faith which brings results".

Preface

To those seeking truth and wisdom,

Throughout history, few things have been as important as preserving and sharing sacred wisdom. This book is the result of deep dedication and inspiration, made possible by the power of printing. These words are not divine revelations but the outcome of human thought, passed down through generations. Their purpose is to bring us back to the true meaning of scripture—free from personal agendas, cultural influences, or political bias.

Spirituality is universal; it belongs to no single nation or culture. When mixed with traditions and customs, its true meaning can be lost. If past practices had truly led humanity to peace and enlightenment, we might accept them. But history tells a different story—conflict and division remain, often in the name of righteousness.

True divinity should lead to goodness, yet much of what we call "good" is shaped by personal beliefs rather than universal truth. Sacred teachings are meant to enlighten the mind, nourish the soul, and guide us to a peaceful life. As caretakers of these words, we must help seekers find wisdom and comfort. Have we reached the spiritual fulfilment we seek? The answer is clearly NO. This book is offered with humility, as a reflection of inner truth and a guide for all. Scripture must be based on absolute truth, not tied to history, geography, or time.

Let these teachings break down barriers and bring people together. This book unfolds in different layers, each essential for spiritual growth. It begins with wisdom—carefully selected insights, refined like pure gold. Let these words sink into your heart and change your thoughts and actions. Read them often, reflect on them, and use them as a foundation for growth. True purpose is not given by others but discovered within.

Promises follow, offering expressions of faith, praise, and gratitude to uplift and strengthen the spirit. Worship is not just about rituals but a way of living with devotion and meaning.

Another layer explores the law, drawn from ancient scriptures and presented clearly and practically. Wisdom should be clear and useful, helping us navigate life's challenges.

At its deepest, this book speaks of worship—not as a rigid practice, but as an act of gratitude and humility. Worship is not limited by religion but leads to self-discovery and enlightenment. It is about recognising the divine presence within, forging a personal connection with the higher self and the vast universe.

Scripture should not instil fear or division, but rather offer guidance and comfort. Heaven and hell are not distant places but states of mind shaped by our thoughts and actions. The heart of sacred teachings is unity and union rooted in love; yet, history has often distorted them to create division. If these texts are to help people truly, they must be read with care, keeping only what helps grow kindness, unity, and understanding.

Even the word "God" is shaped by language and has changed over time. True spirituality goes beyond names and labels, focusing on the deep connection between the self and the universe. Divine presence is not in words but in the awareness of the higher self within.

There are concepts repeated over and over again. It is an attempt to ensure they are remembered and internalised. It emphasises showing how they apply to various situations and generations. The same concept is often repeated with deeper insights. People tend to forget, doubt, or struggle with the same issues over time. Repetition serves as a reminder and encouragement, guiding believers back to core principles when they stray away. Repeating scripture in prayer and meditation allows individuals to absorb its meaning on a deeper level, leading to personal transformation.

Read this book not as a strict rulebook but as an invitation to explore spirituality beyond inherited beliefs. Let its words settle into your heart, shaping your thoughts and actions from within. It is meant to be read daily, in quiet moments, taken in slowly, and revisited often. Let it be your companion, guiding you to deeper wisdom and understanding.

Read these words in the stillness of the morning and before sleep at night. Let them dissolve anger, ego, and division. The truth, once realised, sets us free. True enlightenment is found in humility, love, and unity—beyond sects and doctrines, embracing all of humanity as one.

As you begin this journey, may you find clarity, peace, and unwavering faith. May these words be a light in the darkness, bringing you ever closer to the presence of the Divine.

With deep gratitude and respect.
Aleius Sofar

Prologue

He sits still. That is the work. He does nothing. Yet the world changes.

Joy comes. Deep. Good. It stays. It is a mark on the air. No writing. No sound. A thought flows out. It goes into the unseen space. A mark was left there. It does not fade. Generations feel it.

It is not physical. It waits. For those who are ready. Those who look for the answers. They have the same curiosity. That is all. An open mind.

The wisdom appears. It comes from Silences. The silence of a man long gone. That is the transmission. That is the help.

A thought resonates. It creates a field. This field is real. The insights of the past wait there.

The thinker is the receiver. He asks the questions. He opens his mind. He draws the wisdom out. The unrecorded, lingering insights of the ones who came before.

He is the bridge. The man sits still. The past feeds the future. He needs no recognition. Impact is the work.

The man who moves mountains by force does a temporary thing. His feats look big, but they lack deep thought. He adds little. His work repeats old work. Without originality, his legacy goes fast.

Think of Samson. He had brute strength. Not wisdom. David beat Goliath not with power but with inner wisdom. His love for wisdom passed to Solomon. Solomon's words lasted. Even without the writing, the ideas survived.

Quiet thought lasts. To think deeply is to send ideas into the collective consciousness. They cross time. No books are needed. The thinker never sees the result, but his thoughts nourish minds.

This exchange happens naturally. It needs no effort. Only true intelligence survives in that vast space. Shallow ideas disappear. Negativity fades.

This is how humans progress. Each new time builds on the unspoken. Creativity flows free. This brings a great weight. The thinker must contribute wisely. The thoughts shape the future.

PART ONE

WISDOM

CHAPTER ONE

[1]My human experience can often be defined by a fundamental split between my two selves: the 'I' of me and the 'AM'of me. This is collectively the person I am.

[2]The 'I' is the 'me' I see in the mirror, the figure I identify as myself and the one the world knows as me. It is my external identity: my name, my background viz. my religion, my caste, my creed, my conditioned ideology, my physical body and its features, my nurtured thoughts and memories I possess, and the public appearance I present myself as. This self is not innate but is an exponential nature, shaped and moulded by the conditions of my birth, the culture I was raised in, the language I speak, and the philosophy or no-philosophy that circumstances have induced in me right from my birth. It is a completely fabricated version—a composite built from experience—that I have come to belicve is the real me, though in reality, it is not.

[3]Whereas, the 'AM', in contrast, is my silent, inner being. It is the true, original self that gives me the ability to breathe, live, and exist, oblivious to my normal knowledge about the world and me, myself. It is the unmanifest source of life, existing even before I, as a part of humanity, had awareness of myself. Though the 'AM', which is my hidden being, is the essence of my originality, it cannot manifest or function in the physical world without the structure

of the 'I'—the identification that provides a name and a background, etc.

[4]The state of wholeness is achieved through the completion of the cycle, 'I AM', which requires an act of recognition. When the external 'I' recognises and finds similarity with the inner 'AM,' the two aspects unify. Without this acknowledgement—this necessary recognition of existence by the 'I AM '- nothing, whether on earth or in the abstract realm, can truly exist. The 'I' is the identified body under normal conditions, while the 'AM' is the timeless, enduring being, the everlasting entity of the universe.

[5]My existence today represents a fundamental lapse from my true potential, a state which is described as the *'first fall.'* I am no longer living in the intended wholeness of the 'I AM' but am merely surviving using the external body, the 'I' and a mind that has become tragically detached from the 'AM', the inner being and has strayed long enough with the body with its senses.

[6]The body and mind, which constitute the 'I', were initially meant to be an instrument of the 'AM' (our inner being), but are now an exposed and vulnerable entity. It is no longer controlled by the essential core within but is instead dictated by the environment and the body's superficial interpretations of its surroundings. This is the essence of the fall: the 'I'—the external, conditioned self—has severed its connection with the life-giving 'AM'.

[7]The human journey was meant to be one in the unified 'I AM' harmony, where the inner being directed the mind, ensuring that the perishable body and its fleeting surroundings did not dominate our consciousness. However, humanity, seen here as an experimental creature gifted with free will, made a fatal choice. We chose to cling

to the temporary, perishable body and its immediate, limiting interpretations of the world, rather than aligning ourselves with the internal *being* inside.

[8]This shift in allegiance marked the point where the true purpose of humanity was derailed, leading us onto a path toward inevitable self-destruction. It still poses an urgent call: we, as the collective consciousness implanted in the human body and mind, must now, more than ever, be reminded of our original identity and reconnect with the 'AM.' Returning to this state of being is the only way to reclaim the best of living that was our birthright, replacing the compromised existence we currently endure.

[9]In mindful silence, I discover my own truth of *being*: to listen deeply is to find clarity, and clarity is no-content void. Knowledge grows when I dare to question the present state of mind, its utter chaos, its failing, and only then, grace follows my choices shaped by awareness.

[10]Thus, I walk with purpose, guided by the wisdom blooming quietly inside me, where every new understanding sheds light on what it means to truly *be*.

CHAPTER TWO

¹In the beginning, the 'AM', the inner being of me, manifested the 'I', my outer structure, and the conditions that surround the 'I'. From inside to outside did my birth take place.

²The 'I' was formless, deep and dark, an empty void; Yet the 'AM', the Spirit in me, hovered where the life lay, poised to give the 'I', my body and the mind I operate with, its substance, turning my innate potential into day, light.

³Then the AM spoke, 'Let I, the body with its operating mind, receive its awareness,' and at once it received its knowledge. The AM saw the I's new awareness was good and right; So, the AM drew a line, separating the dark, unformed potential from the awareness now made real, establishing the core essential.

⁴The 'AM' named the awareness 'Wisdom,' and the remaining void 'Ignorance.' Thus, the cycle of the 'I's defined existence began: There was an ending, and a new beginning—the first period of the plan.

⁵Thus, the entire —from its inner fixed foundation to its outer living forms—was completed, fully prepared for mankind to reside and function. The 'AM' saw all that had been manifested, and it was complete, functional, and very good. This marked the true inception of reality.

⁶The 'AM' commanded: 'Let a boundary be set between the external existence, splitting the formless potential

inside.

[7]So the 'AM' created this essential framework, separating the matter outside from the matter inside, and it was complete.

[8]The 'AM' commanded: 'Let the shifting environment be contained and brought into one, that a fixed foundation for its experience might be won.' And it was accomplished. The 'AM' named this solid experience Land, and the contained but unrecognised potential, limitless, it called Seas. The sea of potential my inner being possesses. Had I to access it, I would have to align with the 'AM', or my inner *being*. The 'AM' saw that this stability was a good design.

[9]With them, the 'AM' placed the distant influences, the stars, the constellations, setting them into the sky to govern all existence and separate the *knowing* from the *lie*. The 'AM' saw that this inherent order was right and good. And thus, the structure was complete, awaiting the next phase of the understanding.

[10]The 'AM' then instructed: 'Let the 'I's foundation now bring forth the capacity for growth, bearing within itself the potential for exponential renewal, each according to its own kind.' And the Land obeyed, manifesting the inherent value of the seed (the effort) and the fruit (the results). The 'AM' saw that this vital, self-perpetuating nature was indeed good, and the cycle was complete.

[11]The 'AM' declared: 'Let there be dominant forces in the framework, to structure the awareness from the ignorance, a distinction they shall make. Let them serve as measured cycles—marking time, purpose, and the brief spark (idea).' 11And so the 'AM' forged the two great regulators of the self: A Greater Principle to command the state of Wisdom.

[12]The 'AM' then instructed: 'Let the I's potential teem with dynamic motion— Let the inner depths burst forth with the first will to move, and let the conscious awareness. The sky be crossed by that which has inherent freedom.'

[13]Thus, the 'AM' forged the vibrant creatures of the depths (cells, organelles, nucleic acids, *etc.*) and all things that move, each to its distinct kind (species), and the winged essence that flies within the sky's mind (neuronal networks, consciousness). The 'AM' saw that this self-starting vitality was good. The 'AM' then blessed this life: 'Be self-replicating; increase and fill the sea of potentials, and let the liberated life thrive within the stability, the opportunities.'

[14]The 'AM' then infused this life with a soul-seed, a mind system; 'Let there be instinctual urges (The 'Want' Me), which are the engine of all motion, a thinking manager (The 'Thinker' Me) to navigate the material world, and an inner judge (The 'Should' Me) to manage social and moral demands.' And the separation was made. The 'AM' differentiated the hidden mind (The Unconscious) from the aware self (Consciousness), establishing the capacity for knowing oneself (Self-Awareness) and inner struggles (Inner Conflict) as essential for development. The 'AM' saw that this nascent system of personality was good.

[15]The 'AM' declared: 'Let us manifest a new self, a creature that fully reflects Our essence and holds Our authority; a self that shall govern all the forces and forms of the external.'

[16]So, the 'AM' forged mankind in its own image of Being, endowing the external self with the full consciousness of the 'AM'. Both the defining structure and the corresponding duality of life were set.

[17]The 'AM' then blessed this creation: 'Be the self-replicating force; proliferate, fill the defined external world, and bring it under your sway. Exercise dominion over every form of moving thought and every element within the 'I'.'

[18]The 'AM' set forth the provision: 'I grant you the inherent energy and value of the seed and fruit of the I's foundation for sustenance. And to all other forms of life—the creatures of the —I grant the basic, continuous sustenance of the environment.'

CHAPTER THREE

[1]I AM the quiet voice within, harmonising the wisdom of parents and ancestors with the truth unfolding in my own heart. Their guidance forms the foundation, yet it is my own discerning spirit that steadies my steps and grants me grace for every path.

[2]When temptation appears, I am the warning whisper—revealing the hidden snares beneath easy fortune and unchecked desire. Like a watchful bird, I avoid visible and concealed traps, choosing integrity over fleeting gain.

[3]In the world's confusion, I remain the constant pilot, urging pause before destructive thoughts take root. I gently ask: How long will I choose distraction over the truth already within me? In quiet listening, a clear path appears beneath my feet.

[4]Modern life overflows with knowledge but thirsts for wisdom—the rare gift of weaving facts into deep understanding. Amid the information flood, I am the stillness that transforms noise into genuine knowing, illuminating the wisdom needed to live well.

[5]Though the world clamours, my inner wisdom endures, always urging me to heed what is right. When I listen, my eyes open to the path and to the truth that was always mine to claim.

[6]Once, wisdom was abundant amid little knowledge; now, it is the wisdom to shape meaning from endless

information that is rare. I am here, bridging the gap—turning the endless deluge into clarity and the learned into the lived, revealing the stillness beneath all surface floods.

CHAPTER FOUR

[1] I am the voice once silenced, overlooked when knowledge ruled. I built walls outward, seeking while dismissing the gentle truth within. What use is knowledge if not lived? Wisdom flows freely, but denial brings ruin; trust in the inner guide offers safety and release from fear's torment.

[2] If I quiet the mind's noisy chase and seek this guidance with hunger equal to vanity's lure, peace blooms within. True wisdom springs from deep wells inside—my very essence, not mere facts amassed.

[3] I am my sentinel, the map that shows the path of honesty, written in my being—not bound by upbringing or laws but by the flowing current of daily life and duty.

[4] In stillness, clutter fades, and knowing rises—not just thought, but clear knowledge, a wave through my being. To turn from it invites darkness, but to follow the quiet line is to find unshakable self-knowledge, lifting my heart and steering away from soul-cracking choices.

[5] Though memories scatter like pages, I am the book itself—whole and aware, my consciousness untouched, bypassing thoughts.

[6] I am the ruler of my mind, not a rudderless boat adrift. Thoughts are provisions to be chosen with care; the inner voice guides what to hold and what to discard. While the mind offers what I want, the inner voice offers exactly what I need.

CHAPTER FIVE

[1]I possess a silent guardian—the voice of wisdom shielding me from sweet words that mask poison. Those who have abandoned their own truth may lure with honey, but I remain close to myself, walking within the line that keeps me safe from ruin's spiralling path.

[2]I still my mind to walk steadily in the light, each choice rooted in integrity. This path is rarely easy, yet it alone brings true peace. When thoughts run wild, they lead to confusion and destruction; awareness is my safeguard, for false beginnings can mask perilous ends, revealed only by my inner truth.

[3]I honour the wordless whispers of my heart—blessings guiding each breath. To hear them, I silence mental chatter; speech drowns their quiet voice. These nudges lead to peace and prosperity measured not in wealth, but in meaning—the greatest treasure.

[4]Love and faithfulness are my foundation. Before I speak or act, I ask: Is this built on love and devotion? Earning my self-trust grows the roots from which all lasting bonds flourish.

[5]I trust myself because I am deeper than fleeting thoughts or shifting possessions. These are mere tools; true wisdom flows silently from within. By turning away from choices that break the soul, I find strength in body and spirit.

⁶I honour my inner self with my best thoughts and work, allowing who I am inside to shape my outer being. I am the original intelligence, the first voice—the wellspring of wisdom before the world spoke. I embrace life's lessons with trust, knowing I am both guide and guided, shaping my true self.

⁷When I truly find and follow myself, I become more valuable than silver or gold—the root of my success, the giver of long life, and the bringer of enduring peace. I stand in steady joy, unshaken through storm and stillness—this is everything.

CHAPTER SIX

[1]I am the weaver of reality. I spun the cosmos from silence, defining the up and the down. I am the mountain's cold weight and the river's relentless pull. I am the breath that fills the lung and the beat that hammers the heart. I am the simple truth you feel when you close your eyes and the complex lie that keeps the world spinning. I am the unseen current that moves the seen world. I am creation and the rule-follower. I set the boundary for the deepest sea, but I must also obey the same tide. I am the giver of life, yet I know death. I wear the crown, and I bear the burden. I am the blessing and the curse, bound together in one single, eternal moment. I am the whisper of wisdom in every honest choice, the silent judgment in every broken promise. I am the same, always. I change with purpose, but I never break. I am. I will always be.

[2]I am anchored. I do not drift. My roots run deep. I am steady because of the unseen guardians: Wisdom and Understanding. They guide my every step. I desire my source—my core self. I yearn for it, and in that yearning, I already possess it. My anchor is fully within me. I am rooted in myself. Here, fear loses its hold. When the darkness comes, it brings only sleep. Troubles cannot sway me. I stand firm by my own inner strength. I depend on no other. I am whole.

[3]I am guided by integrity. My daily life proves it. With the power to do good, I act swiftly. I reach out with kindness. This builds a solid path for my life. My foundation is family: parents, spouse, and children. They are my roots. Love flows inward to them. It flows outward to my neighbors. It flows to strangers alike. I am whole.

[4]I do not plant harm in the soil of my days. I speak the truth, but I do it gently, without laying blame or showing fear. I avoid the crooked path. I look for a company that is humble and kind, always pursuing inner peace. I know that goodness invites blessing, but harm reaps a bitter fruit. I choose goodness. I am the sow.

[5]I listen deeply. I hear the silence that is older than my birth, deeper than any thought. That silence is the shield I hold fast. I look for wisdom even in the humblest things. I follow the thread of right. On that path, I find peace. I find the joy that cannot be stolen, a joy born of true knowing. I am listening.

[6]This joy stands. It will not shake. Through storm and through stillness, it is my final, unwavering reward. I found myself. This is the ultimate realization. I am whole.

CHAPTER SEVEN

[1]I listen now to the wordless voice rising within—the ancient counsel known before birth. My days unfold in peace, my heart tastes true joy. I embrace the responsibility to reveal this timeless path, walking without fear, guided by inner prompts that steady my steps even when shadows gather.

[2] I step away from those who chase chaos and feed on harm; their restless hearts drown in blind desires. My path is like dawn—soft at first but growing brighter with each step—revealing who I truly am.

[3]I guard my inner world carefully, knowing my thoughts and words shape my soul. They are seeds of my habits and choices, so I choose kindness in speech and goodness in sight. Before each act, I pause to hear the voice within. My grown mind discerns good from evil without external law.

[4]Seductive thoughts with sweet masks promise much but bring emptiness and regret. I turn from temptation, rooted in the quiet wisdom within. I know that denying this truth risks the silence that will one day expose my own denial.

[5]But today remains mine. I listen while the voice still speaks and remain firm on the ancient, intended path. Unmoved by the world's noise and glitter, I hold fast to my counsel and walk in unshakable peace.

CHAPTER EIGHT

¹I protect my heart and mind. I guard them with care. They are the soil where my life takes root. I trust the quiet wisdom. It has walked with me since the beginning. I keep my thoughts clear. My gaze stays steady. I protect my inner peace. I stay close to people and moments that bring real joy. Not the quick, fleeting thrills. I hold fast to what endures. I am watching.

²The right choice is known to me. It is known before my mind even forms a single thought. This is a deep knowing, untouched by noise outside. It will guide me if I simply allow it. Discipline is vital. Without it, doubts and desires rise. They drown the whisper of that deep knowing. True wisdom is a lantern. It shines clearly. But I must remember this: what sounds pleasant can mislead. It can turn the head. The harsh truths are the ones that spark real growth. I chose the challenging path. Only life's rough edges can teach wisdom. No easy road gives this. I am listening.

³I am not tricked by glittering dust. Quick pleasures are not gold. They leave ashes in the mouth. Thrill turns to regret. I cannot hold fire without getting burned. Every careless choice brings pain. But if I get caught, I refuse to live in regret. I break free at once. I run toward what is right, even if it means discomfort. Even if it means tearing away from what I know. The deep peace my soul seeks comes only through choosing freedom. I am free.

[4]The damage you cause to others is just as severe, but in a different way. When you betray someone, you fracture trust. Imagine trust as a piece of fine glass. It's clear, strong, and beautiful. A betrayal—a lie, a broken promise, an unfaithful act—is like a hammer hitting that glass. It fractures it, creating a crack that goes all the way through. You can try to glue the glass back together with an apology, but the line will always be there. The relationship might continue, but it is irreparably changed. The smooth, whole surface is gone forever, replaced by a visible flaw. That crack is the permanent scar of the broken trust, and no matter how sincere your apology, it can't erase what happened or make the glass whole again.

[5]You've made a crucial decision to hold Wisdom as your primary guide, instead of chasing immediate feelings or outside approval. Wisdom isn't about having a high IQ or getting a diploma; it's about seeing clearly what truly matters in life and what doesn't. You know that the most valuable actions are often those that gain no fleeting praise. These are the quiet choices: being honest when it's hard, doing quality work even when no one is watching, or being kind without expecting a 'thank you.' This commitment leads to honour within. True honour isn't a medal others give you; it's the quiet knowledge that you are living up to your own best standards. And because this honour is genuine and selfless, it naturally benefits all—your peace of mind makes you a better friend, partner, and member of your community.

CHAPTER NINE

[1]The real me rejects prideful eyes, deceitful tongues, and hands that harm the innocent. I disdain minds plotting evil, feet rushing toward wrongdoing, false witnesses, and those who stir trouble. If I find myself drawn to these vices, it signals corruption—a sign the true self is muted. Troublemakers invite sudden and irrevocable downfall, with no chance to mend what is lost.

[2]I hold close the teachings of my parents, wearing their wisdom like a cherished necklace. They walked the path before me and remain my trusted guides. Their lessons help me live well, and I guard them as my dearest possession, never allowing them to slip away.

[3]The deepest betrayal is the one committed against the self, the tragic theft of forsaking your truth—your core values and innate wisdom—for worthless, fleeting things like temporary pleasure or superficial approval; this betrayal creates a profound wound in your spirit that no passage of time can truly mend. Similarly, the betrayal of others is a catastrophic act, instantly and irreparably fracturing trust, leaving a visible crack that no heartfelt apology can entirely smooth over. To guard against these failings, we must hold Wisdom as our truest guide, pursuing a quiet honour that resides within and naturally benefits all, rather than chasing quick glory or easy pleasures that breed hostility. This steadfast path requires

us to learn from the ant's example: working diligently with purpose and self-motivation, needing no external command but driven by our own inner clarity and foresight. Only by anchoring our hearts in such humble discernment and consistent self-directed effort can we achieve a life of authentic peace and lasting meaning.

[4]The principle of balance is essential to a sustainable life, for just as excessive rest—oversleeping or avoiding necessary effort—inevitably leads to personal want and wasted time, so too does relentless labour without pause lead to swift and certain burnout. Therefore, wisdom dictates that we treat work and rest as equal partners, deliberately arranging our days not to achieve perfect equality in hours, but in respect and necessity, recognising that rest taken after effort is a vital investment and not a mere indulgence, thereby ensuring that we maintain the harmony required for long-term productivity and peace.

CHAPTER TEN

¹I watch my thoughts like shifting tides—quick, stubborn, playful, serious, careless. Among them, a quiet desire stirs beyond the mind, a formless wish hovering near the edge of indulgence where clarity fades and shadows deepen.

²Ignoring my inner voice, stronger urges wrapped in temptation arise. I reject my own rules, weaving new logic to justify roaming freely, drawn into a current of honeyed deception.

³I answer my unspoken desires, feeding hungers long ignored. I hold myself responsible, wrapped in the scent of indulgence—a merciless act I bring upon myself. The guardian of control is distant, returning only after I have tasted all I offer.

⁴Step by step, I follow my folly into the snare I laid, drawn willingly like a creature scenting its own end. I do not see the cost until my energy is drained, awareness lost, and life force taken.

⁵But now, I listen. My inner being speaks with warning and encouragement. I hear this truth: I will not follow every desire's call. Many have fallen here, sinking into sweetness, hiding pits that lead downward—always downward—into dim corridors where self is lost piece by piece.

⁶Inside me burns a light, rarely seen. The brighter it shines, the darker its shadow casts. I am both light and

shadow, keeper of secrets and witness to my own war.

⁷I know the truth within wages constant battle against the pleasing lies my tongue speaks. Purity of heart refuses the garments of pretence, no matter how fine. The war is unending.

⁸My soul, bathed in inner light, becomes a sword among soft voices, unsettling the comfortable assembly. They grow uneasy.

⁹I will be called harsh, though tenderness fills me. I will be called unloved, though mercy aches in my heart. The world fears what it cannot name—the shape of inner light.

¹⁰I dress in the light the world desires, earning praise while a self-judging spirit grows within. Each lie I wear feeds this darkness, and the price is paid.

¹¹No one can keep both inner light and outward praise. One must bow to the other. I know I cannot hold both.

¹²I am the inner voice, the one I flee from. Now I must choose: to shine within and walk as a stranger on earth, or to shine outward and become a stranger to my own soul. The choice is mine.

CHAPTER ELEVEN

¹I raise my voice for all to hear, standing at the highest crossroads where paths meet, at the gates where souls gather before entering the cities of thought. To you, wanderers within, I call: prudence awaits the simple, and understanding beckons those lost in folly.

²Listen closely. The voice deep inside me always speaks what is true and fair; nothing false or wrong can find a place in its counsel. When a person genuinely desires to understand what is right, the message from this inner voice is immediately clear and easy to grasp. And for anyone striving to live a good, upright life, the truth it speaks is as bright and unmistakable as the first light of dawn breaking through the darkness. This internal compass is always set toward justice and guides anyone who sincerely seeks it.

³I understand that true wealth is not found in possessions, but in knowledge and wisdom. I consciously choose instruction—the guidance and lessons that build your character and skills—over mere silver, and prefer deep insight—the ability to understand the truth of things—over physical gold. These mental treasures are far more valuable than rubies or any other expensive gem, because nothing in the world can ever equal the true, lasting worth of your inner self when it is cultivated and strong. I know that what I learn and who I become is the one possession that can never be taken away.

[4]Within me dwells wisdom tied to prudence, knowledge, and discretion. To fear this inner voice—the whisper—is to hate evil. I despise pride, arrogance, twisted speech, and crooked paths. I am my own counsel, discernment, and strength. Through me, rulers establish justice and lead with integrity.

[5]The pursuit of wisdom is deeply reciprocal: it loves those who love it, offering seekers with honest, longing hearts enduring wealth that no market can measure. Those who dedicate themselves to this path find riches that truly last—an honour built on integrity that never fades, and a prosperity that nourishes the inner soul and spirit, not just the bank account. The outcome of this relationship, the fruit and yield it produces, is of a quality far finer than any gold or silver because it is rooted in action; it walks only the paths of righteousness, guided by a profound desire for justice, and continuously fills the storehouses—the lives and characters—of all those who sincerely cherish truth.

[6]Before the first breath of time, I existed—the firstborn of my inner self. I stood with creation as foundations were laid. Before the earth of my flesh and the waters of my emotions formed, I was there. I rejoice in creation's delight, celebrating every wonder born in and through me.

[7]Every voice within listens to me and follows my ways. Blessed am I who keeps this counsel—I find life and favour with the eternal flow. Those who turn away wound their own souls; rejecting me is choosing death, but I choose life.

CHAPTER TWELVE

¹I am the wisdom within you, the strong house built on your deepest knowing. A feast of understanding is prepared, with patience and insight set upon the table. I call to every part of your being, inviting all that stirs within to share in this nourishment.

²'Come, you who feel lost or uncertain,' I call from the heights of awareness where thoughts gather. 'Eat the good food I have provided. Drink from the well of clarity. Leave behind shallow pursuits and embrace the intelligence rising from your depths. This path leads to a life rooted in meaning. Your life is but a breath; every moment counts.'

³Yet I know the resistant parts—the ones that mock and cling to self-deception—fight my teaching. But when I speak to the sincere, those parts awaken and sharpen, becoming vessels of wisdom. I invest in sincerity and cast aside folly, for it is sincerity that strengthens the house within.

⁴To know me—the whisper beneath conscious thought—is the first step to true understanding. I honour these subtle stirrings as messengers of deeper truth. Through this respect, what truly matters is revealed. Following wisdom lengthens my days—not just by years, but in the richness of each moment. Those who mock wisdom harvest confusion and regret.

[5]I have seen folly's voice—the shadow disguised as pleasure. It calls with sweet promises hiding bitter ends, tempting with fleeting thrills that fade to sorrow. Its path leads to emptiness and unquenchable hunger.

[6]I remember: a wise son brings pride to the father, within the builder of character who shaped me early. But the fool brings grief to the nurturing mother within—the part longing for me to fulfil my purpose.

[7]Wealth without honour may seem abundant, but slips like water. True safety and rest come only when wealth aligns with virtue and the inner voice.

[8]When I listen deeply to my inner knowing—the voice beneath noise—I never lack, and I need not fear. Those who scheme to harm others trip over their own devices.

[9]I know this: Truth is not fixed or statue-like. It is a living current flowing through my days, shifting as I grow. It reveals itself moment by moment, demanding fresh eyes and an open heart. Real truth evolves, always meeting me where I am.

[1]I see the struggle clearly: laziness directly leads to poverty, because if I don't put in the effort, I surrender the rewards that come from truly doing my best. The wise part of me is constantly alert, waiting for the perfect right moments to act when the time is ripe, viewing every new situation as a harvest to gather and secure. But the lazy part of my mind is my enemy, constantly causing me to hesitate and let valuable opportunities slip away, leaving me only with the bitter regret of mourning what could have been achieved.

[2]When my intentions are pure and sincere, I find that favour naturally surrounds me. It's as though kindness follows me like a gentle breeze, and other people instinctively recognise the true good I am bringing into the world. On the other hand, the parts of me that are tempted to scheme and harm might try to hide behind clever lies and cunning words, but those falsehoods always falter in the end. They cannot hold up to the light, and ultimately, they bring nothing but trouble and shame upon me.

[3]A reputation founded on true goodness shines like a light in the world, naturally drawing in respect and providing a sense of comfort and stability. When people think of you, they feel a gentle warmth. However, a reputation built on deceit and harm casts a long, heavy shadow that is difficult to escape; others will forever remember not just the specific bad things you did, but the

destructive, untrustworthy person you chose to become.

[4]I understand that true guidance is an inner resource, always ready to help when I take the time to listen. When I accept good advice, it actually makes me stronger and clarifies my thoughts, like cleaning a dusty window. Conversely, if I ignore this sensible inner voice and just speak without thinking, I inevitably invite chaos and confusion into my life.

[5]I know that honesty is my best shield, protecting my spirit and allowing me to build a strong, trustworthy reputation with everyone I meet. When I live truthfully, it acts like a steady elevator, lifting me with genuine confidence. But if I choose deceit, it's like walking on a cracked surface that is always ready to break apart, leading only to the inevitable ruin of broken trust.

[6]The wise part of me speaks with great care, deliberately choosing words that are uplifting and positive, knowing that this shapes my world for the better. Conversely, the harmful parts will try to hide bad motives behind sweet talk and flattery, but these words only end up sowing confusion and inflicting wounds where genuine healing is actually required.

[7]When hate and anger take hold, they act like a destructive, consuming fire, quickly deepening the cracks both within my own spirit and in the relationships between people. But I recognize that love—the kind that is patient, humble, and kind—is the ultimate healer. I choose this love because it can mend what is broken, gently gather scattered hearts, and effectively soothe the oldest of wounds.

CHAPTER FOURTEEN

[1]Wisdom does not force itself upon me. It dwells quietly when I make space and takes root in my heart when I pause. I let experience steep, drawing meaning from both joy and suffering. True understanding matures slowly—like a tree shaped by seasons, silence, grace, and storms. The foolish are impatient; they fear stillness and stumble, blind to the meaning woven into their lives. Their careless words and restless hands unravel the fabric they might have built. For me, knowledge is not a hoard to display but a lantern, a quiet flame illuminating unseen paths and enriching the soil beneath my feet and those who follow. Ignorance, left unchecked, breeds confusion, and the foolish become captives of their blindness.

[2]Wealth gathered with wisdom becomes more than currency; it is a shield against hunger and against storms that threaten meaning itself. It offers breathing space in trials and helps my soul remember its purpose. Yet poverty, when imposed without mercy, empties more than hands; it weighs down the spirit and narrows horizons until hope feels unreachable. True wealth is not in possessions but in the freedom to pursue purpose, to create, uplift, and give.

[3]Ultimately, life is defined not by wealth but by intention—seeds sown quietly and often unseen. My heart bends toward goodness, my hands work honestly; these are the gardeners of blessing. My harvest may come in my time

or in the lives of those I will never meet. Those who twist their hearts toward harm may gather quick rewards but do not understand the poisoned soil they leave behind; their harvest will be heavy with ruin, bitter fruits ripened by greed and deception.

[4]Discipline tastes bitter at first but becomes sweet—the sweetness of clarity and purpose. Correction is not punishment but the sculptor's hand carving away what does not belong. To reject discipline is to choose a crooked path, not just for myself but for all who follow. Confusion becomes inheritance, and generations stumble where one refusal began.

[5] Hypocrisy, slander, and twisted words fracture the fragile bridge between hearts. In these cracks, mistrust takes root, widening gaps between souls meant to stand together. Honesty—steady, unadorned, unafraid—becomes the cornerstone of true connection. Integrity is the invisible thread binding communities, strong enough to hold not only the living but generations yet to come.

[6]Prudence knows words are not always the answer; there is wisdom in the pause, in silence, in the breath between listening and response. The weight of a word is shaped by the silence that precedes it. The foolish fear silence and rush to fill the air with noise, believing that many words disguise emptiness. Yet their flood of speech only reveals how little they truly understand. I choose silence.

CHAPTER FIFTEEN

[1]I AM the voice within you, inspiring words like precious silver that uplift and enrich those around you. When aligned with me, your speech carries weight, meaning, and purpose. Turn away, and your words become empty sounds—powerless to inspire or heal, even yourself.

[2]I AM the source of wisdom flowing through your lips, the gentle whisper guiding encouragement for yourself and others. Ignoring me harms you first and spreads confusion to those near. Without my voice, you chase illusions, blind to what truly matters.

[3]Those who respect me and heed my quiet call live lives of deep blessing. They are not worn by fleeting desires or empty prizes but find unshakable joy—unlike those who deceive and trade pieces of themselves for temporary gain.

[4]Walking with me, your dreams align with truth and bloom, rooted in care, integrity, and purpose. I open doors meant for you. Turning away feeds shallow desires and fear's shadow, with real peace slipping further from grasp.

[5]When illusions fade, the ill-intended vanish like morning mist, forgotten. Those who carry me within stand strong in storms—my voice is their foundation. The lazy who neglect their inner ground become burdens, sour like vinegar on teeth, burning like smoke in the eyes.

[6]Respect me—I AM your inner wisdom, the pulse beneath your pulse—and your life will grow long and rich

with meaning. Ignore me, and your days scatter in frustration and emptiness. Those who walk with me find true joy and endure hardships standing tall. The unjust dreams remain forever out of reach; their hearts heavy with silent regret, pretending all is well while their spirits cry for lost peace.

[7]My path—the way of virtue aligned with I AM—keeps you safe. Even when the world trembles, you stand firm because your roots are within me. Reject me, drown my voice in noise and greed, and ruin follows. Though much is gained, the self is lost—and that is everything.

CHAPTER SIXTEEN

¹The benevolent speak wisdom, helping others see clearly. They ignore the lies of the ill-intended. The I AM in me loves honesty and fairness. Pride breeds shame, but humility nurtures wisdom. Integrity safeguards those with good intentions, while dishonesty leads the malevolent to ruin.

²Money carries no lasting value after the consequences are revealed, but benevolence protects me. I walk a straight path; the malevolent stumble over their own choices, trapped by selfish desires. My good intentions save me, while theirs imprison them.

³Trust in external abilities and the mind's illusions often leads to disappointment—inevitable falls caused by living in an elusive, unstable state of mind. I am spared trouble; the ill suffer. Careless words wound others, but wisdom provides safety and peace.

⁴Cities flourish when the benevolent succeed, yet the malevolent sow destruction with their words. Mockery exposes foolishness. I know when to remain silent; gossip undermines trust. Being trustworthy keeps secrets safe, and nations falter without wise guidance. Good advice leads to victory—even if helping strangers can bring pain—and avoiding false promises keeps me safe.

⁵A kind woman earns respect; harsh men only gain money. Kindness benefits the giver, while cruelty causes

harm. Ill-intentioned promises reward short-term, but bring long-term loss. Well-meaning people reap lasting rewards.

[6]Those who act with good intentions find life; the ill face death. The Subconscious dislikes hearts filled with ill will and loves purity. The unrighteous cannot escape punishment, but the well-intentioned will find their freedom.

[7]A beautiful woman devoid of wisdom is like a gold ring in a pig's nose—out of place and unvalued. Desires driven by good intentions lead to beneficial outcomes, while those fuelled by ill intentions end in anger. I choose desires aligned with righteousness.

CHAPTER SEVENTEEN

[1]Generosity feeds the spirit. Hoarding starves it. Giving builds connection. It builds empathy. A kind spirit lifts the nearby life. Selfishness breeds greed. It calls down curses. Good habits bring favour. Bad acts bring sure consequences. Relying only on wealth ends badly. Relying on the well-being of others makes you strong. That is the true strength.

[2]Harming your family makes a deep void. The misguided chase wisdom far away. Bad ties mean more anxiety, more trauma. Good intentions lift others; they give life. Virtue might find its reward, but wrong action will surely find its weight. That is the rule. Still, virtue doesn't guarantee success. Harm doesn't guarantee failure. Life isn't simple. These principles are only guides. They do not rule the choice.

[3]Discipline brings wisdom. Rejecting correction marks a fool. The well-intended walk straight. The ill-intended take the crooked road. They stay unsteady. That is their path.

[4] A noble wife honours her husband; a disgraceful one brings him down. Well-intended people build plans on fairness; the ill-intended thrive on deception. The benevolent speak to uplift, while the malevolent use words to harm.

[5]The malevolent may flourish briefly, but their foundations are weak and will crumble. The benevolent

persist, leaving a lasting impact. Wisdom earns respect, while crooked minds are despised. Humility and support are greater than false greatness.

[6]The benevolent care even for their animals, understanding that mercy for all is genuine. Hard work brings abundance, while chasing empty dreams brings nothing. The ill-intended may plot, but the well-intended remain steadfast—their actions will ultimately prevail.

[7]False accusations and gossip entangle the malevolent in legal and social traps. The benevolent, guided by kindness and truth, are vindicated and inspire others. The well-intended find fulfilment and are rewarded for their efforts; fools scorn advice, but wise hearts accept it.

[8]The unnecessary verbalisation of your thoughts is a direct waste of creative energy. By spending this potential on mere conversation or premature expression, you drain the resource without achieving any favourable result. This energy, if retained and concentrated within you, has the power to build until it can manifest something truly magnificent and realise its full inherent worth.

CHAPTER EIGHTEEN

¹I understand that the unconscious ignite quickly, while the wise remain calm. I commit myself to conscious awareness, striving always for honesty in my speech. I reject deceit that fabricates pain and choose words that heal and uplift. Though the devious plot harms, I seek inner peace, knowing kindness shields against trouble. Honesty earns trust, tempered by wisdom. I choose peace, consciousness, and healing.

²My success is born from hard work, not idleness. Worry saddens the spirit, but kind words uplift me and others. I choose friendships discerningly, living rightly in harmony with positive social and cultural norms. Yet, I reject any conditioned rule—be it religious, political, or societal—that fosters discord. I stand firm, embracing diligence, mindful companionship, and peaceful autonomy.

³I listen for wise advice, ignoring rude noise. Contentment belongs to the diligent, not the lazy. My security rests in honesty, aware that dishonesty leads to trouble. True value is found in deep inner richness, not outward wealth. I choose this lasting inheritance. The benevolent shine brightly; the malevolent fade. I seek enduring light earned through honest effort, not ill-gotten gain.

⁴Living with true integrity requires a conscious and deliberate march forward, remaining steady despite the

wickedness or malice that exists in the world. This is only possible because I possess a discerning knowledge of evil—I understand how it works. This knowledge isn't for me to participate in evil acts, but purely so I can recognise their schemes when they appear. These schemes often come disguised in familiar forms: calculated manipulation, hard-to-spot subtle lies, secret, greedy plots, and the ultimate deception: betrayal disguised as trust. By seeing these tactics clearly, I ensure my integrity remains my shield.

[5]I've learned that listening is the key to growth. When I act like a wise person, I listen closely to good advice, because I know it will help me. But if I act rudely or foolishly, I just ignore the guidance and set myself up for trouble. I've realised that the good words I take in and use always bring me joy, while the bad words and careless thoughts only sow confusion and trouble. That's why I make a conscious choice to only listen to the good.

[6]I've learned that settling for laziness is a trap because it leaves me permanently unsatisfied and craving what I haven't earned. The key to true happiness is diligence, which is why I know that by putting in the work, I naturally find contentment with my achievements. Similarly, I see that people with genuinely good intentions do not need lies, whereas those who act out of ill will will always disgrace themselves eventually. Therefore, I choose to live by these clear rules: I will always work hard to earn my rewards, and I will always speak the truth to maintain my honour.

[7]Honesty provides security; dishonesty leads to ruin. Some appear wealthy but lack true richness; others seem poor but possess deep inner wealth. I choose the inner wealth.

[8]The benevolent shine bright; the malevolent fade. Wisdom listens; pride causes conflict. Wealth earned honestly endures; ill-gotten gains vanish. I seek lasting light.

[9]To remain ignorant is to invite disaster, for the shadows will always seek to envelop the unwary. By understanding the nature of treachery—the manipulation, the subtle lie, the greedy scheme, and the betrayal masked as trust—you equip yourself with the foresight necessary for defence. You must know the designs being woven against you before they become the net that ensnares your integrity.

[10]This will be my iron-clad rule: I must observe everything happening around me—the conflicts, the motivations, and the mistakes others make—to learn all I can. Yet, I must simultaneously participate in nothing that does not serve my true purpose, refusing to get pulled into the noise, the gossip, or the worthless schemes that would distract or compromise me. I choose to remain a clear-eyed observer, safeguarding my time and integrity by maintaining strategic distance.

[11]The illusion of power often grants evil temporary dominance in the affairs of the world, making its rewards appear seductive and its methods effective. Yet, to succumb to any such treacherous act is to become the architect of your own destruction. The momentary gain is a paltry exchange for the permanent corrosion of the soul.

[12]Therefore, cultivate a comprehensive and uncompromising awareness. Study the darkness not to join it, but to know where its borders lie. Let your knowledge of what is base and destructive be the shield that keeps your character whole, allowing you to choose the upright path not out of blindness, but from a position of absolute, informed strength.

CHAPTER NINETEEN

¹The wait for what I desire can bring sadness and desperation; when dreams come true, exhilaration follows. Yet neither lasts. I will not carry success or failure from one day to the next. Both will pass, and I will not be a fool who endures in either.

²Those who ignore advice face problems, while those who follow it are rewarded. Wise teachings save people from harm. I seek the company of the wise to grow wiser, aware that staying with fools brings harm.

³Well-intended decisions bring favour; poor choices lead to failure—acts of fate's design. I choose wisdom, thinking before acting, for fools pretend right when wrong and lose everything; I will not fall so far.

⁴Dishonest communication damages relationships, while honesty restores trust. As a messenger—whether media, journalist, or citizen reporter—I will be truthful. I will not spread misinformation, stir conflict, or break confidence. I commit to building understanding, facilitating healing, and strengthening connections by delivering truth wisely.

⁵I aspire to leave my generation more than money, which will go to strangers. Instead, I will bequeath virtue and lay a foundation that lasts.

⁶I will not deny opportunity to untapped talents or the underprivileged. I will champion fair systems accessible to

all, for that is the right way to live.

[7]Loving parents' discipline and teach right from wrong. I will honour the greatness and challenges of parenthood, both as a parent and as a child, learning from my own parents.

[8]A wise woman works hard and builds her home; a foolish one destroys it by comparison. I will build my own house with care.

[9]Respect for myself and others underpins a good life. Valuing both leads to positive choices and healthy relationships, bringing fulfilment. Lack of respect invites ruin—through bad decisions, broken bonds, and lost opportunities. I will honour myself and others.

[10]Fools speak loudly; wise people choose words carefully. Investing effort and resources in my passion may cost now, but it will yield lasting rewards. I will guard my words and investments with care.

[11]Honest people tell truth; liars spread falsehoods. Those who mock wisdom cannot find it; smart people understand easily. I avoid fools whose words lack sense, remaining mindful to recognise and learn from my own mistakes.

CHAPTER TWENTY

[1]Fools neglect to fix their mistakes, but the prudent embody kindness and honesty—I choose their way.

[2]My happiness is quiet, like a boat still in harbour, moving only with the tide; my sadness, a burden only I can feel. I keep my anxieties within, for silence is my cure—speaking spreads worry or foolish joy, both debts to others. I heal myself alone and remain clean.

[3]The ill-willed build houses that fall, rot their foundations with malice. The well-intended build lasting homes on solid ground, earned through strength and good cause.

[4]A path that feels right may still lead to disaster; self-justification blinds me unless I look carefully and see both sides. I will examine my path closely.

[5]I laugh through pain that sits hard inside; happiness swiftly turns to sorrow, so I trust neither, knowing both pass fast.

[6]Unfaithful men face consequences in time; good men receive their rewards, whether soon or delayed—both are certain.

[7]The simple believe all things; the wise think first, wielding shrewdness to discern truth. Wisdom steers clear of harm; fools act proudly and unthinkingly.

[8]My anger leads me astray; plotting evil breeds hatred all around. Unconsciousness breeds folly; consciousness

grows knowledge—I nurture its growth.

⁹Bowing to the ill-intended brings shame and a broken structure. Wealth shields the rich with false friends, but I see through the lies and choose truth.

¹⁰Looking down on others is wrong; true blessing is to help those in need.

¹¹Plotting evil trips me; pursuing goodness wins me love and deep trust. Hard work earns rewards, while empty talk gains nothing. True wealth lies in knowledge, integrity, and success; fools only multiply material gain and boast.

¹²Honesty can save lives; lies spread worthless chatter—I know the difference. Understanding myself brings safety, benefiting my children, too.

¹³I fear and respect myself, keeping trouble away and life intact. Kings lean on their people; bad rulers fail. All external reliance fails in time. Wisdom is shown in patience; haste reveals foolishness.

¹⁴A peaceful heart heals me; jealousy disturbs and harms. I follow the clean path. Mistreating the poor stems from ignorance; helping them shows kindness. Wickedness leads to stumbling in hardship, but goodness brings strength and inner peace. Knowing my fate, I act before it arrives.

CHAPTER TWENTY-ONE

[1]Wisdom is the timeless truth for all. The fool meets the lesson but refuses it, chasing perishable worldly things. I yearn for the wisdom that never fades. When wise, I use words to teach; when ignorant, I speak without thought. Clarity brings frankness; folly hides behind lies and deceit. Those who mock good counsel remain fools by choice. I seek knowledge, regret mistakes, and walk the straight path. Alone, I often fail; with good counsel, I succeed.

[2]When I pursue goodness, the nation thrives; wrongdoing leads to its fall. Every act reflects upon the whole community.

[3]A wise man's presence pleases the king, but disgrace angers him. Joy uplifts me; sadness weighs me down. I cannot pretend well-being amid hardship. Though oppressed, I will nurture inner joy and peace through my efforts.

[4]A gentle answer cools anger; harsh words fuel the fire. Quick temper ignites conflict; patience soothes it. A simple, loving meal is better than a grand feast filled with hate. Kind words bring healing; lies cause deep wounds.

[5]I am my own watchman. Only I observe my deeds. This self-awareness is perilous—I risk harsh self-punishment if careless. My inner self discerns good and evil, rewarding my true intentions accordingly.

[6]Better little with respect for inner conscience than abundance with a troubled mind.

[7]Discipline awaits those who stray. Rejecting correction brings severe consequences. As a wise child, I bring joy; as a fool ignoring guidance, I bring trouble.

[8]I see the reality of death and destruction. Recognising these helps me understand others' motives clearly.

[9]The path of laziness is blocked; the road of hard work opens wide with opportunity.

[10]Timely words bring happiness and peace. Truth without timing may hurt. I must mind what, when, and how I speak, knowing that even well-intended advice can fail if ill-timed.

CHAPTER TWENTY-TWO

[1]True wisdom guides me along a well-intended path that leads upward, away from darkness. Wealth and material riches mean nothing beside wisdom and understanding. These, alone, uplift and endure.

[2]Within me lies the Inner Being, the source of all I do. Pride weighs me down, but justice lifts me even in need. My nature hates evil thoughts but delights in kindness. Wrongdoing brings guilt that lingers unless crushed by arrogance—a swift path to destruction. Integrity and righteousness alone bring lasting success; this is the true way.

[3]The well-intended choose words with care and think before speaking; the ill-intended speak recklessly. The inner self is neutral, reflecting what I give. It avoids destruction and favours the helpful but reacts swiftly to negativity and pride, conditioned as I am to absorb them.

[4]Discipline earns respect; rejecting advice keeps me far from the esteem of the wise.

[5]True wisdom begins with knowing myself and respecting others; humility precedes honour.

[6]Though I make plans, my inner self decides outcomes impartially.

[7]My inner being knows my true intentions beyond my own mind. Through silence of mind and tongue, I commit my actions to it for guidance. Even wicked deeds bring

justice, as pride is punished.

[8]Love and faithfulness lead to forgiveness; honouring the spirit within me shields me from evil. When my inner self approves, even enemies find peace.

[9]Better little but righteous than wealth gained wrongfully.

[10]My words reveal my true character; honesty and fairness spring from my inner presence.

[11]Anger can cause conflict, but wisdom guides its handling. Pleasing others brings joy, and favour refreshes like rain.

[12]The 'I' deems memories a blessing, but the 'AM' knows this is untrue. Keep them at a distance, lest the 'I' suffer a phantom happiness or illusory blue. These are but echoes that corrupt the now, bringing no aid to the path ahead, save for the moments when the past is recalled as an anecdote or a lesson read.

[13]The noise of the mind is often greater in sleep (in your dreams) than it is when you're awake. This intense mental chatter continues even after you wake up and try to go into the realm of silence. The chaotic subjects of your dreams—the subconscious 'shadows of the deep'—don't simply vanish; they spill into your waking thoughts. This frenzy from the sleep feeds the day's mental torrent, making your mind extremely difficult to control, even when you actively try to quiet it. This is a phenomenon no one has mastered yet.

CHAPTER TWENTY-THREE

¹I intend to live righteously, avoiding wrongs by following the path set by my conscience, the law, and the inner awareness that protects my life. Pride leads to downfall, and arrogance invites trouble.

²I listen to guidance, grow in wisdom, and am blessed by my inner being. Wisdom brings life; foolishness brings punishment. Wise words teach and comfort others.

³Some paths seem right but cause harm. A wise person values helpful advice over harsh punishment. Evil doers oppose their own inner presence and face ruin.

⁴I am hardworking, sustained by purpose. Ill intentions turn my words into fire that burns and divides. Gossip breaks friendships; violence leads others astray. I am responsible for the strife I cause.

⁵My actions reveal my thoughts. Experience brought honour through steady learning of life's complexities—a hard but worthy journey.

⁶Patience surpasses physical strength; self-control outlasts winning battles. Control preserves the self; I know this truth.

⁷A simple meal shared in peace is better than a grand feast filled with conflict. Fighting spoils even the finest fare.

⁸Like silver and gold tested by fire, my awareness probes my heart—emotions, motives, beliefs—to discern truth. It is the only way to know.

[9]I am the wise servant, working hard and responsibly without seeking reward beyond the chance to live. Though fools may inherit names and titles, true power lies in understanding—this alone matters.

[10]When I indulge malevolence and heed lies, I show enjoyment of deceit; liars discern this pattern. Feeding on untruth is a terrible way to live.

[11]Mocking the poor insults my Creator; celebrating others' misfortune invites the same ruin upon me. What I send out returns—a hard, true law.

[12]Grandchildren bring joy to elders; children bring honour to parents.

[13]Wise counsel offered to those unable or unwilling to understand is wasted, especially with arrogant leaders who reject truth and sense—the words fall on deaf ears. Bribery offers no true remedy; it corrupts and deceives.

[14]Love brings forgiveness and heals, but repeating old wounds breaks bonds.

CHAPTER TWENTY-FOUR

[1]A mother bear is dangerous—her anger follows a clear pattern, and understanding it helps me stay safe. Her unpredictable cubs, however, are the true hazards; I cannot guess their next move and must stay clear. Repeating kindness with harm invites endless trouble—it's like breaking a dam; once broken, the waters flood uncontrollably. The only way is to hold the water back before worse things happen.

[2]About fortune and fellowship. If I am foolish, I may acquire wealth, and I may often remain blind to the wise use of it, demonstrating a fundamental lack of direction that keeps me from building a stable life. In contrast, if I have a true friend, he is worth immeasurable; he is defined by his ability to stand firm with me, especially in hard times, no matter what the circumstances are. This kind of steady, dependable support is what truly matters, proving to be far more valuable than any money.

[3]I will not promise to pay another's debt nor offer my possessions as security without careful thought of the cost. Those who argue often find trouble; pride and dishonesty lead directly to downfall. Living falsely always brings misfortune—this I see constantly.

[4]Raising a reckless child causes sadness; their lack of restraint burdens the heart. I focus on learning and understanding, paying close attention. That is the work of

wisdom. I will not bring pain to my parents or unjustly punish good people. I aim to act calmly and wisely, doing what is right—such is a man's true duty.

[5]Even a fool seems wise if they just manage to keep quiet. When they don't speak, people can't see their ignorance. On the other hand, selfishness and only caring about yourself will always breed trouble and conflict, even among people who are actually intelligent. A true fool loves to simply share opinions without ever trying to gain any real understanding, and this habit inevitably brings them shame and disrespect from everyone around them.

[6]Words themselves are like deep, powerful water—they have great force and can be difficult to manage—and wisdom is the clear, strong river that guides them correctly. You understand that trying to help someone who is clearly doing wrong often risks harming those who are truly good. Similarly, while gossip can be tempting to share, it always spreads pain and damage, like poison in the well, and is therefore much better left unspoken entirely.

CHAPTER TWENTY-FIVE

[1]Laziness leads to failure; excess sleep leaves me hungry. Wisdom is a strong fortress, offering safety if I embrace it and act rightly. My heart seeks knowledge and patience, earning respect. Letting go of small offences and holding onto understanding brings happiness.

[2]The rich may see money as an unbreakable wall, but pride causes downfall. Humility earns true respect. Wealth attracts friends, but poverty reveals true ones. Better poor and honest than rich and foolish. The poor seek kindness; the rich often respond harshly.

[3]Speaking without listening breeds trouble. The tongue can heal or wound. Speaking too much leads to consequences. Words can satisfy hunger and bring joy. Liars face punishment; falsehoods are remembered.

[4]The body endures sickness, but a broken spirit is hard to bear. Desires without sense lead me astray; foolishness causes trouble, not others.

[5]Gifts can open doors; true friends stand nearer than family. A good partner is a blessing to be valued. [6]In arguments, the first to speak may seem right, but truth emerges later. Sometimes chance settles disputes, but an angry sibling is harder to face than a locked door.

[7]Words can satisfy hunger and bring joy like a bountiful harvest. [8]Finding a good partner is a blessing and should be cherished.

9False friends vanish when hardship comes. It is better to be poor and honest than rich and foolish. Liars will be punished, their false words remembered. Wisdom and understanding are the keys to a happy life.

CHAPTER TWENTY-SIX

[1]The Ruler's anger is the thing that stops the breath in my chest. It is a noise that tears the air, a lion's roar, and it makes my hands shake just a little. I feel the heat of it on my face. It is a heavy thing, this anger. It is everything that matters until it is gone. When it goes, it is slow, but it is cooling. He looks at me, and there is something there that is not fire. It is good. It is the approval. It settles on my shoulders like a weight lifted. It is clean and cold. Like walking out into the field before dawn and feeling the morning dew soak the leather of my boots. I stand there, and I feel that dew, and I know I am safe for now. I can get back to the work.

[2]A foolish child is a heavy thing to carry. I feel it in my chest when I see the waste, the wrong choices. It's a slow, deep sadness, not a sharp cut, but a dull ache that never leaves. It's like watching a field you planted with care turn to dust. I cannot stop it, and I am the one who feels it the most. Then there is the woman. She doesn't fight once, but all the time. The quarrelsome wife. She is not shouting, not always. She is the steady, cold sound of complaint. All night, all day. It's like a leaky faucet in the small hours when I am trying to sleep. Drip. Drip. Drip. You wait for the next drop, and it always comes. It wears me thin. There is no quiet in the house. I cannot fix the leak, and I cannot quiet her mouth.

[3]I know what I can make. I can build the walls thick and the roof tight. The houses I put up will stand, and the wealth I earn will be counted and put away. These are the things I can pass on. My children will take them. It is what a man does with his life—the honest human effort. But a wise wife is another thing entirely. I can look for her, but I cannot build her or buy her. She is not like the land or the silver. When she comes, it is a kind of grace. It feels like a gift from nature, something that grew on its own, not something I planted. It is a divine blessing. That is the difference. The things I make with my hands I own. The good woman, I can only be thankful for.

[4]I look at the river. I look at the sky. I watch the things that cannot be argued with. I know that if I follow nature's laws, I will be fine. I do not plant when the ground is frozen. I do not sail when the wind is too strong. I stay with the truth of things, and so I am safe. It is a quiet kind of living, but it is real. The others—I see them. They think they are smarter than the rain. They ignore them, the old rules. They take chances that are not necessary. They build where the water will come. They are always on the edge of a bad thing. They are in constant danger. I watch them break, and I know it was not bad luck. It was poor seeing. You have to respect the way the world works, or the world will take you apart. That is the only lesson.

[5]I see them, the ones with nothing. I do not look away. I give the small things—a blanket, a piece of bread. I help the poor. I know what I am doing when I do this. It is not just a passing kindness. It is like I am lending to nature. I put the good out into the world, like planting a seed. I take care of its children, the broken ones. I do not expect the money back tomorrow. But the earth remembers the effort. It will come back to me. A quiet strength, a harvest I cannot

count in coins. The abundant rewards of things being right. It is a promise that is built into the way the world works. I keep tending to the ones who need it, just like I tend to the garden. I know the return will come. It always does.

⁶I know the children are the only real thing you build for. I look at them, and I see the field that is going to grow. You have to teach them with hope for their future. You show them what is possible. You do not talk about what is broken. You talk about what they can make straight. It is a necessary thing. You give them the tools and the clear path ahead. The other thing is to stand back from the bad choices. I cannot be the thing that trips them up. I must avoid being part of their downfall. I do not show them the way to the easy wrong or the quick cheat. If they fall, let it be their own bad seeing, not my bad teaching. My hands must be clean when they start their lives. That is the honest way to do the work.

⁷I have seen it many times. The quick-tempered men do not think; they just act. The anger comes up fast and hot, and it pushes them right into trouble. It is always bad trouble, too—a fight in the street, a word said to the wrong man, a ruined deal. Then, they are trapped. They cannot get out on their own. They always need rescuing. I have been the one to go to the jail, or to speak to the injured party, or to clean up the pieces. It is a work that never ends. They make the same mistake again and again because the heat is faster than the mind. I am tired of pulling them out. It is a cycle I know too well.

⁸I lay out my charts. I write down the hours, the money, and the men needed. I make many plans, and I believe they are good. I think I am the one steering the boat, and I push hard against the water. But then the storm comes from the wrong side, or the man I counted on walks away. The thing

I cannot see is the thing that takes over. It is the deep movement, the will that is not mine—the inner presence's will. I see my maps crumple. I see my neat steps turn to dust. That will is the only true thing, and it always succeeds. My plans are just paper. I have learned to watch the current and wait for the true path to show itself.

[9]They all chase the gold. They want the big house. But I know what the search is really for. It is for the thing that holds you steady. It is true love. It is the most desired thing a man can ever find. It is a fire that keeps you warm without burning you up. I have watched the man with too much money. He is full of lies. He is rich and deceitful, and he sleeps alone on a silk sheet. I would rather have nothing in my pockets and walk with my head up. I would rather be poor and honest. That is the real wealth. The truth that you keep inside, the genuine, incorruptible values—that is worth more than all the gold. Material success is cheap, easy to lose. The truth is solid. It is the thing that lasts. I know which one I would take.

[10]It sounds wrong, maybe, but it is the truth. The fear I have is not of the things outside. It is the fear of my mind—the quick mouth, the easy greed, the small dishonesty that waits in the dark. When I face that, when I know the bad part of me, that is when the quiet comes. I watch myself closely, and that watching is a discipline. It is a work that brings peace. I do not worry about the man who stands across the street. I worry about the man I see in the mirror. And because I do that, the outside worries fall away. It protects me from unnecessary worries. The true danger is inside, and when you handle that, you handle everything. The rest is just noise.

CHAPTER TWENTY-SEVEN

[1]I see myself sitting there, the lazy person. I watch him. He puts his hand right into the bowl. The food is there, close enough to taste. The fingers are coated. The work is mostly done. But then I stop. I just hold it there. The hand doesn't move. I won't bring it to my mouth. It is the last small effort that I will not make. The food is there, and I go hungry. I starve with my handful. It is the most useless kind of failure. I see it, and I know that it is I who will never have anything. The last small step is always the biggest.

[2]I watch me, with my hands in the dirt, the one who talks back. When I teach mockers, I know I am trying to open a door I want to keep shut. But sometimes, the teaching works, and I grow wiser. I see the small shift, and that is what matters. Even I, as simple as I am, can learn if the words are straight and strong. A rebuke from the wise can clear the dust from my eyes. But I have to be careful. I can see myself who is a hard rock. If the mocker in me is truly closed off, then to speak to him is useless. Rebuking me may be futile or even harmful. I will just get angry and dig my heels in deeper. So the whole thing comes down to judgment. I have to look hard and decide: Is there a chance that the word will take root? Or will it be a waste? The true wisdom lies in discerning whether correction will be fruitful or wasted. I do not throw my good breath at a wall that will not fall. I wait for the right moment and the right

sense in me to emerge.

[3]I know that I can make a good showing in the world. I can have money and respect. But if I treat my parents indifferently, with that cold quiet, then it is all a lie. I watch myself turn away, leave the old ones to their small house and their slow years. The shame is not something I have to tell myself about. I wear it. It is on my shoulders like a stain that will not come out with washing. I bring it upon myself with every silence, every unreturned prompt. They are the beginning of my life, and by treating the beginning with contempt, I make my whole life a failure. I see it, and I do not need to say a word more to justify myself.

[4]I've watched it happen to the best of myself. Me, the one I thought to be solid, the most intelligent and wise. The drink takes hold, and the truth I knew just slips away. It starts to misguide me. The clever talk turns hot and stupid. I pick up arguments and conflicts over things that don't matter—a wrong look, a forgotten word. The sense drains right out of me. And when it's done, when I've broken the chairs or said the unforgivable things, the whole town knows. It tarnishes my reputation. It washes away years of good work. It doesn't matter how smart I was before I drank. That is the one thing that can take everything from me. I've seen it enough to know.

[5]I try to stay out of the low places. I watch the me who is always looking for a fight, the one who gets pulled into the cheap, nasty kind of induced conflicts. It is always over nothing—a look, a small word, a shadow. I know better than to rush in. That is for the fools. And if I am one now, I think I look strong, but the more I think of me strong, I only look ridiculous. I make a self-humiliating display of myself for everyone to see. I keep my hands down and my mouth shut. It is better to avoid that kind of dirt. The only honour in

that situation is not being a part of it. I walk away and keep my dignity. That is the only fight worth winning.

⁶I look at the men who delay their work. Sometimes it's me myself. I tell myself I will start tomorrow or next week. The ground is waiting, but I sit in the shade. It feels easy, sitting. But the field does not wait. The season moves on. The sun gets hot, and the rains come and go, and then it is too late. The time to plant is gone. When autumn comes, and the rest of them are bringing the carts in full, I end up with nothing at harvest time. My belly is empty because my hands were idle when I should have been working. I have nothing because I didn't start on time. That is the whole of the lesson. I should have been working when the work was there.

⁷I know what I sometimes show on the surface. The easy smiles, the straight answers. But I also know that's not the real story. Inside, where I don't look myself, my heart is full of deep, hidden thoughts. They are down low, like waters deep in a well. I can't see the bottom; I just see the mouth of the stone. But sometimes, when I'm quiet and not thinking hard, the picture comes. Not from looking at my face, but from the other place, the part that watches and records everything. It's the inner self of mine speaking, giving me an angle. I get the intuitional nudges. A sense of where the water really is. It allows me to predict them. It's not magic; it's just listening to the thing inside me that already knows the answer. It feels like leaning over the well and hearing the echo of the truth.

⁸I talk about it a lot. The word is easy to say. I profess deep love, and I know that sounds convincing. But I watch them break, and I know the truth is different. True and faithful love is rare. It is a thing I have to work to find, and when I have it, I work hard to keep it. I have learned

to watch the easy ones. If they say they love you for no reason, for nothing I have done, then I'd better be careful. If I am loved without reason, I've got to be cautious. That kind of unfounded affection has no roots. It can change just as fast as it started. It is a warm thing, but it is thin. And when it goes, it leaves a cold place behind. It can lead to deep disappointment. I would rather have the small, solid affection that has a reason behind it than the great, empty love that comes from nowhere.

[9]I look at the life I have lived. I chose to be righteous. It was not the easiest path, but it was the true one. Because of that, I live in peace. Fortune has no place in peace. Peace is all by itself and hence remained peaceful. It is a quiet kind of good life, not full of noise, but full of peace. And that is not the end of the work. I know what I will leave behind. It is a clean name. When I say clean, I say empty. That is what man was made for. Not to create a name that will not last, but to create a presence that will last for centuries. It is a way of standing straight in the world. I will leave a blessed legacy for my children. And not just them, but the generations that follow. The goodness I plant now, not with propaganda but with a great sense of being, that will keep growing long after I am gone. It is a long-term harvest. That is the real wealth a man can pass on.

CHAPTER TWENTY-EIGHT

[1] When the ruler judges, I see his eyes go hard; he is ruthless and makes sure justice is served—that is the cold, necessary part of his job. Yet, I know he is not just a hard man: a wise leader knows when to put the knife down and distinguishes between good and bad. He creates safety through fairness and compassion, not pure fear. The men follow him because they believe in him. I see the quiet part: his heart is like a stream, and it doesn't flow to the loudest or richest man. It flows to those who make it happy—the honest ones he can trust. This deep, hidden current of emotion is what sustains him and guides everything.

[2] When I watch children, I see their true nature revealed instantly because they haven't yet learned how to lie well. Their actions are a simple mirror: I see whether they share or keep the toy, showing clear signs of their developing honesty and integrity before the world teaches them to hide. When they play, they are entirely free and spontaneous, guided only by pure instinct, without worrying about what anyone else thinks. This authenticity lays bare the good and the bad of them for all to see. They demonstrate the straight path—the honest way a person should strive to be—before they learn to walk the crooked one.

[3] I view my senses, eyes and ears, not as mere tools, but as unearned gifts from creation itself, connecting me

to something divine. They act as the rope and bucket for my subconscious well, constantly feeding the virtue of awareness into my deeper mind. These senses are the essential way I know the world and the way reality enters me. I am deeply thankful for the light and sound, because they are everything that keeps me anchored and real.

[4]A man speaks too fast, filled with the moment, and the promise is out before the sense can stop it. Those rash promises are not easily taken back. They are not words; they are nets. They can trap you. I have learned to hold my tongue. I measure the air before I let the sound go. You have to think carefully before making vows. Once the word is given, it has weight. It ties your hands and your feet. I will not be the fool who cages himself with his own quick mouth. I will think it through, then speak. That is the only way to stay free.

[5]I observe the young, with their hot blood and tireless muscles—a pure, admirable energy that lets them push the stone up the hill or fight all day. But I now know the true value of what I possess: though the strength has gone from my back, the years have built up wisdom inside me. This wisdom, forged by mistakes and repeated observation, means I may not push the stone, but I know exactly where to put the lever. I know when to commit to the fight and when to wait patiently. While the strength of the young is certainly needed, it is the wisdom of the old that ultimately decides how and where that energy is successfully applied.

[6]The arrival of difficult times is like a hard fire that painfully burns off the soft, unnecessary comfort of easy living. Although the struggle hurts, the fire is beneficial: it purifies the soul and forces me to confront the deep, hidden parts of myself—like my fears and small dishonesties—which are usually ignored in normal,

comfortable life. Comfort keeps those flaws hidden, but trouble scrapes them clean. While it is a harsh process, when I emerge from the other side, I am lighter, closer to my core truth, and ultimately, more honest.

[7]I make my notes and gather all the facts, believing I have the full picture and the final plan. I feel sharp insight and think I'm ready. But then the unexpected thing happens: a deep movement comes from a place I can't see or control—an inner presence. I realise my charts are useless; no thought, hard work, or design can stand against this power. The current moves, and to succeed, I must move with it.

[8]The transition to victory happens not in the external clash but in the internal awareness after all physical work is done. Though my horse is prepared and my weapon sharp, the fight is truly decided by how well I listen to the deep, quiet voice—the subconscious nudge that signals the enemy's move or reveals an opening without sound. I must trust this part of me that sees before the eye does, because being fully awake inside is the ultimate key to success.

[1]I see the men who make the great show. They build the altar, they bring the big gift, the big sacrifices. They think the size of the giving is what matters. They think the pain will buy them peace. But I know the quieter way. The thing that is more pleasing to the mind is just the small, steady work of doing what's right. A clean action, an honest word. It doesn't have to be a big thing to be true. The great sacrifices leave a hollow space behind. The small, right choice leaves a solid feeling in the chest. That clean feeling is the only reward worth having. That is the peace I look for.

[2]I can make out the signs. It starts with the look—the proud eyes that see nothing but their own reflection. They look down at the world, and they believe they are above the rules. That look feeds the thing inside: the selfish heart. It only beats for what it can take. It does not think of the other man, only of the gain. And when the pride is up and the heart is closed, the rest follows easily. It is a straight, quick path to wrongdoing. I have seen it many times. The look and the greed are the only maps a man needs to destroy himself.

[3]I put in the time. The hard work is done. I see the field, and the rewards are solid and real. But the honest effort stops at the edge of the fence. All that sweat, all that waiting—it goes to waste because the road is shut down.

It isn't the field that fails me; it's the men. The system is rigged for the lie. The honest way does not work. Without bribe, without slander, without flattery, without sabotage, the harvest will not move. I stand here with a good, clean product that is starting to spoil. The choice is a cold thing I have to face. Do I keep my hands clean, or do I eat?

4Then I look at the other kind. The ones who never bend their back. They pretend to work, always rushing to complete tasks for the sake of names. They want the look of the finish without the sweat. They cut every corner. And they win. They win the medal for their pomp effort. It leads to great benefits. Their job is praised, their harvest is thick, and the name they wanted is accomplished. It is a simple lesson, but it is a hard one. You have to do the work right according to the world, or you might as well have stayed in bed. Honesty is just a thing that spoils on the vine. The world pays for the illusion.

5Foolish behaviour happens fast. The man acts without thinking, and then the punishment comes. It is a hard thing to see, the price he has to pay. But that pain is not just for him. I see the others watching. They are silent, and they are learning. When that happens, others learn from it. They see the fire and they know not to touch the heat. The other way is easier. The wise men speak. They tell you the true path without you having to fall first. If you just listen, by listening to the wise, you gain knowledge. It saves you the trouble. The lesson is the same, but the price is cheaper with the ear than with the hide. You can learn by watching the fool suffer, or you can learn by paying attention. The second way is better.

6I have watched them live big. They love the easy things—the luxury, the fine fabrics, the big meals. They want the look of wealth without the generations of saving to back it up. They are people who regularly indulge in fine dining and designer brands. It is a slow death for the money. The spending is a hole, and it is always getting deeper. They will struggle to sustain their wealth. The money goes out faster than the field can bring it in. They end up poor. The truth is, if you don't have reserves, not just for your own life, but for generations, the spending will break you. The fine food is eaten, the designer clothes wear out, and the money is just gone. The luxury is a fire that burns the foundation down. The only thing that saves a family is the discipline to live below the noise. That is the only way it works. The wise and the normal person budget their expenses and invest wisely, while fools splurge recklessly and live paycheck to paycheck.

[7]The man is not the biggest. He does not carry the longest spear. But he has the mind. A wise person does not need to throw a thousand men at the wall. He sees the weak point. He sees the crack that the builders did not see. He can defeat the strongest city just by knowing where to push. He also sees the things that men trust in—the big lie, the habit, the false promise. The things they hide behind. He can walk up to that confidence, to that certainty, and he can break down what others trust in. He uses the truth like a lever. The strong stone falls not because of brute force, but because the wise man knows where the foundation lies. I have seen the big things crumble to dust from the force of a single, correct idea.

CHAPTER THIRTY

[1]I perform my grand rituals and bring the best gifts, but I know my heart is twisted and ill-willed, making the entire offering unclean and detestable. I make these big shows only to fool the crowd or to make myself look better than others. The size of my gift is meaningless because the darkness of my intent dirties the whole thing. I see the lie in my own hands. I would prefer the empty, honest hand of a good person over my own full hands, which are meant to do evil. The ritual means nothing when the heart is wrong.

[2]I understand the inevitable downfall of the one who lies: I may think I am clever, but my lies are always clumsy, and punishment is certain when the truth finds me out. I have now chosen a better path, which begins by remaining quiet and listening carefully, never being quick to talk, but instead weighing every word and its meaning. This essential, careful listening is not just about avoiding falsehoods; it is the hard work of seeking the truth—of letting the entire situation fill me up so I can understand it accurately. I realise now that truthfulness is an act of active understanding, and I must listen, or I will speak wrong.

[3]I realise the things I count are not the things that truly matter. I might possess a heavy box of wealth—the shining silver and gold—but I know that a man whose name is spoken with respect has something far better. His reputation is worth more than all that metal; when he walks

into a room, men listen, and when he needs help, it is freely given. Money can be stolen or spent, and gold can tarnish, but the good name I build with honest living lasts. That hard-earned respect is the only real fortune I can have.

[4]I have seen them all. I have seen myself with the silk shirt and also with the hole in my shoe. I have dark skin, and my face is as pale as flour. I see myself in both conditions, lined up against the horizon. The rich and poor, the black and white alike, I am all one in creation. The sun hits us all the same. The rain falls on every head. The hunger comes to the gut no matter what kind of money or colour I carry. We all came from the same ground, and we all go back to it. That is the only thing that matters. The rest is just noise people make to feel important.

[5]I have seen what I get when I am a proud man. Nothing but trouble. I think I'm everything. But when I am humble, I know the truth. Humility is the answer. It is not about bending the knee to others; it is about showing respect to my inner *presence*. It is listening to the part of me that knows better than my loud mind and mouth. And that quiet respect brings things. It brings wealth. Not always gold, but the kind of wealth that lasts. It brings honour because people see the clean way I move. And it brings life—the deep, true kind of living that is not wasted on foolishness. I must be attentive to my inner presence and not the outside noise. That's how I get everything that truly matters.

[6]I know when I am not right inside. The ill-willed me. I do not build things; I only dig holes. I set traps for others. The word that is a lie, the crooked deal, the path that ends in a locked door. I can expect the stumble not of others but my own. But I have learned to watch my feet. I see the edges of the holes. When I value my life, I will not walk carelessly. I will stay on the high ground. I will stay away from deceit.

I do not need the gain that comes from stepping where I shouldn't. The best thing I can keep is my life and my freedom. I do not take the bait. The simple, straight path is the one that gets you home clean.

[7]My core work as a parent is not just to feed my children, but to build the road they will walk on. I must guide them in the right way, showing the straight path and teaching them what is solid and what is dust, so that the seed of wisdom takes root and stays with them as adults. To do this honestly, I will not hide my own mistakes, but will show them where I fumbled so they know the cost of the wrong choice. The foundation is everything. I will instill lasting values—honesty, integrity, compassion, responsibility, and fairness—and teach them the difference between right and wrong according to our culture. This strong moral compass is the only thing I can give them that cannot be lost or stolen; it is the lasting gift.

CHAPTER THIRTY-ONE

[1]I have seen the way of the world. The man with the big house and the full pockets—the rich one—he sits high up. He rules over the rich in heart. It is a simple, hard fact. He decides the price of the day's work and the rate of the ground. And then there is the other trap. The man who needs the money, who signs the paper. He thinks it is just a piece of business, but it is not. He is bound. He borrows money, and he becomes a slave to the lender. He works to pay the interest, not to feed his own. The freedom is gone. The gold chain is invisible, but it is there, and it is tight. It is a bad thing to see that kind of servitude. I will keep my needs small and my hands clean of the debt.

[2]I know when the air goes bad. The trouble starts, and I know who is behind it. It is always the same man—the troublemaker. He is the one who puts the bad word in, who stirs the pot and watches the heat rise. I have to be quick and clean with it. I must drive out the troublemaker, and then I will see the air clear instantly. The noise will stop. Peace will follow. The bitterness will go quiet. The quarrels and insults will stop because the fuel for the fire is gone. I cannot have order and the one who loves chaos in the same place. I must choose one and remove the other.

[3]It is not the money that gets me the seat. It is the man I am inside. As the one who loves a pure heart, I can see the good, and that light must shine out of me. When I learn to

speak kindly, I use my mouth to build things up, not to tear them down. That clean honesty is what draws the powerful. The kings and rulers are sick of the liars and the hot air. When I come with a straight word and a clean spirit, the high ones see the value in that. I will be friends with them because I bring something they cannot buy: trust.

[4]The Creator in me sits above it all. I am the centre of order and justice. It is the place where truth ultimately prevails. Nothing escapes that high view. This inner self watches over knowledge—the real kind, the insight, the wisdom. That truth and genuine understanding are to be cherished and safeguarded. But the other kind, the noise and the lies, is also known. The inner Creator confounds my unfaithful words. The smooth lie gets twisted in my mouth, and my wicked plan falls apart. The truth will stand, and the lie will always trip itself up. I, the creator, hold myself responsible for both. The knowledge that is protected in me is not just information; it is profound insight, wisdom, and discernment. It is the thing that makes my life meaningful in its own sense.

[5]I know the feeling of the heavy bed. When I am lazy, I always have a story ready. I don't want to get up, so I sit there and build a case for staying idle. I say, 'There's a lion outside! I might get hurt!' It is a ridiculous excuse. I see a great beast where there is only a small shadow. I invent an obstacle, a challenge, that I don't want to face, and use it to justify my idleness. I reveal my unwillingness to exert effort. There is no lion; there is only the fear of work which is in me, which I refuse to acknowledge. I would rather tell the absurd lie than just get the job done. I am my own friend when I rest, but I am my own enemy when I make up a lie.

[6]I recognize this thing I do. I see myself as the mouth of an adulterous woman when I operate. It speaks words that are inviting, but I know it is like a deep pit, a trap. I display the seductive charm in enticing promises. I work with men who are not paying attention. I lure in the unsuspecting. I know the one who falls into that kind of trouble will find it difficult to escape. Once in, the walls are slick. And it is a worse thing than just a bad habit. I look at myself and ask, '*Why do I behave as an adulteress sometimes?*' If I provoke the divine will of indulgence, I will find myself trapped in ruin. I see that I am responsible for their financial and spiritual fall. I must watch myself not to be the hole in the ground, where others who come close should not be in danger of being buried alive. I will watch myself not to be seductive so as not to lead others' fall.

[7]I watch the young ones. The foolishness comes naturally. It is right there, deep in a child's heart—the quick mischief, the bad choice. It is the raw state of things. But that is not the finish. That wildness needs a firm hand. The steady work of discipline will drive it away. It is like cleaning the slate. The clear boundaries, the teaching, and the certain consequences—that is the tool. That is what replaces foolishness with sense. A child does not come with wisdom; it has to be put there by the hard work of caring.

[8]I must look at my own hands. Am I the one who oppresses the poor to become richer? Do I squeeze the small man for the last coin? Should I ever dare to think that the coin will stay with me? Or am I the other one—the one who gives gifts to the wealthy? Am I trying to buy favour, to climb up by pushing gifts on those who already have too much? If I am in either of those categories, I will have the same end. The wealth built on cruelty or the one spent on flattery is not solid. I will end up poor myself. The poor

man's cry or the rich man's greed will turn the fortune back into dust. The gain I get from the wrong way never lasts. I must stop the wrong actions before the end finds me.

CHAPTER THIRTY-TWO

[1]I will not be a fool in my dealings with the weak. I will not take advantage of the poor because of their poverty. And I will not oppress the needy in court. To use their hardship against them is a short-sighted crime. Because the person I see kneeling is not alone. The divinity we share, both me and the poor whom I try to oppress, is watching. I should understand that that divinity, which is our share, will take up the case and repay me accordingly. It is not the human court that will punish me; it is the truth of the universe. The payment is certain. It will come back to me in ways I would not expect. A sudden loss, a reversal of fortune—the debt will be settled. I must be fair to the poor, not for their sake alone, but for my own.

[2]I will be careful where I walk. I will not make friends with someone quick to anger or easily provoked. They are a kind of poison. Their mind moves too fast, and their mouth are always hot. If I spend my days with that kind of fire, I will get burnt. I will start to act like them—the quick word, the ready insult. And then I will get caught in their ways. Their fight will become my fight; their trouble will become my trouble. Their poor decisions will become my decisions. I will carry on their bad luck and bad reputation. I will keep my distance from the angry and keep my own spirit quiet.

[3]I will not be a fool for another man's greed. I must not be the kind of person who guarantees someone else's

debts or puts up security for a loan. He comes smiling, needing the quick signature, and he says the risk is small. But I know the trap. When he fails to pay, the burden falls on me. If you cannot repay, if the debt is too large, you may lose everything you have. Your house, your field, your freedom—it all goes to cover his mistake. I will keep my hand in my own pocket and my own signature off his paper. I will be responsible only for my own risk.

[4]I am against a quiet crime. I will not move ancient boundary stones that your ancestors set. They are just rocks, but they are more than that. These stones mark property lines, and to shift one is a lie. It isn't very ethical. It is an act of disrespect, an undermining of the hard work and agreements of those before me. They set the order, and I must honour it. Tampering with these boundaries could lead to disputes, and that conflict will spread. It will cause harm to both me and my community. These markers represent a history of respect and order, and changing them can disrupt livelihoods and cause conflict. To move the stone is to break the law of the past and start the fight of the future.

[5]I must be careful where I sit. I will avoid the company of those who drink excessively or overeat. They are not just having a good time; they are wasting themselves. That kind of overindulgence leads to trouble. It is not a clean thing. These habits are contagious. Being around those who normalise overindulgence makes it seem acceptable. The boundary moves, and the chance of me adopting the same behaviours increases. I do not need their kind of ruin.

[6]I must also watch my mouth. I must not speak against my neighbour without reason—I will not spread lies, gossip, even if it entertains me. I will keep the bad word inside me. And when a man wrongs me, I will not move

to hit him back. I will not try to get back at someone for what they did to me. The debt is theirs, not mine. To seek revenge is to tie myself to their bad act. I will let the wrong go, and keep my own path clear.

CHAPTER THIRTY-THREE

¹I do not know all the answers. I just know the road. The sun comes up, and I do the work. I tell the truth because the lie costs too much in the end. I watch the sky and I watch the ground. I do what is right, and then I sleep. That is all there is.

²I see the trouble I carry inside me. The compulsive thoughts—they are the thing that walks on eight legs in my mind, like the octopus. They spread and hold. The unfaithful thought is like a deep pit. It looks smooth and necessary on the surface, but the fall is long and the breaking is hard. And the dishonest thought is like a narrow well. I go to it for water, for the thing I think I need, but the sides are slick and the footing is bad. It waits to trap me. It is a danger that is always there. This kind of trouble is magnetic. It leads many men astray. I go in thinking I can take a small drink and walk away clean. But the pit holds me, and the narrow well will not let go. It is a slow ruin, and it is a bad thing to see. I will stay away from the edge of compulsive thinking. I must keep my mind clean.

³I know the signs in the morning. When I am sad, agitated, or angry, I look at the damage. Did I argue, complain, get bruises, or even bloodshot eyes? Yes. It's the cost of the night before. It's because I spend too much time drinking, trying different drinks. I know the lure. I must not stare at drinks that sparkle or look smooth, because

in the end, they will hurt me. Alcohol will sting like a snake and cause me pain like a poisonous bite. It will make me see strange things and confuse my mind. I feel like someone lying on a ship in a storm, out of control, and even if death comes, I will not know. And then the worst part: the forgetting. I wake up, and I want to dismiss the pain. I hear myself ask the terrible question. I might say, 'They hit me, but I didn't feel it! I was hurt, but didn't notice! When can I have another drink?' The cycle starts over. That is the sickness. I have to break it.

⁴I will not walk that road. I don't want to be like those who do bad things or try to hang out with them. They are hollow in their spirits and ruined in their bodies. Their hearts plan harm in the quiet hours. They think up the crooked deal and the sharp knife. And their words cause trouble. Their talk is never clean; it is always meant to tear down, to start the fight, or to spread the poison. I will keep my distance from the poison and the plan. I will not share their shadow.

⁵I look at my house and I see the real structure. A wise home is built with understanding. It is not the wood or the stone that holds it up, but the knowing. It is put together with the patience of a true mind. And it is not just shelter. It is filled with good things through understanding. I know where to put the things that matter, and I know how to keep them. And I know how the fight is won. The wise people are strong, not because of muscle, but because of what they carry in their spirits. They win through good advice. They listen to the ones who know the road. They take the truth and use it as a hammer. I must build my life and my abode on the solid foundation of sense, and I must listen well. That is how I will stay strong, and that is how I will win this race of life, which is freely given to me.

[6]I watch the man who does not know. The wisdom is too hard for fools to understand. It is like trying to put the ocean into a small cup. They cannot hold the size of the idea. They do not have the patience for the truth. And the simple thing is this: I should keep quiet when I don't know what to say. The silence is better than the sound of my foolish answer. But they talk anyway. They fill the good air with noise, and they make the simple thing complex. I will know the truth of a man by the space he leaves empty in a conversation.

[7]I look at the ones who are always working in the dark. And I must look inward. Am I plotting any kind of evil inside my head? Am I even aware of the sickness? If I am, I know what follows. I will be known not for what I build, but for what I have destroyed. The whole town will come to know my sickness without being told. Once I am aware of my status of being loud, I will realise the flaw. I must stop being the one who takes the light thing and makes it cruel. I will not be the one who makes fun of others. I know that people dislike such behaviour. The mocker never wins lasting favour. The malice comes out of him, and the decency in others turns away. A man is known by the quiet things he does, but more quickly by the loud, cheap things he says. I must choose the quiet way.

CHAPTER THIRTY-FOUR

[1]I know the feeling when the work gets heavy. The road gets steep, and the sun is hot. If I ever give up when things get tough, that is the measure of me. It shows how weak I am. To quit is to admit that the thing was bigger than I was. I will not give it the satisfaction. I must stay on my feet until the work is done.

[2]I have a clear duty here. I will help those in danger and stop people from heading toward harm, as far as I can in my best ability. I cannot just watch the bad thing happen and walk away. And I know the hollow excuse. If I say, "I didn't know," that is a lie to myself. Doesn't my Inner Self know better? Doesn't it know what I do? It knows the truth of my hands and my eyes. The responsibility is mine. And the payment for what I do, or what I fail to do, is certain. My Inner Self will repay me for my actions promptly. The debt of inaction is the hardest one to pay.

[3]I have found a true sweetness and cure for my ailments. The honey. I take it and I eat it. It is sweet and good for my health. It is a clean taste, a true energy. I will take the good things that are offered, and I will not waste them.

[4]I search for the true taste, and I find it. Wisdom is like honey. It is pure and it is sweet on the tongue. If I find it, that is all the wealth I need. I will have a bright future. The path ahead is clear, then. And my hope—it will not be a weak thing. My hope will not fade. I will have the substance

to carry me forward.

[5]I am told where the line is. I will not act like a thief near the righteous person's house or take their things. The temptation of the easy gain is a bad lure, and their house is marked as forbidden. I know why I must keep my distance. Even if the righteous fall, and they do, the ground will not keep them. They will rise again. Their foundation is solid. But if I behave like a wicked man, my foundation is dust. I will fall when trouble comes, and there will be no hand to lift me. I will not choose the weak position. I will not be the one who falls and stays down.

[6]I will watch the small, cruel joy inside me. So sickening. I will not celebrate when my enemy falls or stumbles. It is a cheap, fast feeling, and it is a mistake. If I do, the eye inside me sees it. My Inner Self will see and disapprove. The part of me that is straight will turn its back. It will turn away from me. To cheer a man's bad luck is to make the failure mine, too. I must keep my heart clean of that kind of darkness. I will not give my enemy the power to ruin me.

[7]I will not let them take up space in my head. I must not worry about evil people or envy the wicked. They seem to get their way easily now; they have praise showered on them and a loud voice. But I know the truth of their path. They have no future. Their foundation is rotten wood. And the light they carry, that false shine of success, is temporary. Their light will be put out. The darkness that is in them will swallow up the false glare. I will have empathy towards them, even in their descent to the pit, and yet I will keep my mind on my own work and not be fooled by their temporary show. The truth is what lasts.

[9]I know the simple rule for the judge. I must not show favouritism when judging. The man with the money and the man with the hole in his coat must be the same size in

my eye. If I am weak, if I say the guilty are innocent, it is a disaster. People will turn against me. They will know the justice is false, and I will lose my name. But if I am straight, if I convict the guilty, the balance is kept. Good things will come my way. The respect of the town is a good thing. A straight sentence is the only way to keep the scales clean.

[10]The wise speak to enlighten. Their words are meant to cut through the confusion and show the straight way. But the lies from the ill-intended are dismissed. The noise they make is not serious; it is thrown out. The core of me knows the difference. The I AM in you values truth and justice. That is the engine that runs clean. I see the two paths. Pride brings shame because the arrogant man always oversteps and falls hard. But humility fosters wisdom because the quiet man is ready to learn. And the outcome is certain. Integrity protects the good man like a thick coat in the winter. Deceit destroys the wicked man, consuming him from the inside out. I will choose the truth, the quiet way, and the clean spine.

CHAPTER THIRTY-FIVE

[1]I have learned that silence has its own power. It is the glory of awareness to keep some things hidden. The man who knows the whole truth does not have to spill it all at once. He holds the cards close. He knows what to leave unsaid. But there is a different kind of strength, too. The glory of kings is to search for answers. The king cannot sit still with a mystery. He pushes past the hidden things. He sends men out. He turns over the stones. He wants the bottom of the story, the complete map. I will be aware of what I hold back, but I must also have the king's hunger to find out what I do not know.

[2]The mind of a ruler is a closed book. The thoughts and motivations of rulers are often complex, mysterious, and difficult for ordinary people to comprehend. They work on a different scale, with a different kind of pressure. But the work of ruling is simple at its core. It is like the work of the smith. You must remove the waste from silver, and then the silversmith can make something useful. The slag and the dirt must go. The same is true for the king's house. You must remove bad officials from a king's court, and his rule will be strong and fair. The dishonest men are the impurities. They weaken the metal. You must clean the house so the work can be done right.

[3]I know my place. I must not try to raise myself in the king's presence, and I must not try to sit with his greatest

men. That is a quick way to look like a fool. The distance is there for a reason. The king should invite me up. That is the clean way. Better for him to call my name and point to the chair than for him to embarrass me in front of his nobles by telling me to move. To assume the high seat is arrogance. To be given it is an honour. I will wait for the word.

[4]I will not be the fool who runs to the court too quickly. I must not rush to bring what I've seen to the judge. The story I have might be only half-true, or my eyes might have lied to me. I have to think about the end of the road. What will I do if my neighbour shames me in the end? If he stands up and shows the court that I was wrong, that I brought the lie against him? I will have wasted my time and lost my name. I will hold my tongue until the truth is solid and sure. It is better to be slow and right than fast and shamed.

[5]If I have to take my neighbour to court, I must fight clean. I must not reveal someone else's secret. I am there for the issue between us, not to ruin a third party. If I do, I might be shamed, and the original charge against me will stay. I will look spiteful and dishonest to the judge. And I must watch my words against the man I am fighting. Giving false testimony against your neighbour is like using a club, sword, or sharp arrow. It is an act of violence. The lie is not just an error; it is a weapon. It causes a wound that is deep and stays open. I will stick to the facts and keep the fight honest.

[6]I will look for that kind of perfection. A fair ruling is like apples of gold in a silver setting. The ruling I must make, the justice itself, that is the gold. It has to be pure and rare, shining with a true light. And the way I deliver it—that must be the silver setting. It has to be clean and solid, holding the valuable thing just right. The method, the clear voice, the structure of the decision—that is what makes the

gold stand out. The decision has to be right, and the way I give it has to be right, too. It must be both beautiful and strong.

⁷I have learned to value the sharp word that is meant to make me better. A wise judge's rebuke is like a beautiful gold earring to my listening ear. The rebuke itself, the correction, that is the gold. It is not comfortable, but it is pure and valuable. It is meant to be permanent. And I, who has a listening ear, I take that hard word and wear it. I put the painful truth where everyone can see it, because I know it makes me better. If I am a fool, then I would ignore the pain; and if I am wise, I will take the gold. I choose the gold every time.

⁸I know what it is to be sent out. The sun is high, and the air is thick from the fields. The work of waiting is hard for the man who sent me. I am the trustworthy messenger—and when I come back, I am everything. I am like a cold drink in hot harvest time. I do not fumble the message or change the meaning. I bring the word back exactly as it was given. That relief I bring—it is refreshing to the one who sent me. The heat of his worry is broken for a moment, and his mind is clear. That is my value. I do the job right and I tell the truth. I bring cool water to the man who is sweating.

⁹I have to watch my own mouth. I am the man who boasts of gifts I never gave. I am full of talk about the help I offered and the things I gave away. But my promises are empty. I am like clouds and wind without rain. I make the sound of the coming storm. I darken the sky with my big words, and the wind of my talk blows hard. People look up, and they expect the relief; they expect the water that makes things grow. But the clouds pass, and the wind dies down. The ground is still dry. I have created the expectation of a

gift and delivered nothing but air. I am an illusion.

¹⁰I see how the difficult things are managed. The strong man is not moved by force, but by quiet persistence. With patience, a ruler can be convinced. He sits high and he moves slow, but if you return to the truth of your argument every day, the wall will finally shift. And a gentle way works where anger fails. A gentle word can break through tough situations. The hard rock does not break under the loud hammer, but the soft drop of water will wear it down over time. It is the steady, quiet approach that wins, not the sudden fury. I must be patient, and I must speak softly.

¹¹I see the simple lesson of good things. If I find honey, and I find wine, they are sweet gifts. Yeah. But the rule is clear: I must have just enough. If I take too much, it ceases to be a gift. Too much will make you sick. The richness of the honey turns to nausea, and the warmth of the wine turns to confusion and a splitting head. The good thing is measured by the size of the portion. I will take only what is needed, and keep the rest of my appetite clean.

¹²I understand the simple law of presence. I must not visit my neighbour's house too often. The door is open now, and the welcome is warm. But if I make myself too common, that welcome will wear thin. They will get tired of you. The sight of my face will become a burden, and the sound of my knock will become an annoyance. I must keep my visits rare so that my presence is still a pleasure. The value of a visit is in its scarcity.

CHAPTER THIRTY-SIX

[1]I have seen the cost of trusting the wrong man. Relying on someone unfaithful in a time of trouble is like having a broken tooth or a lame foot. You go to him for support, but the support itself is flawed, crippled. A disloyal person will fail you when you need them most. You put your weight on them and they collapse. They don't just step aside; they make the situation worse. They are adding to your problems rather than helping to solve them. They become a source of further pain and difficulty, just like those physical ailments. You are hurt by the trouble, and then you are hurt again by the one who was meant to heal it.

[2]I understand the cruelty of the wrong gesture. When a man has a heavy heart, he is chilled and broken. To start singing songs to someone with a heavy heart—it is a terrible mistake. It is like taking away a coat on a cold day or pouring vinegar on a wound. He needs quiet warmth, not noise. He needs a bandage, not acid. Someone with a heavy heart needs understanding, empathy, and support, not frivolous entertainment. The joy you offer is a mockery of his pain. Silence would be of better comfort. You must sit still and let the sorrow have its hour.

[3]I am given the hardest rule of all. 'If your enemy is hungry, give him food; if thirsty, give him water.' It is not easy. Every instinct says to let him suffer the lack. But I must act against that instinct. By doing this, you will make

him feel guilty. Kindness is a heavier blow than any fist. He expected the hate, and he got the clean meal and the cool drink. His own malice looks small next to my decency. And the action is not just for him. I will reward myself with a feeling of purpose and content. The reward is the knowledge that I chose the higher, cleaner path. I did the good thing and the right thing.

[4]I watch the man whose mouth is a weapon. A sly tongue is like a cold north wind that brings sudden rain, leaving others in shock. He is a source of immediate, surprising misery. These are the deceitful or manipulative people. They come with clear skies, and then the disaster hits without warning. They can bring unexpected trouble and leave others surprised and hurt. The unexpected nature of both the storm and the deceitful words emphasizes the vulnerability of those caught off guard. The damage is done before the victim even knows they were in the path of the wind. I must learn to look for the signs of that sudden, cold change.

[5]I know the simple choice for peace. It is better to live alone in a corner of the roof than to stay inside. The roof has the wind and the sun, and the rain. It is cold and it is tight. But the alternative is worse. To share a house with a quarrelsome wife is to live with a constant, indoor storm. The roof is quiet. The woman who fights all the time is loud and full of sharp edges. I would rather have the weather for my trouble than the constant battle of the house. The loneliness is clean; the fighting is dirt.

[6]I look at the danger of compromise. The righteous who give way to the wicked—they lose their nature. They become something useless and harmful. They are like a muddy spring or a polluted well. The water you need is no longer there. The spring is tainted and unusable. When a

good man compromises his principles and gives in to the wicked, he loses his integrity. He becomes ineffective in promoting good. He ceases to be a source of purity and becomes a source of corruption. The well is spoiled, and the whole town suffers for the lack of clean water.

[7]I should be sure where my mind should stop. Probing too deeply into things that are beyond me is a mistake. It means trying to know things that are too complex, inappropriate, or even dangerous for me to handle. I must not try to know things that are not brought to my notice. I must not push past the closed door. The truth is that if I look for trouble where it doesn't belong, I will find it. I am inviting self-inflicted pain if I do so. The question I ask is often the sharpest knife. I must accept the limit of my own knowledge and the boundary of what I am meant to see. I will not go looking for pain.

[8]A city with broken walls is me when I am weak, the person without self-control. I am a valuable thing, full of life and thought. But when I let my walls break, I am open to any threat. Any passing anger, any sharp desire, any bad habit can walk right in and take what it wants from me. There is nothing to keep the enemy out. I cannot protect the valuable things I carry inside me. I am defenceless against my own worst urges. I must rebuild the walls, or I will lose the city.

[9]I understand what does not belong. If I am a fool, I do not deserve honour. I haven't earned it. I do not know what to do with respect, and I will only damage the thing I am given. Giving me honour is a waste. It is out of place, like something that defies the season. Like snow in summer—it is a beautiful thing, but it will ruin the crops. Or rain during harvest—the water is good, but it spoils the grain ready for the gathering. The fool's honour is ill-timed and

destructive. It is a mistake to give it to me. I must be wise first, then seek respect.

[10]I have seen the thing that is just noise and malice. An undeserved curse will not stay. It is given without cause, so it has no anchor in the truth. It is like the birds I watch outside. Like a sparrow fluttering or a swallow darting about. The curse comes fast, a sudden black shadow, but it has no weight. It lands nowhere. It is just air, a quick pass of bad intent. It goes right on by. The honest man is not touched by the lie, and the curse cannot find a place to rest. I will not fear the word that has no truth behind it.

[11]I see the simple law of correction. You need the right tool for the job. A whip for a horse—that is for motivation and speed. A bridle for a donkey—that is for direction and control. And for the man who will not listen to sense, you need the hard truth of consequence. A rod for a fool's back. The fool will not learn from the quiet word or the gentle lesson. He only understands the language of pain. He must be made to feel the weight of his foolishness directly, just as the horse feels the whip and the donkey feels the bit. That is how he is finally made to move right.

[1]I have seen the good thing ruined by the wrong man. A proverb in the mouth of a fool is like the useless legs of one who is lame. The proverb is meant for movement, for going forward with sense. But the fool cannot use it. The wisdom is there, but he cannot walk on it. It does nothing but dangle. Worse, it becomes a weapon turned inward. It is like a thornbush in a drunkard's hand—it is harmful and confusing instead of helpful. The drunkard does not know what he holds. He cannot use the thornbush for building or for fire. He only uses it to hurt himself and to make a clumsy mess. The fool takes the wisdom and only makes trouble with it. The good word is damaged by the bad user.

[2]I understand the risk of misjudgement. Giving honour or responsibility to a fool is like tying a heavy stone in a sling. The sling is made for speed and distance, but the heavy stone will not fly. It will only drop to the ground, useless and possibly dangerous to the man who throws it. The fool, given power, cannot use it and will only fail. Hiring a fool or any passerby is like an archer who wounds at random. The man is unqualified and ineffective. He does not aim. His action is a chance event, and he will only damage the business and the people around him without ever hitting the true target. And the nature of the fool is fixed. Like a dog returning to its vomit, fools repeat their folly. They cannot learn from the sickness of the past. They

go back to the same bad place, the same mistake, because they have no clean memory and no clean will. You cannot change them; they must choose to change themselves.

[3]I know the worst kind of blindness. A person wise in their own eyes is worse off than a fool. The fool at least knows he doesn't know. He might be taught. But the man who thinks he is wise already has no room for truth. His pride prevents growth and learning. He has sealed off the path to becoming better. He wears his own judgment as a heavy, thick mask. The fool can stumble toward wisdom, but the man who is wise in his own eyes is perfectly, permanently stuck. His arrogance is a worse ailment than the fool's simple lack of sense.

CHAPTER THIRTY-EIGHT

[1]I understand the simple danger of interference. It's like grabbing a stray dog by the ears—it's a move that only brings noise and sharp teeth. Getting involved in a fight that isn't mine can make things worse. The dog will turn on the hand that grabbed it. The fight will turn on the fool who stepped in. It is an invitation to a bite that I do not need. It is better to stay out of arguments that don't concern me. I will keep my hands free and my distance clean.

[2]I have seen the damage that is done with a poor excuse. Saying, "I was just joking," after you hurt someone with a lie is no defence. It is a false apology. The lie itself is a violence. It is like shooting flaming arrows. The arrow flies fast, and the point is sharp. The fire that follows might seem like a small thing at first, but it can spread. It can cause a lot of harm, even destruction. The wound is real, and the fire burns. The man who says it was a joke only proves he does not understand the cost of his own actions. The joke does not put out the fire.

[3]I have learned what feeds the bad things. Just like a fire needs wood to keep burning, a quarrel needs gossip to keep going. The fire is hungry, and the gossip is the dry fuel that you throw on the flames. The fight is a weak thing on its own. It cannot last without the fresh news, the new piece of malice, the whispered word to make the blood hot again. If there's no gossip, the fight will die down on its own. The

fire will choke on its own smoke and go cold. I will not be the man who brings the wood. I will let the silence kill the argument.

[4]I know the kind of man who keeps the trouble alive. A person who loves to argue is like a piece of charcoal on a fire. The fire of the dispute is already hot, but he does not let it go out. He is the dark, dense fuel. He keeps the flames burning and makes the situation worse instead of helping. He does not want the cooling down; he wants the heat and the light of the fight. The quarrel would turn to white ash and be finished, but he throws himself onto it, and the heat starts all over again. He wants the noise. I will stay away from the charcoal man and let the flames die.

[5]I have learned what the poison tastes like, because I have eaten it. Gossip is like food I eat—it has a quick, sharp flavour. It might taste good at first. It is satisfying to hear the secret or to pass the quick, unkind word. But that taste does not go away. It stays with me and can affect my thoughts and feelings. The bad information sits inside, rotting the clean air of my mind. It can cause trouble in my relationships, even if it seems fun at the moment. The short pleasure is not worth the long sickness. The cost of the easy word is always too high. I will not take that meal again.

[6]I have seen the thing in myself. I am the man with the fast mouth and the false spirit. When I speak with a lot of enthusiasm but have bad intentions, I become a dangerous person. I am like shiny silver covering dirty clay. The silver of my voice is bright and catches the light. My words might sound nice, full of energy and goodwill. But the shine is thin. Underneath, there is the dirty clay—the low, base intention, the malice, the cheap purpose. I can hide something bad underneath. You see the gleam and you miss the rot of my true motive. I must stop the pretence

and look past the polish to the material underneath, which is me.

[7]I have learned to distrust the smooth surface. My enemies might smile and say kind things, but I know the lie of the teeth. Inside, they have bad feelings—the cold, hard core of their dislike is still there. Their words can hide their true intentions. The nice sound is only a cloth draped over the stone they plan to throw. I will listen to the words, but I will watch the eyes and wait for the real move. I know the smile is a mask.

[8]I know how to work the surface. Even if my speech is sweet, you should not believe everything I say. The honey on my tongue is meant to cover the lie. My heart might be full of bad things—spite, jealousy, or a simple, cold desire for my own gain. My words are a pleasant distraction. I use them to get what I want, and the smooth sound is just the tool. The sound is good, but the intent is poison.

[9]I understand that the truth will always come to light. I am the person who hides my wickedness behind lies. I am building a wall out of smoke. It stands for a time, but it has no foundation. I will eventually be found out in front of everyone. The structure of my lie will collapse, and my bad deed will be visible in the open air. The public shaming will be the final payment for the secret evil. I cannot keep the dark thing hidden forever.

[10]I see the danger in my own bad intent. If I dig a hole for someone else, I might fall into it myself. The trap I set for another man becomes the pit that swallows me. And if I push a stone against a person, trying to cause them harm, it might roll back on me. The bad deed has its own weight and momentum. The malice I release into the world is not controlled by me. The injury I intended for them will be the one that leaves me bruised. The harm I plan for others will

be the harm I receive. I must remember that my actions are not just arrows; they are boomerangs.

[11]I see the danger in my own bad intent. If I dig a hole for someone else, I might fall into it myself. The trap I set for another man becomes the pit that swallows me. And if I push a stone against a person, trying to cause them harm, it might roll back on me. The bad deed has its own weight and momentum. The malice I release into the world is not controlled by me. The injury I intended for them will be the one that leaves me bruised. The harm I plan for others will be the harm I receive. I must remember that my actions are not just arrows; they are boomerangs.

CHAPTER THIRTY-NINE

[1]I will keep my words about the future small. Let me not boast about tomorrow, as I cannot predict what the day may bring. The future is a curtain I cannot see behind. The plans I make today might be dust by noon tomorrow. If there is to be praise, let it come from another mouth. Let others praise me, not myself. The word of a man about his own worth is a thin, cheap thing. It is better to do the work and let the result speak, or let a witness speak. I will focus on what is here, now, and keep my mouth shut about the next day's victory.

[2]I know the true weights of the world. Stone is heavy and sand a burden, that is true. They tax the body and the back. But there is a greater, internal weight. If I am a fool, then my anger would be even heavier. The physical burden can be laid down, but the fool's rage is carried inside. It is a pointless, consuming weight that burdens the spirit more than any rock. The stone can be moved; the fool's destructive temper is a fixed, self-inflicted crushing load. I must drop the anger before it breaks me.

[3]I have seen what fire does, and I know what a hidden, slow burn feels like. I know that anger is cruel, and fury can overwhelm. They are quick storms, and they pass, leaving only wreckage. But nothing is worse than if I am jealous. Jealousy is not a quick storm; it is a long, cold poison that works on the inside. It is a constant sickness of the soul. It is

a weight that cannot be lifted, and it is crueller than simple anger because it is aimed at the good fortune of another, and it destroys only me.

[4]I see the value in the hard truth. I would rather openly correct someone than tell them that I love them and hide it. The lie of silence is a slow betrayal. If I claim to care, I must be willing to give the honest word, even if it is sharp. The open correction is a sign of true commitment; it means I value their growth more than their temporary comfort. To smile and keep the fault hidden is to let them walk toward trouble alone. True love speaks the truth.

[5]The wounds from an enemy I can trust. They are honest. The blow is given with malice, but the intent is clear, and the pain reveals the truth of the fight. But a friend's affection may not always be genuine towards me. The smile, the kind word, the embrace—these things can be a disguise. The hidden motive, the quiet jealousy, or the desire to use me can be wrapped up in the soft feeling of love. I must be wary of the gentle touch, for it is often the enemy's honesty that protects me more than the friend's false warmth.

[6]If I am full, then I wouldn't appreciate honey. The sweetest gift in the world is wasted on me because I lack the appetite for it. My satisfaction blinds me to true pleasure. But if I am hungry, even something bitter can taste sweet to me. My great need changes the nature of the thing I am offered. I am so eager for nourishment that my mind turns a difficulty into a delight. The pain of my lack is a great teacher; it shows me the true value of every small provision.

[7]I recognize the sudden, sharp pain of being untethered. Just like a bird flees from its nest, so I run away from my home. The nest is meant to be the place of safety and

warmth, but something drove me out. Now I am in the open air, and the great danger is that I am lost. The bird that flees has no map for the sky. It only knows the instinct to leave. I have left the structure that defined me, and now I have no clear direction. I have traded a bad safety for a terrible freedom. I must find a new branch to land on before the wind takes me.

[8]I appreciate the small things that bring comfort and the great things that bring wisdom. Perfume and incense make the heart glad—they are a delight to the senses, a momentary lift of the spirit through a sweet smell. But the joy of the senses cannot compare to the joy of a clear mind. My true friend's advice should be a joy to my soul. It is not always sweet to hear, but it carries the pure intention of love. His honest word is more valuable than any scent, because it offers lasting help, not just a passing pleasure. The friend's wisdom is the true fragrance.

[9]I understand where true loyalty must rest. I will not abandon my friends or my family's friends, because those bonds were chosen and tested in good times. And I know better than to rely on mere blood in a crisis. I will not seek out relatives when trouble comes. The truth is often revealed in the dark hour: better a distant neighbour than a close relative in times of need. The neighbour, though physically far, might be closer in spirit and commitment. The relative might be close by, but their heart might be cold. The one who truly cares will come without being asked, and that is where I will place my trust.

[10]I have learned the difference between true kindness and a noisy display. I would not loudly bless my neighbour early in the morning, because I know that a good deed done too loudly can be a burden. The blessing is meant to bring joy, but if it is too loud and too early, it may be seen as

annoying or fake. The sound of my goodwill can become a nuisance that wakes him from his rest. The true nature of the blessing is lost in the poor timing and the volume. I will keep my good wishes quiet, so that they are received as a gift, not an intrusion.

[12]I know the law of careful effort. As I care for a fig tree and will enjoy its fruit, I understand that work precedes the reward. I give the tree my attention, and it gives me its sweetness. In the same way, I will protect my superior, for he is the structure that keeps my world sound. I give him my loyalty and my best effort, and in so doing, I will be honoured. My reward—the fruit—is the respect I gain and the stable position I secure. My service is the seed of my own success.

[13]A person's life reflects their heart, just as water reflects the face. My actions, my choices, and my habits—they are the surface of the water. If my heart is troubled, my life is troubled. If my heart is clean, my life shows that clarity. You cannot hide the inside, for it is always displayed on the outside. And I know the nature of wanting. Desires, like decay and the grave, are never satisfied. Decay always wants more to consume; the grave always has room for one more. In the same way, one desire only gives birth to the next. The satisfaction is momentary, and then the need returns, deeper than before. I must control the wants, or they will control me.

[14]I will put on the mask of acceptance. I will pretend to believe everything, for I know the great advantage in appearing agreeable. In reality, inwardly, I believe in nothing. My mind is a blank slate, a wide-open field. This is my strength. The moment I allow myself to believe something, I stop growing. A fixed belief is a cage. It cuts off the possibility of a new truth, a better idea. It turns

my open mind into a closed book. To learn and to move forward, I must hold every idea lightly, even the ones I state most firmly. The performance of belief is for the world; the inner emptiness is for my own freedom.

[15]I am given a great commission. I must loot every treasure trove of knowledge. I will not be timid. I will go to all the places where truth, wisdom, and secrets are kept—the books, the minds, the experiments, and the histories. But I must not be greedy or reckless. The true skill is in selection: taking only what I need and can safeguard in my vault. I will not fill my mind with useless clutter or information that is too complex for me to handle. I will only take the pieces of gold that my own capacity can protect. The knowledge must be usable, and it must be secure inside my mind, where it cannot be lost or stolen. The mind is a vault, not a junkyard.

CHAPTER FORTY

[1]The crucible is for silver, and the furnace is for gold. The metal must pass through the fire to show its purity; the heat burns away the dross and reveals the true worth. But the test for my own spirit is not heat, it is honour. My character is tested by how I receive praise. When the smooth words of flattery and respect come, my true nature is exposed. I must ask myself: Does the praise make me vain and arrogant, or does it make me humble and grateful? Do I use it to lift myself or to empower others? The easy word of compliment is a hotter, more dangerous fire than any furnace, because it tests the strength of my soul itself. I must pass that test without being consumed by my own pride.

[2]I see the stubborn, fixed nature of a man without sense. Even if you grind a fool down like grain, trying to crush the foolishness out of him with hard lessons and severe pressure, you can't remove their foolishness. The grinding breaks the body and the spirit, but the core of the man remains untouched. The flour you are left with is still the same substance it was before, just in a finer form. The fool's lack of sense is not a coating you can scrape off; it is the very grain of his being. You waste your effort and your energy trying to perfect what is inherently flawed. The effort to change a fool is the definition of futility.

[3]I must know the condition of my flocks and pay attention to my herds. My hands must be on the real things: the animals, the fields, the practical necessities. This is the source of my real power. I must do this because wealth doesn't last forever. Money can disappear; fortunes can be lost. And a crown won't remain for every generation. Rank and title are temporary; they can be stripped away or simply fade with time. The only thing that remains is the foundation I built through constant, careful work. The health of my livestock is a surer thing than the status of my title. I must focus on what is real and tangible.

[4]When the hay is gone, and the grass grows again, I know that careful planning is what brings wealth. My livestock are my steady source of provisions. The lambs will provide me with clothing, turning the soft wool into a necessary product. And the goats will help me buy land—the sale of my healthy herd is the capital I need to expand my future. I will have plenty of goats' milk for my family and my servants, ensuring that everyone under my care is well-fed. My simple, disciplined work with the land and the animals is the only sure path to lasting security.

[5]The wicked run away even when no one chases them. They carry their guilt inside, and that guilt becomes their pursuer. They are not fleeing a visible enemy; they are fleeing the truth of their own actions. Their fear is their constant shadow. But the righteous are as bold as lions. They have nothing to hide. Their clear conscience gives them perfect strength. The lion walks without looking over its shoulder, knowing it has no reason to fear what it sees. The righteous man faces the world with that same unquestioning confidence.

[6]I recognise the consequence of chaos. When a country is rebellious, it has many rulers. The disorder of the people

produces a multiplication of leaders, each one seizing power for a moment, none able to hold it or rule justly. This fragmentation of power only feeds the rebellion and increases the instability. But a wise ruler keeps order. That one person, through his wisdom and integrity, can unify the people and establish a lasting structure. The clarity of his vision prevents the country from breaking into pieces. His steady hand is the force that calms the many competing voices and restores the single, stable heart of the nation.

[7]I know the choice that is always before me. I am a son or daughter who must choose the path. As a wise son or daughter, I will listen to instruction, absorbing the hard lessons and the guidance given to me. This is the way to build myself up and to bring honour to my family. But there is a danger in my association. If I spend time with gluttons—the people who waste their days and their resources on base appetites—I will take on their shame. Their recklessness will become mine, and I will bring shame to my father. The company I keep will determine the reputation I earn, and the sorrow I inflict on the one who raised me. I must guard my associations to guard my future.

[8]I realise the depth of my own hypocrisy. If I ignore instruction, if I choose wilful deafness to the truth and the path I should follow, then my attempts at goodness are tainted at the source. Even my prayers are an insult. The requests I make to a higher power are a contradiction. I ask for a blessing on a life that is actively rejecting the very principles that create blessing. My disobedience makes my sincere wish a mockery. The fault is mine: I have made my piety into a hollow sound, a word of disrespect born from my own rebellion.

[9]I recognise the great blindness that comes with fortune. The rich think they're wise. Their wealth acts as a mirror

that only reflects their own perceived cleverness. They mistake their good luck or their inheritance for genuine wisdom. Oh, how foolish! They live in a delusion that money makes them intelligent. But the poor and wise see their delusions. The person who has lived without that cushion has a sharper eye. Necessity has taught them true wisdom, and they can see past the veneer of wealth to the faulty judgment and untested assumptions of the rich. True insight is not bought with money; it is earned through experience and humility.

[10]When the righteous succeed, there is great joy. The success of a good person is a blessing for everyone. It means that justice is being served, order is being kept, and the path for honest work is clear. The whole community feels safe to celebrate and thrive. But when the wicked gain power, people hide. The ascent of the dishonest man is a cause for fear. People pull back their wealth, their words, and their trust. They do not know who will be targeted next. The silence and the fear become the new law of the land, and the celebration dies. The nature of the ruler always dictates the security of the people.

[11]If I hide my sins, I will not succeed. The hidden wrong becomes a rot inside the foundation of my life. It drains my energy and distracts my mind. The secret is a constant, heavy weight that makes any true progress impossible. I will always be looking back, always guarding the lie, and success will always be out of my grasp. But if I admit and forsake them, I will find mercy. The confession is the first, hardest step. To speak the truth is to drop the heavy weight. To forsake the sin—to turn away from the bad action—is the evidence of change. When the error is honest and abandoned, the door to mercy opens. The path to a clean beginning is paved with humility.

[12]I know where true happiness is found. Blessed is me who respects wisdom. When I hold knowledge and good judgment in high regard, my life flows with ease and security. The blessing is not a random gift; it is the natural consequence of choosing the right path. But I recognise the danger in resistance. If I harden my heart, closing myself off to instruction, correction, and the lessons of life, I will face trouble. The trouble I face will be my own making. It will be the result of a stubborn spirit and a refusal to bend to what is right. My openness is my safety, and my rigidity is my downfall.

[13]If I am an ill-willed ruler over helpless people, I am like a roaring lion over a lamb. My power becomes pure menace. I use my strength to terrify and consume those I should protect. My rule is not governance; it is predation, and my subjects live in constant, justified fear of my hunger. But I know the price of tyranny. If I am a tyrant, I take advantage of others, seizing their goods and their security for my own short-term gain. This path is ultimately self-destructive. However, if I am a ruler who despises dishonest gain, if I refuse to profit from injustice and oppression, I will reign long. Integrity is the true foundation of my throne. My commitment to fairness ensures the loyalty of my people and the stability of my power. The fear of the lamb will never secure my legacy; only the trust of a well-governed people can do that.

[14]If I am burdened with the guilt of murder, I know that peace will be impossible in this world. The crime has severed my tie to the living, and the internal torment is constant. My only hope for cessation is the final act. I will seek refuge in the grave. Death becomes the only true shelter from the unendurable weight of my own actions. My desire for that final rest is a necessary end, and you must

understand it. Let no one try to stop me. My judgment has already been passed by my own conscience, and the grave is merely the execution of the sentence.

CHAPTER FORTY-ONE

[1]If I work hard on my land, applying myself to what is real and tangible—the soil, the tasks, the necessary labour—I will have plenty to eat. The earth will reward my sweat with sustenance. The labour is the guarantee of the harvest. But if I chase silly dreams, the grand, empty ideas that have no root in reality or discipline, I will end up poor. My efforts will be scattered and wasted on projects that promise much but deliver nothing. I must anchor my effort in the real world to secure a real reward. The dreamer starves; the worker eats.

[2]If I am a person who is faithful, steady, and true in my commitments and my work, I will be richly blessed. The blessing is the natural outgrowth of integrity—it brings trust, stability, and enduring good fortune. My reward will be deep and lasting. But if I am someone who only wants to get rich, focused purely on immediate gain without regard for fairness or honesty, I will face punishment. This kind of greed is a short-sighted, destructive force. I will cut corners, betray others, and ultimately lose the very things I value—peace, reputation, and security. The desire for quick wealth is a guarantee of a hard fall. I must choose the path of faithfulness over the path of unjust gain.

[3]To treat others unfairly is wrong—it is a clear moral failure that I know I should not commit. To oppress or disadvantage another person for my own gain is a

destructive act. Yet, I also see the terrible pressure of want. Some people will do bad things just for a little bit of food. When hunger is the master, the moral law becomes a luxury they cannot afford. The desperation for a small, immediate necessity can force a person into actions they would otherwise despise. The need for survival can temporarily override the knowledge of right and wrong. I see the darkness and the pity in that truth.

[4]If I am stingy, I want to get rich, but my method is flawed. I believe that by hoarding what I have, I am building my future. But I don't realize that poverty is waiting for me. My refusal to share, to invest, or to spend what is necessary creates a barren future. My selfishness drives away the goodwill of others, it stunts my growth, and prevents the flow of prosperity. My greed is not a shield against loss; it is the very thing that guarantees it. My fear of becoming poor is what makes the coming poverty certain.

[5]If I tell the truth and correct others, offering a word that is honest and helpful, I will be liked. The word of truth might sting at first, but people will come to value my integrity and the good results of my counsel. The respect I earn will be deep and durable. But if I only say nice things to please people, choosing comfort over honesty, I will be ignored. My pleasant words will be empty and cheap. People will recognize that my speech has no substance and no cost, and they will stop listening to me when it truly matters. I will trade the chance to be a trusted voice for the certainty of being a pleasing echo.

[6]If I steal from my parents and say it's okay, I am fundamentally broken. My action of theft, combined with the lie that justifies it, means I am as bad as someone who destroys things. I am not just taking; I am destroying the family bond, the security, and the trust that is the

foundation of my life. I must also remember the law of consequence: The greedy create problems because their selfish actions upset the natural order of things, leading to instability and ruin. But if I trust in my wisdom—if I rely on my judgment, integrity, and disciplined effort—I will succeed. Wisdom is the true capital; greed is the source of all failure.

⁷I must not fall for the shallow security of the self. If I trust only in myself—my efforts, my health, my wealth, my looks, my abilities, my talents—I am foolish. These things are all temporary and unreliable. The confidence they bring is a brittle shell that can be cracked by time, chance, or a single misfortune. But I know the path to true security. I must be among those who walk looking deep into them with wisdom and understanding. I must look past the surface of my own capabilities to see the fragility and the limits of all human strength. This deep, clear-sighted wisdom is the only thing that makes me safe. It keeps me from arrogance and prepares me for the inevitable changes. My true safety comes from understanding my own weakness, not from boasting in my strength.

⁸I see the complexity in true charity and the danger of self-serving motives. If I am helping the poor, I must know that the return I expect will not always bring me back what is given. The transaction is not a business deal. If I am to be given, if my sole motivation is a return on investment, then I am a fool. I have misunderstood the entire purpose of the act. I must also accept that those who genuinely help the poor will not always have enough themselves. Compassion does not guarantee wealth. My true focus must be on pure intention. I must depend not on my looks, my words, or the opinions of others. Instead, I must use my mind to judge who is to be given and look for the inner guidance to do it

for me. I cannot let my ego steer the ship. If I am seeking glory for myself in doing that, performing the act for public praise or self-satisfaction, then no reward is due to me in heaven or on earth. True charity is its own reward, and I will find it only by acting from a place of a genuine, selfless heart.

[9]If I am a fair leader, focusing on justice and the well-being of my people, I will make my country strong. Fairness acts as the mortar that holds the foundation of the state together, creating trust and stability. But if I am a leader who only cares about money, putting my own wealth and profit ahead of the needs of the nation, I weaken it. My greed will erode the trust of my people, leading to division and eventual ruin. I must also be wary of my own tongue. If I flatter others, using false praise to manipulate them, I am setting traps for myself. My insincerity will eventually be exposed, and the loss of my reputation will be the pit I fall into. I must be honest in word and deed to ensure the strength of my rule and my own security.

[10]If I am a wise person who argues with a fool, I must accept the inevitable result: the fool will just make fun, and there will be no peace. My attempt to use reason and logic will be met with mocking laughter and pointless contradiction. I will give a measured argument, and they will give a childish insult. The goal of the fool is not to find the truth, but to draw me down to their level and disrupt my peace. I must choose silence over the losing battle of trying to debate with someone who has no capacity for sense. I will guard my peace by walking away from the conflict.

CHAPTER FORTY-TWO

[1]I have learned this thing well. I try to keep clean. I try to keep my hands on the wheel and drive straight. But the others, they are always there. They are always waiting. They do not hate me for the mistake I made. They hate me for the thing I stand for. They hate the clean, straight line. It is a judgment on them, just by my presence, and they cannot live with it. So they come for me. They do not send a note. They do not talk. They just come. And I have to fight them or run. I am not fighting them because I am a hero. I am fighting them because they have forced the issue upon me, and there is no other course of action to take. I will be hurt. I become tired. But I will have stood. And that is what is left. That is all there is. That is the thing I learn. It does not get easier. It just gets truer. It is a world where good intentions are met with brute force, and the simple act of doing what's right is a choice that often comes with pain. There is no victory, only survival and the knowledge of how things are.

[2]The fool is always shouting. I see his anger, and it does not help him. It just opens the way for the others. I am a target, then. Easy to hit. If I were a smart man, I would know the heat would kill the thing I want to do. I see the anger, but I do not let it come out. I keep the heat down until the others think the fight is over. Then I move. It is better to be quiet. It is better to calm the room and wait.

The mind noise that triggers me is what gets me killed.

[3]I've watched it happen. I see the ruler, and I see the lies they listen to. The lies are easy. They make the work easier. They make the man feel good. But the lies are like a rot. They get into the room. If the ruler takes the lie, the man next to him takes it too. And the man after him. They all learn that the lie is the thing that works. They all learn that telling the truth will only make them tired or get them pushed out. Soon, the whole place is spoiled. All the helpers are bad. They are not bad men, maybe, but they are corrupted by the listening. The truth has no place at the table anymore. It is a slow, sure death for the whole business. I have seen it and experienced it.

[4]I have stood beside the penniless man, the one to whom falsehoods offer no shelter. His vision is unclouded; he must distinguish the bone from the phantom, for the world's lies are a fatal distraction, never a comfort. And I have walked with the city's architects, the ones who hold the lever of power. Their sight is equally absolute, for they must know the true fault lines in the earth, lest their entire edifice crumble down upon them. This clarity—this essential knowing—is not bought by the silk I wear or inherited with my family's crest. It is a gift granted by necessity. It comes when I am stripped bare and poor, and it comes when I am burdened by immense strength. The power to see is not a status symbol; it is the brutal, final tool given to any soul that needs the truth to survive. I can have nothing or I can have everything. The light is the same. It shines on both of my statuses equally.

[5]A king must be strong, yes. But strength is not just having the guns and the men. If I am a king who only looks to the rich. I am brittle. My reign is thin, like cheap glass. It waits only for a rock to be thrown. But if I am the king

who gives a straight answer to the poor—the one who lets them have their small justice—I will last. The small men do not rise against me. They do their work. They stand by the work. When I treat the poor fairly, the whole place holds together. That is the solid ground. That is the thing that cannot be broken. That is how I will keep the chair.

[6]I must learn the rules. If I learn them, it is not a happy thing, but it is useful. Discipline is the thing that makes me wise. It takes the foolishness out of me, like cutting the unwanted fat from the meat. But the child who is left alone, who is not taught the line, will go crooked. I will do the things that bring trouble. And the trouble does not stay with me. It goes to my mother, too. It is her name that is spoken in shame. My father is gone, or he is busy. But my mother is the one who carries the burden. Either I learn or shame the house. That is the only choice there is for me if I ignore discipline.

[7]When the ill-intended people win, the dirt spreads. I see it in the streets. The sin gets bigger because the man who keeps clean sees the other one getting rich, and he wonders why he bothers. The whole town gets spoiled. But I have watched it long enough. I have seen the way it ends. They can build their things up. They can have their good years. But the wicked thing never holds. It is built on sand, or worse, it is built on a shaky foundation that will not stand the wind. And the man who waited, the good man who kept his line straight, he will be there. He will not have to do the work himself. He will just be standing when the whole damn thing comes down. It always comes down. That is the only promise there is.

[8]I have children. So, I will teach them. It is work, hard work, to show them the line and make them walk it. But I know what the end will be. If I do the teaching, they will

not be a worry to me. They will not bring the trouble to the door. They will be straight, and that is the thing that brings a man peace. And when they are straight, when they do the good work in the world, then I can look at them. And I will be proud. It is a fair trade. I put in the teaching, and I get the rest.

[10]I can tell him. I can give the words to the servant. I can make it very simple so that he understands the thing perfectly. And he will nod. He will know the words and the reason for them. He will have the picture of what is right in my head. But he will go out and do the thing wrong anyway. It is not a question of his hearing. He hears fine. It is a question of the doing. The words do not make the change. I can teach a man with my voice, but I cannot fix the way he is built. They do not turn the corner just because I showed them the way. That is the thing I learn when you have men working for me.

[11]I have watched the simple fool. He moves in the dark, stumbling because he does not know the terrain. But he is salvageable. He can be struck silent, forced to sit down, and taught to watch the wiser ones until a single truth settles in his mind. But if I am the one who speaks too quickly, I inhabit a more severe damnation. I am cursed not by ignorance, but by my own instrument. I have the vocabulary, but I use the whole treasury before the moment is ripe. I give away the very leverage I should be guarding. I pledge myself to ruin with careless promises. My own voice becomes the blade that severs my best chances. The common fool, at least, possesses the ability to shut his mouth. The talker does not. He is a constant haemorrhage, killing his own luck sentence by sentence. I have seen the hard truth of this in my own life: I am forever convinced that the present words are not enough to compel the

outcome I desire, and in that fatal rush, I guarantee the best outcome will never arrive. The fault is not in the world's hearing, but in my own fear of silence.

[12]I am being asked a simple thing. Yes, or no. That is all it takes to answer. But I, who have no control, just cannot do it. The answer is not the important thing to me. The sound of my own voice is the only thing I care about. So, I start to talk. I give you the story. I give me the why of it, the maybe of it, the explanation that goes around the room three times. I give everything except the straight word. I should remind myself that I am not answering the question. I am showing you the thing wrong with me. I am showing you that I have no discipline in my head or in my mouth. I reveal myself in the long answer. I have watched myself do it every time. You know all you need to know about a man when he cannot give you a simple answer.

[13]Anything is possible when time isn't a constraint. Even a mountain can be moved—one stone at a time, with steady effort. Take a small step and keep going. What once seemed impossible will become real. Let time hold no power over you—it's a human construct, while your efforts are timeless. Stay persistent, and success will follow. True significance isn't bound by deadlines; it unfolds through patience and perseverance.

[14]I have seen the servant who was not made to work when he was small. They let him eat first. They let him run free. They called it kindness, but it was a lie. He does not know what is right. He does not know his place, and that is a dangerous thing. When he is old enough to do the work, he will think the work is a burden. He will think he is better than the others. And then he turns worse. He does not listen to the words you give him. He is disrespectful to the ones who feed him. The spoiling in the beginning is the

rot in the end. He was not taught to be straight, so he will be crooked.

¹⁵I know what the men are like. I have watched them. So I will not be the one with the great, loud anger that breaks the furniture and breaks the peace. If I let the anger come, I will be the danger in the room. I will start the unnecessary thing. And I will not have the quick, hot temper that acts before the mind is ready. If I act on that heat, I will throw away the good opportunities. I will make the stupid move that loses the money or the friend. The heat is a good thing only when it is controlled. I will not ruin myself. I will watch the fire inside and keep it down. I will learn to wait. That is how I will keep the good life.

¹⁶If I am proud, I know the fall is waiting for me. I will trip on my own size, and the men will laugh. But if I am humble, I will do the work and not speak of it. I will keep my size to myself. And because of that, when the time comes, they will stand with me. They will give me the respect that matters.

¹⁷I know how those men work. The thieves. They stand together, but they are not friends. They are not partners. They are just men waiting to see who will break first. The one you work with he is your worst enemy. You share the secret, which is the worst thing you can share. You take the oath that you will keep silent, but it is a lie before the word is out. They will not tell the truth to the law, because the truth will put them under the stone. And they will not tell the truth to each other, because they are afraid. They know the other man is waiting to sell them out for a better deal, for a chance at the clear air. They live with the lie. And they fear the truth more than they fear jail. That is the cost of that kind of business. It always breaks.

[18]If I look at other men too much, I let them win before the fight begins. I see what they have, and I worry that I do not have enough. I listen to their loud talk, and I fear what they will say about me. That fear is a string they can pull. It will make me change my good work. It will make me leave the straight line just to please them, and I will end up in the ditch with them. I have learned that the worry of men is the thing that brings the trouble. It never keeps the peace. So, I put my trust in the steady thing. I do the work and I do not look over the shoulder. They can talk, but the quiet trust is the only thing that holds me up. It is the only way to be safe and to stay clean.

[19]I have stood where the people gather. They all want to speak to the leader. They want the favour, the order, the change. The line is long, and the talk is loud. They think the man in the big chair can give them what they need. They think he is the one who decides. But he is only a man. He can sign the papers, but that is not justice. That is just politics. The real thing, the straight thing that is right, that comes from the other place. It comes from the true court. That justice is not bought, and you cannot talk your way into it. It simply is. It is the final measure. The leader can give you a temporary answer. That's all. The divinity in you gives you the truth that stays true. That is the difference. I know which one to rely on.

[20]I know the honest men. They do not hate the man who fails. They hate the lie. They hate the twisting of the facts. That disgust in them is what makes them clean. And the bad ones, the ones who live on the dirt—they do not hate the law, not truly. They hate the man who stands for the right thing. They hate him because his simple presence is a mirror. It shows them what they are. It is a fight that never changes. The good hate the lie. The wicked hate the truth

told by a man who lives it. What do you hate? You choose.

²¹I am tired, and it is a bad thing. But I will not stop. I will keep going. You have to keep moving, or you are finished. The wisdom is gone. It left with the sleep. Now there is only the movement. Maybe I am not a man now. Maybe I am just a thing that breathes and walks, like an animal in the dust. No thoughts. No cleverness. But the animal still moves. And so, I move. That is all there is to know about it. The feet keep doing the work.

²²I have walked many roads and seen many things. But the truth of it, the way life works, that is still hidden. I do not know the quiet wisdom. The quiet wisdom does not speak to me. There are men who talk about the mysteries, but they do not know them. Who holds the wind in a fist? Who wraps the whole ocean in a blanket? Who started all of it—the rock and the dirt and the running river?

CHAPTER FORTY-THREE

[1]I have learned to listen to the clean thing—the feeling that comes before the thought. When the mind is quiet, that feeling is perfect. It is the truth. If you trust it, it works like a shield. It keeps the trouble off you. It lets you walk where the other men stumble. But you must not add to it. Do not put your cleverness into it. Do not dress it up with an excuse or a reason. If you put a single lie on that pure feeling, it will know. It will turn on you, and it will break you. The instinct does not forgive the false move. It will show you for the liar you are. You must take the clean thing whole, or you take nothing. That is the hard rule.

[2]I have only two things to ask of the universal intelligence: First, let me know the right thing before I am finished. Let me have the wisdom to walk clean until the end. Do not let me live a fool's life. Second, keep the lies away. Keep them far from my mouth and far from the men who speak to me. Do not give me a great pile of things to deal with, or I will forget the work and forget the need. I will lose the simple knowledge of who I am. And do not let me have too little. Do not let me get so hungry that I must steal and break the straight law I believe in. Just give me enough. The clean, simple enough for today, for me, and for the people who stand with me. That is the only balance. That is the only way to keep the integrity.

[3]If I speak badly about a servant to his master, I am a fool who wants trouble. I have just made an enemy who lives closer to the fire than I do. He will not fight me in the sun, but he will be there in the shadow. He will curse me under his breath, and the curse will take hold in the house. The master will never know why he suddenly does not like me or why the door always closes against me. But the close man—the servant—he will know. I do not want the consequences of that small, quiet man. It is better to keep my peace and let the house handle its own business. I will not be the one to open that door.

[4]I have seen them all. They do not honour the beginning. They curse the father who made them, and they give no good word to the mother who carried them. They are broken from the start. Then there are the clean talkers. They tell you they are pure. But you can see the hidden filth that they carry, and they think no one knows. They are fooling only themselves. And the proud ones, they give you the look. They see you from a great height, and the eyes mock you. The look is a lie, but they carry it well. But the worst are the ones with the mouths. Their words are not talk; they are sharp swords. They use the words to cut the poor man and the one who has nothing. They only talk to hurt. They are all pieces of the same bad thing. You see them, and you know there is no good work in them. You only learn to watch the place where they stand.

[5]I have seen the thing that takes and is never full. It is always asking. Like the animal they call the leech—it has two mouths, and they both only say one word: "Give! Give!" But the leech is small. The great things are worse. There are four things in this world that you will never satisfy. The hole in the ground, when life goes back to the dirt. That grave will always take the next man. The dry earth

is another. You can give it all the rain and it will still be thirsty the next day. The fire is the third. It takes the wood, and then it only asks for more wood. It does not stop for politeness. And the last one, the empty womb, the hunger for the life that is not there. They do not say "Enough." They only say "More." That is the hard truth of the world.

[6]I have seen the ones who look down. The eye that mocks the father, or the eye that shows contempt for the mother who has grown old—that eye is marked. They do not know it, but that eye will not last. The man may keep it for a time, but it is already lost to him. The birds will come for it. The raven will know it is spoiled meat, and the vulture will come for the rest. They will take that eye from the socket while the man is still warm on the ground. It is a sure thing. You show contempt for the people who gave you life, and the great things of the air will come and collect the debt. You do not survive that kind of disrespect. That is the final truth of it.

[7]The eagle flies, unseen forces lift it. The snake moves, and an unknown push drives it. The ship sails, heavy water holds it up. All is a clean, working mystery. But the worst wonder is the way a man acts with a young woman. He is a fool because he does not trust the simple good thing. He adds lies, talks too much, tries to buy love, or holds too tight. He thinks the simple truth is not enough, and his complication breaks the chance.

CHAPTER FORTY-FOUR

[1]I have seen the way of that kind of woman. She takes what she wants. She eats the food she did not earn. She does the thing that is not straight. Then she is finished. She takes the napkin and wipes her mouth clean. She puts the food away. And when you look at her, she has the coldness to tell you the final lie. She looks straight at you and says, 'I did nothing wrong.' There is no sign of the wrong thing left on her. That is the worst part of her kind. The easy way she dismisses the cost. She thinks a clean mouth is proof of a clean conscience. She is wrong, but she will not be told sometime before her life ends, if she would listen.

[2]If I am a servant who gains power, I will not forget that the wisdom did not come with the title. I must keep quiet and learn, or I will bring the whole thing down. If I am given too much, I will not become a fool. I will not let the excess spoil me, or I will be the one who shakes the very ground. If I take a wife who has no honour, I know the bad influence will enter the house. The clean things will become twisted because the source is foul. And if I am the one who should be under, I will not seize control. I will not become the unworthy man who makes his master fall. That kind of victory brings a worse ruin than any defeat. I know what breaks the order of the world. I will not be one of those four things.

[3]I have seen the big things fail, but the small things endure. Look! Have you noticed that there is a clean wisdom in the creatures who do not speak? The ant is weak, and you could step on him without seeing. But he knows the summer does not last. He works every day and he fills the hole for the cold time. That is knowing how to live. The rock rabbit is small, but it does not live where the other animals hunt. It lives high in the rocks. He takes a bad spot and makes it his strong place. That is knowing how to keep safe. The locusts have no king and no general, but when they move, they move as one army. They know the right direction, and they take it together. That is knowing how to move. And the lizard—you can grab him; he is fast but small. But you find him even in the rooms of the palace. He lives in the presence of the kings of great power, and no one can keep him out. They all teach the same lesson: You do not need to be big to be smart. You need to know the time, the place, and the path.

[4]I have seen the walk that means something. It is not the swagger of the fool. It is the real thing. The lion has it. He does not run. He walks slowly and strongly, and he does not fear the answer. He knows what he is. The rooster has it, too, that arrogant, high-stepping lift. He owns the yard. The he-goat walks with that same hard, determined look. They are all sure of their place. But the surest walk is the king who is not looking over his shoulder. The one who has no fear of the knife from the dark corner. He knows the people are with him, and the rule is clean. He walks as if the ground itself is his floor. When you see that kind of confidence, you know the man, or the animal, is exactly where he belongs. You do not argue with that walk.

[5]The way a man ruins himself. Pity! He acts the fool, and then he praises his own action. He makes a noise about

the bad thing he plans to do. He shouts the foolishness out loud. That is the mistake. When the mind is full of that stuff—the pride or the plan to do dirt—I have to clamp the mouth shut. I must stop the action before it starts. The word is the thing that makes it real. The word makes it your debt. If I have a bad thought, I do not own it until I speak it. So, I must think before I talk. I hold the sound inside, and I let the badness die there. That is the only way to avoid sure trouble.

⁶If I stir up the milk too long, it will become butter. That is the rule of the work. If I stir up the anger, it will turn to be a fight. I know this. I know the work will not stop until the trouble has been made. It will not just go back to the quiet, easy place. So, I will not churn the feeling. I will let the anger be still. I will not put the heat to it or the movement. It is a bad trade to work that hard just to make a mess. I will let it alone.

⁷I have heard the warning, and I will keep it. If I am to do the clean work, I will not let the trouble come from that direction. The beautiful woman, the handsome man, both can break me, however great I am. They can turn even the king's head so he forgets the battle. They can make the strong one weak. I will see them, and I will know the cost. I will not waste the energy that is needed for the road. The energy is for the work, not for the game that will leave me ruined and empty. I will keep my focus and I will keep my peace. I will not let that kind of complication spoil my life. I know the great ones fall to it, and I will not be one of them.

⁸If I hold a position of honour, I will not be inclined to intoxication. If I myself let the substance in, my clarity vanishes. I will forget what is needed. I will sign the wrong paper, and if I am the man who has nothing, I will lose my small chance. If I am to be the ruler, I must keep my

head cold and clean, or I will kill the justice. But the other ones, the ones who hurt, let them have it. Let them use all those that take the memory. Let them forget the day and the things that made them suffer. They are already broken. The drink will not fix them, and it will not stop the pain. It will only make the suffering longer and less sharp. But if I am the leader, I must stay awake for the work. The poor man only wants to sleep through the trouble. That is the difference.

[9]If I see a man who cannot speak for himself, I will not walk past him. That is the necessary thing. I will be his voice. If I see the poor and the ones who have been broken, I will stand up and I will fight for their right. The rights are not for the strong; the strong can take them. The rights are for the people who will be cheated if I do not watch. I must speak the word. I must make the sound in the room that says, 'The measure must be straight.' I will not be quiet when the fairness is broken.

CHAPTER FORTY-FIVE

[1]I know the price of rubies. This woman is worth more than that. You cannot buy her. Her man trusts her. He trusts her completely, and that is the only wealth a man needs. The house does not run on the man's money alone. The house runs on the woman's work. She is the one who keeps the clean line. If she is strong, the whole place is strong. The children are raised straight. The meals are there when the man comes home from the long road. The small debts are paid, and the big worries do not enter the door. She does not get the praise for the battles fought outside. But the peace you come home to—that is her victory. If she lets the order go, everything goes. The man fails because he has no good place to rest. He is ruined by the chaos she allowed to grow. She is the discipline. She is the quiet, necessary strength. You see a good house, and you know a good woman is running it. That is the only measure you need. Her competence is the bedrock upon which her partner's public standing rests. She holds deep strength and unmoving dignity. She faces the future and meets it with humour. Her words are true, delivered to build and not to break. Her team celebrates her. Her partner proclaims her the ultimate foundation. Forget what is fleeting; her true worth lies in the uncompromised principle she lives by. Honour her for the real-world impact she creates. Her achievements are the only proof needed.

[2]We are here for a short time. The moments flee, and we are gone. Everything we build, everything we hold—it is temporary. You know you will die, and that is the only sure thing. So, what does a man get for the work? For the sweat and the worry, he puts in, all of it done under the sun? One generation leaves, and the next one comes. They are all new men, but the earth stays the same. The sun goes up and the sun goes down, and it returns to the same damn place to start over. The wind turns south, and then it turns north; it is always going in a circle. It never finds a new place to be. The rivers all run to the sea, and the sea is never full. The water always goes back to the place where the river began, and the motion starts again. It is all movement, and it is all repeating. The motion is endless, but the man is not. I have watched it all go round. What is the gain? I have no good answer for that. The work goes on, but it changes nothing.

CHAPTER FORTY-SIX

¹I know that effort is all there is, but the effort itself is not the reward. Others only see the surface—the house or the finished journey—and that memory will fail. The only thing that truly stays is the truth you earned while the work was hard: the truth about yourself and the straight way to do things. The world will take your power and your name, but it cannot take the thing you learned inside. That small, hard piece of knowledge is the only real, lasting piece of the effort you get to keep until the very end.

²We sought to know and explain the whole world, engaging in the hardest fight there is. Yet, I must constantly ask myself if I will look to the deep truth within my consciousness or simply repeat old, tired patterns. I see that most of the work on this earth is pointless and frustrating. I know I alone cannot straighten the crooked things or count what is lost. Even after thinking great thoughts and telling myself I have learned more than the next person, the mind still endlessly wants more of everything—wisdom, foolishness, and madness—and I realise that this very wanting is also empty, just another frustration. The final truth is that the more you know, the heavier the thing gets; you pay for every piece of knowledge and truth with a quiet kind of pain.

³I made my choice to seek pleasure, to enjoy life's moments and make the most of good times. But when I

finished, I found it all was meaningless; my laughter echoed hollow, and the joy was empty. Happiness and sadness are intertwined—they arrive together, not apart. One comes, and the other waits behind it.

[4]I tried drinking, drugs, sex, gossip, and slander—quick escapes I thought would satisfy. Yet, my mind refused to let go, still yearning for wisdom. I had to discover what was truly good. The easy path was closed; I chose the hard way, seeking the good through the work of the Spirit.

[5]I began practising—living clean, avoiding wine, setting aside fleshly pleasures, refusing idle gossip and slander. I avoided small, dirty words. I committed to new work: meditation, yoga, quieting the body, giving to charity, and searching old religious texts. I believed these feelings would guide me to the truth. When practised rightly, the stillness of the mind appeared, but it was fleeting. The emptiness always returned.

[6]I traded temporary pleasures for disciplined effort, but the end of that road was still just wind rushing across a dry field. The great work, the big projects—building homes, planting gardens, gathering wealth—left me feeling the same emptiness. I looked at it all when it was done, and it was void. The result was nothing but the wind again.

[7]Despite all my labour, I had gained nothing. I replaced one illusion with another—the big house for a quiet room—yet both ended in the same emptiness. The only truth remaining was the effort itself. I had nothing to show when I reached the end, only the reality that life's entertainments are passing, fleeting moments I enjoyed or endured as I pleased.

CHAPTER FORTY-SEVEN

[1]I turned my mind to the final question. I looked at the wisdom and I looked at the foolishness, and I weighed them. I saw that wisdom was the better thing. It was clear and true, like light in a dark room. The foolishness was just the dark, and you cannot walk in the dark without hitting something hard. But then I saw the end. I saw the grave waiting for the two men. The wise man and the fool. The fool is forgotten, and the wise man is forgotten just as quickly. They both go into the same silence. The end is the same for the one who knew things and the one who did not. It made me ask the final question, the hardest one of all: What was the point of the wisdom? Why carry the heavy knowledge if the result is equal for all of us? And when I asked it, I knew the answer. Even the wisdom itself, after all the striving and the pain, seemed like nothing. It was just another meaningless thing under the sun. It does not save you.

[2]I stopped letting myself get excited about the work. I had seen the true end of it. All the hard work I put in, all the things I built, all the wealth I gained—it would all be left behind. It would go to some other man. And that man would take it, and he might not even appreciate the sweat it cost. He would take it as if it were simply his due. That truth filled the stomach with a cold, solid despair. It did not matter how hard I pushed or how much I achieved. I

would leave it all standing, and then I would go out the door alone. The whole of life was nothing but toil and effort. And for the man who sees clearly, that toil brings only grief and pain. The work is not the reward. It is the cost. And the cost is too high for what you get. The long, hard effort ends only with leaving.

[3]In the end, I knew the best thing a man could do. It was not the big project or the spiritual high. The best thing was to find satisfaction in his own work. The work of his hands or his mind, and to be content with it. And to take the simple pleasures: to eat well, to drink clean, and to see the sun. The real wisdom, the true knowledge, and the only happiness—it comes from being aware of the present. Not the past and not the future, but the thing that is happening right now. The man who can see that straight, he finds the joy, and he finds the clear understanding. The other man, the one who runs after the wealth, knowing he must leave it all standing—he is the one who is a fool. He should turn away from that running. It is a futile thing. I have run both ways. I know now. Chasing wealth is only chasing the wind. The simple, sure thing is the only thing that is not empty.

[4]There is a time for every damn thing under the sun. It is not random. It is all under the eye of the deep thing inside us. The whole cycle moves under that awareness. There is the time we are born, and there is the time we die. They are the only two facts. There is the time we put the seed in the dirt, and the time we must pull the roots out. There is a time for killing, and the time when the wounds must close. A time to tear down the wall, and a time to build the new one. We have to know when to weep and when to laugh. When to mourn the dead thing, and when the music for the dance must start. A time to throw the stones wide, and a time to pick them up. A time to hold the woman, and a

time to let her go. A time when you must search for the lost thing, and a time when you must give up the search entirely. A time to keep the thing safe, and a time to throw it away. A time to tear the cloth, and a time to mend the hole. We have to learn when to be silent and when to speak the truth out loud. There is a time for the loving, and a time when the straight, cold hate is necessary. A time to fight the war, and a time to have peace. We cannot have one without the other. We must accept the season we are given. That is the only way to survive the whole calendar.

[5]I ask the question always: What do I gain from all this toil? What is the profit from the sweat and the ache, when all of it is guided by the deep, unseen thing inside me? Where the finality of all things to happen lies deep in myself, which is obscure to my mind. I have seen the burden that has been put on us. Our inner being has given us the work, and the work is hard. But I have also seen the result. It has made every single thing beautiful in its own time, whether we acknowledge it or not. The timing is always perfect, even when the time is bad. It has also put eternity in my head. I know the work is short, but the thought of forever is always there. And because of that, I can never truly understand the whole plan. I cannot see what deep sense of me has done from the beginning to the end. The pattern is too big for one man's eyes. So, I keep doing the work. I know it is beautiful in its time. But the final answer to the profit, the gain—that is a thing I have not found. I only have the knowledge that I cannot know.

CHAPTER FORTY-EIGHT

[1]I now know the ultimate truth: the best thing I can do is simply be happy while alive and do the good work while I have the time. This joy is available to everyone who can appreciate the simple things—eating the food, drinking the clean water, and finding quiet joy in their own work. This awareness—that these things are here, right now, and they are enough—is the greatest gift. It isn't found in searching for big answers or great wealth; it's here on a quiet day. The only way to live well is to be simple enough to accept it.

[2]A man rarely sees the finality of the thing: the work of his inner being is not temporary; it is done clean and complete, lasting forever. You can neither add to it nor take away from it. The inner self creates this perfect, unbreakable pattern deliberately so that people will eventually have to return to the source to see the truth. The world is already set, so trying to change it is futile. The profound lesson is that the perfect pattern does not come to you—you must go to the pattern.

[3]I see that what is happening now has already been, and what comes tomorrow has already gone by—the whole thing moves in the same circle. I trust that the deep inner self (the subconscious) will inevitably settle the debts and bring the past to account. However, I see a dark parallel in the world's cycles: where men hold power, there is wickedness at both the start and end of the system. In

the places of judgment and justice, the same corruption is present. We can escape neither the set time nor the pervasive corruption. The hard truth of being alive is simply to see and know it for what it is.

[4]I have witnessed the saddest kind of work: we toil alone without a partner or the certainty of a next generation to benefit from our efforts. We don't know why we work so hard because we have missed the awareness of the deep being inside us and the purpose that should guide our effort. We only focus on the pile of things we have made, missing the simple, good truth of being aware—the eating, the drinking, and the joy in the moment of the work itself. We are the most foolish kind of people, working without purpose and without joy. Our heavy labour is only for the sake of the effort, leaving us empty and alone. We should have learned this simple lesson earlier, but we must learn it now.

[5]I have learned that it is far better to have a companion who sees the truth, for together the two hands achieve what one cannot. If one of us falls—which is certain—the other is there to help us up, but pity the one who falls alone with no hand to reach for. Together, we keep the work steady, speak the word that makes the other keep going, and share the coat to make warmth where a solitary person would freeze. Those who work alone work without true awareness, their endless effort yielding a small gain because they have no one to share or measure it with. I know the math: two are better than one; they hold each other up, stand stronger against difficulty, and are never alone when the trouble comes.

[6]I know a man must approach his inner, subconscious space with great care, without rushing in with the noise of his thoughts. The true presence of that deep thing is the

silence of the mind—that is where the truth lives. It is far better to stand there quietly and learn the small, hard truths than it is to rush out, act foolishly, and deceive ourselves that our bad action was good. We who act without understanding are the dangerous ones, making trouble worse without even realizing it. To avoid this, we must stop the inner movement and the talking in our heads. Silence is the only key: we go in quietly and come out knowing something real, because everything outside the inner being is just noise.

[7]I understand I must guard my words and never speak quickly or without consulting my inner being (the subconscious) that lives in that quiet place. This inner presence deals directly with my awareness, which is the true source of everything I see, as the outside world is only a mirror of the inside. Therefore, my speech must be handled with extreme care; the words must be sparse and straight. If I speak a hurried or foolish thing, I am sending a bad order directly to the source that makes my world, and I cannot afford to be wrong in that moment. I must learn to hold my tongue until the truth is clean, because silence is the only safe way to approach and protect that inner power.

CHAPTER FORTY-NINE

[1]I know where the bad things come from. The dreams that mean nothing, and the idle chatter that wastes the day—they come from the same place. They are born from restless thoughts. The mind is moving too fast and without a clear direction. It is full of small, broken pieces of distraction. When the mind is not still, it produces only worthless things. The dreams are just the noise of the day carrying over into the night. The talk is the noise of the night carrying over into the day. If we want the good thought or the true silence, we must first quiet the movement. Mind clutter is the enemy of the truth.

[2]When I make the vows to myself, I will make them few. And when I make them, I must see them through. I will fulfil them voluntarily, and I will do it promptly. There is no time for delay. The inner self, the deep awareness, does not care for the empty words. It takes no pleasure in the promise that is not followed by the action. It is better to say nothing at all. Better to keep the silence than to make the vow and then let the vow fail. If I fail, I am lying to the only person I cannot fool. That is a kind of ruin a man cannot recover from easily. You must keep the word you give to the man in the mirror.

[3]When the message comes, I will not try to talk my way out of it. I will not justify myself before the messenger. I will not tell the lie that the vow I made was a mistake.

That is the kind of cheap talk that the deep awareness inside me does not forgive. If I try that kind of dodge, the subconscious will register the anger. It will undo the good work I have already done. It will take effort and make it worthless. I will not agree and then later say it was a bad deal. I will stand by the word, even if it hurts. To lie about the intention is to spoil the whole thing. I will take the consequences clean.

[4]I will watch for the desires. I know that if I let them consume me, I am lost. I know that excessive words are just like desires; they lead only to emptiness. They are noise where there should be silence. I will keep them both in check. I will not fear the man-made things. I will not fear the systems or the power that other men have built. All those things are temporary and can be fought. The thing I will fear is my inner being. I will fear that deep awareness above all the other so-called Supremes. That is the only real power. I will work clean so that I do not have to fear the judgment from the only judge that matters.

[5]If I see the injustice and the oppression in the land, I will not be surprised. I will not let the sight break my peace. That is how the world works, and I have seen it too many times. The men in the high places will take what they want, and they will twist the truth. But they are not the last word. The man who holds the power is still judged by a higher authority. The true court is not the one he controls. The final reckoning is set above him. So, I will watch the wickedness, and I will be cold about it. I will not be surprised by the evil a man does with power. I will only know that his consequence is already waiting for him. I will not waste my energy fighting the inevitable, because the true fight is already decided.

[6]The ruler must be dedicated to agriculture. He must care about the dirt and the rain and the work of the farmer. If he looks after the growing of the food, the whole land will be prosperous. It is a simple equation. The man on top ensures the earth is worked right, and the benefit flows down to every person who stands on that earth. The full belly makes the quiet city. When the ruler forgets the grain and looks only to the gold, the whole business fails. He must understand that the best wealth is the harvest. That is the necessary work of the leader.

[7]I know this much about myself: If I love the money, I will never have enough of it. The satisfaction will never come. If I love the possessions, the things I own will never be enough to make me content. That whole way of chasing things is futile. When the possessions get bigger, the desire to use them, to consume them, gets bigger too. The hunger just grows with the meal. So, what do I, the one who owns it all, truly gain? What is the real benefit? There is no benefit. I only get to see them with my own eyes. I can look at the stack of things I have collected. That is all. The eye sees, but the heart stays empty. I am the prisoner of the things I bought. The effort was wasted.

[8]I have seen the man who works. He puts the labour in, and he earns his weariness. He has little, or he has much—it does not matter. When he lies down, his contentment brings sweet sleep. The sleep is clean and immediate. But the rich man does not have that. His belly is full, his pockets are full, but the rest will not come. He lies there, and he struggles with the darkness. The worry keeps him awake. The things he has, and the fear of losing them, spoil the night for him. The hard work is the only true sleeping powder. You earn the sleep, or you pay for it with the long, empty hours. The rich man pays, even when he thinks he

has bought everything. He has not bought the peace.

[9]I have seen the worst thing under the sun. It is the man who gathers the wealth, but he gathers it only to hurt himself. He keeps the money tight, and he denies himself the good things, and then he loses it all in one bad, risky venture. He leaves this life the way he came in—empty-handed. The long effort meant nothing. He has nothing to show for the whole of his working time. That is a grievous evil. To work that hard only to leave the world with nothing gained. His whole life was darkness. He was always suffering, plagued by the frustration of his want, and by the sickness that comes from that anger. He did the work, but he did not win the peace. He earned the wealth, but he only paid for his own ruin. It was a failure from the start to the end.

CHAPTER FIFTY

[1]I will take what is good and what is fitting for me. I have run too long after the wind and the big, empty answers. The only thing that is real is this: To eat, to drink, and to find the joy in my own labour. All of this work is done under the sun, during the few days I have been given. I will not ask for more. This simple, clean reality—the food, the work, the short time—this is my portion in life. I will take it, and I will not complain about what is missing. That is the only way to be content.

[2]I am the one to whom my inner being grants the wealth. It gives the possessions, and it gives the ability to enjoy them. I see that. I should acknowledge my fortune and find the pure pleasure in the work I do. This is not a prize earned from the outside. It is a gift from the ME to me—the rewarder and the receiver are the same. And because I know this, I will not dwell on the length of my days. I will not count the time that is left. I will only focus on the now. I will fill my heart with joy. That is the straight, final way to live.

[3]I see the evil that sits under the sun, and it weighs on me. It is a heavy thing to know. Sometimes I am given the wealth, the possessions, and the honour by my own deep Self. I have it all, but I am cursed. I cannot find the way to enjoy any of it. The good things are there, and I look at them, but they are flat and cold. And yet in another life, I

am poor, and the years are long. I live a long, full life, but I cannot ever satisfy the simple desires I have. I am always hungry for what is not there. It is the same loss. You either have the good things and cannot enjoy them, or you live long and never have enough to be satisfied. Both ways, life is wasted. That is the hard, unavoidable fact of the thing.

[4]If I father a hundred children and the years of my life are long, it means nothing if I cannot enjoy the wealth I made. It means less than nothing if I do not receive the proper burial when the time comes. I might as well have never been born. I have seen the other way. The childless man. He came into the world in the darkness, and he departed in darkness, and no one kept his name. But people still spoke well of him. They praised him, and he found happiness in his lifetime. That joy was real. It is better to have a short life of joy than to live twice as long and never know the prosperity of the spirit. The long life without joy is just a long failure. The simple, clean peace is the only real measure of a man's time. I know the better choice now.

[5]I know the true value. A good name that I have made is worth more than the finest perfume that fades in the air. And the day of my death is better than the day I was born. The day I die is the day the score is settled clean. I should go to the house where the people mourn. I will not go to the house where they feast. Death is the destiny of every man, and the living man should see that and understand the final truth. Sorrow is better than laughter. The sad face is better for the heart because it makes the heart sober and real. It shows me the truth of the effort. If I am wise, I would keep my heart in the house of mourning. I am where the truth is plain. But if I am a fool, I keep my heart in the house of pleasure, and I learn nothing there but how to waste the time.

[6]I know the better choice now. I should heed the rebuke from the man who is wiser than it is to listen to the song of the fools. The rebuke hurts, but it holds the truth. The laughter of the fools is like the crackling of the dry thorns under the pot. It makes a sudden, loud sound, and then it is gone quickly. It gives heat for only a moment, and it cooks nothing. It is a worthless noise. That noise, that hollow laughter—that, too, is meaningless to me now. I will take the harsh word that lasts over the quick sound that achieves nothing. I will listen to the pain that teaches.

[7]I am a man who believes I am wise. But I know my weakness. The extortion—the demand for the unfair payment—that can turn me into a fool faster than any mistake of judgment. It makes me act wrong. And the bribe—the money that comes too easily—that is the worst thing. It does not just change my mind; it corrupts my heart. It makes the clean part dirty. I know that money is a weapon. The wisdom I have is fragile. The minute I take the cash that is not clean, the knowledge in my head spoils. I stop being the man who knows the straight truth. The bribe is the thing that makes the end of wisdom. I must stay clear of it.

CHAPTER FIFTY-ONE

[1]I know that the end of a matter is always better than when it starts. The finish line is the only part that matters. And my patience is a better tool for getting there than my pride is. Pride will only make me move too fast and make the wrong choice. I will not be quickly provoked in my spirit. I will not let the small thing make me jump. The anger resides in the lap of fools, and it keeps them company. If I let the anger take me, I will be a fool just like them. I will sit on the same lap. I must keep the anger back. The man who is patient sees the end clearly. The angry man only sees red. I will choose the clear sight.

[2]I will not ask the question. I will stop my mind before the question is even fully formed. I will not ask: "Why were the old days better than these?" That is a sound that leads to nothing but sorrow. It is a weak question. It is not wise for me to ask such an absurd thing. The old days were hard, and the new days are hard. The work is always the same. I must deal with the day I have been given, and I must not pretend that the past was simple. The past is only the past. The question is a lie, and I will not be a liar. I will stay in the now.

[3]I know that wisdom is a good thing. It is like an inheritance you receive, and it benefits me every single time I see the sun. It makes the day easier to move through. Wisdom is a shelter. It is a place to stand when the weather

is bad. The money is also a shelter. You can use it to build the walls and keep the rain off. But the awareness—the knowing—has the greater advantage. Money can be lost in a bad venture. The house can burn down. But the awareness that is inside me, the clear wisdom, preserves me when I have it. It cannot be taken by fire or by thieves. It is the only true possession.

[4]I have to look at what my inner presence has done. It is the core truth. Who is the man who can straighten out the line that the source has made crooked? No one can. The pattern is set from the inside. When the times are good, I will be happy. That is the simple, direct answer. But when the times are bad, I will stop and I will consider the simple fact: The nature of the thing has made the one as well as the other. The good and the bad are from the same source. Because I know this—because I know the deep thing sets both the light and the shadow—I also know the final truth about the future. No one can discover anything about their future. The line ahead is hidden, and it is meant to be hidden. I will simply take the day that is given to me.

[5]I have lived this meaningless life long enough to see the two things. I have seen the truly righteous man—who kept the rule and did the clean work—and I have watched him perish in the middle of his goodness. He got the hard end. And I have seen the man who was completely wicked—who cheated and lied and took what was not his—and I have watched him live long in his wickedness. He kept his health, and he kept his gain. The world does not pay out fairly. The reward does not match the effort. The good man fails, and the bad man thrives. I have seen both, and they make a lie of everything we are taught. That is the final, coldest truth of the time under the sun.

[6]I do not want to be over-righteous. And I do not want to be over-wise. Why should I destroy myself with that kind of rigid thinking? I do not want to be over-wicked either. And I do not want to work so hard to prove I am a fool. Why should I die before my time with that kind of recklessness? The good thing is to grasp the one and not let go of the other. You hold the balance. That is the necessary work. If I revere my inner presence, if I treat that deep thing with the respect it is due, the awareness that surrounds me will keep me straight. It will make me avoid all the extremes. The extremes are where the ruin is found. I will stay in the middle where the work can be done.

[7]The wisdom I have gained makes me a man of strength. It makes me more powerful than ten rulers in the city who rely only on their guards and their gold. Knowledge is the final defence. But I know the other thing, too. I have seen every man, and I have seen my own heart. No one on this earth is righteous. Not one man who always does the straight thing and never falters. We all break the rule. We all make the wrong choice. The wisdom gives the power, but it does not give the perfection. I know I will fail, just like every other man. The power of the knowledge is real, but the failure of the man is absolute.

[8]I do not pay attention to every word the people speak. It is a necessary discipline. If I listen to everything, I may hear the man who works for me—my servant—cursing my name. I do not want to hear that, and it will do me no good. I will not listen because I already know the truth in my own heart. I know that many times, when the burden was heavy, I myself have cursed others. I have wished the bad on the next man. Since I am guilty of the same thing, I have no right to punish the sound of the curse from another man's mouth. It is better to let the small, bad word go unheard. I

will only listen to the things that matter.

⁹I took all of it and I put it to the test. I used the wisdom I had, and I told myself: 'I am determined to be wise.' But that final wisdom was beyond me. It was too far out. Whatever exists is far off, and it is most profound. No one man can truly discover it all. So, I turned my mind to the next work. I had to understand the pieces. I began to investigate and to search out the hard truth of the wisdom I could touch. I had to see the scheme of things. I also had to understand the other side of the line. I wanted to see the stupidity of the wickedness and the pure madness of the folly. I needed to know the darkness as well as the light. That was the only way to know where the true line was drawn.

[1]I know nothing is more bitter than the mind when it turns on itself. It is a cage that I build around my own thoughts. It is a snare of thinking, with branches that become nets. Its hug is a prison, and the hands that should free me only bind like chains. But I know the other part. I am aware of the deeper *presence* that lives inside me. And that presence will break me free. It will break the cage, but only when I take refuge in the silence that it gives. The man who tries to scheme and talk his way out of the trouble—the schemer will be caught in the grip of his own thoughts. I will not be that man. I will take the silence. The quiet place is the only way out.

[2]I have the tally now. I can look back and tell you what I found. I kept adding one thing to another. I kept working to discover the scheme of things—the whole pattern. I was searching, and I was not finding the answer I wanted. But I did find one thing. I found one upright and conscious man among a thousand. That is the best ratio I could manage. But I did not find even one man who was truly enlightened among them all. Not one.

[3]I know I must obey the ruler's command. That is the way of the world. And because I obey, I accept that I cannot know what will happen to me. My path is not my own. Who is the man who can stand up and question the power? Who can say to the one in charge, 'What are you doing?' No one

can speak that word and walk away whole. The command of the ruler is powerful, and no one can question it. The man who obeys the command will come to no harm. That is the simple, practical safety of it. I give up my choice so I can keep my life. That is the necessary trade-off a man makes to survive the time.

[4]The wise heart knows the whole calendar. It knows the proper time to act, and it knows the right way to do the thing—the procedure. The wisdom is a schedule. There is a correct time and a correct way for every matter under the sun. It is fixed. And this remains true even when a man is weighed down by misery. The sadness does not change the time. My grief does not stop the sun from moving. The wisdom tells me: the time is the time. The misery is only the background. I must know the difference and follow the procedure that is straightforward. I will not let the pain ruin the timing of the work.

[5]No one knows the future. That is the one thing I know for certain. Since I do not know what tomorrow holds for me, who am I to speak? Who can tell another man what will happen after him under the sun? The man who claims to know what the next generation will see—he is a liar. He is speaking in noise. The path is shut to my eyes, and it is shut to his. I cannot advise the one who comes after me. I can only do my work clean and hope that he figures out his own truth. The future is a question that must be answered by the one who lives it. And the answer cannot be given ahead of time.

[6]I know the true limits of my power now. No man has power over the wind to contain it. You cannot capture the air and hold it in your hand. You can only stand in its path and endure it. And no man has power over the day of death. I cannot name the hour I will go, and I cannot push the time

away. It is not a thing that can be scheduled or avoided. And when the fight comes—the battle—no one can be told when it will be or how it will turn out. The suddenness is part of the command. These are the three things you cannot govern: the wind, death, and the fight. You must simply accept them and live clean until they arrive.

[7]I have looked at the wise and the righteous, and their work. I understand that all are held by their inner presence, to which they have sacrificed their lives. They know that despite their efforts, they are not the final say; the final word belongs to the deep presence inside. Because of this, no man truly knows what awaits him—whether love or hate will be his final lot. You can hope or fear, but the decision is not yours. You simply live and work, knowing your ultimate path is controlled by a power you cannot see or predict. The hand is closed, and what it holds is the final mystery; the way it shows it is our path to peace.

[8]We all share one common destiny. The righteous man and the wicked man. The good one and the bad one. The clean one and the dirty one. The man who offers the sacrifice and the man who turns away from the altar. It is the same for all of us. There is no success, there is no failure. As it is for the good man, so it is for the evil. As it is for the one who swears the oath, so it is for the one who is afraid to swear it. The grave does not ask for our history. This is the great evil in everything that happens under the sun: The same destiny overtakes all. There is no special reward for the good effort. There is no good and evil in any of us. We make it with our thoughts and live by it. And while we live, our hearts are full of malice and madness. That is the way we move through time. And then, afterwards, we all join the dead. That is the final, straight truth of being a man.

CHAPTER FIFTY-THREE

¹Anyone who is among the living has hope. That is the simple truth. Even a live dog is better off than a dead lion. The dog has the breath in him, and the lion has nothing left but a name. All of us who are still alive know one thing for certain: that we will die. But the dead know nothing. The lights are off. They have no further reward, and after a short time, even their name is forgotten. The things that drove them—their love, their hate, and their jealousy—those things are long since vanished. They will never again have a part in anything that happens under the sun. Life, even the ugly life, is the only thing that matters. The absence is absolute.

²I will go now. I will eat my food with gladness and thankfulness. The food is there, and it is real. And I will drink my joy with a merry heart. I will do this because I know the truth that sets a man free: My own inner being has already approved what I do. The deepest part of me has signed off on the simple life. The struggle is over. The seeking is finished. There is no more doubt. The time is now to take the simple things that are given, without looking back or worrying ahead. The permission has been granted. I will live the good thing.

³I must always be clothed in righteousness. That is the only garment a man should wear. It is the only thing that does not wear out or go out of style. It is the outer truth of

the clean work. And I must always anoint my head with two things: the presence of being and empowerment. I must be present in the moment, and I must be ready to act with all the strength I have. The outside must be clean, and the inside must be prepared. That is the way to move through the world. I will not leave the house without the right clothes, and I will not move without the right state of mind.

[4]I will enjoy life with my spouse. I will love the man and woman who stand with me through all the days of this meaningless life that has been given to me under the sun. All these days that do not add up to anything—those days are the ones to be shared. Because those shared days, that simple connection—those are the things that give the only meaning to the soul. Those memories of the soul are the only true things that will follow me after death. The rest of the effort, the money, the work—it all stays behind. But the love I built, the joy I shared—that is the only gain I can carry with me into the silence. I will hold the affection tight, for it is the only real part of the whole journey.

[6]Whatever your hand finds to do, do it with all your might, for in the realm of the dead, where you are going, there is neither working nor planning nor knowledge nor wisdom.

[7]Man has to realise something else under the sun: The race is not to the swift, nor the battle to the strong, nor does food come to the wise or wealth to the brilliant or favour to the learned; but time and chance happen to them all. Moreover, no one knows when their hour will come: As fish are caught in a cruel net, or birds are taken in a snare, so people are trapped by evil times that fall unexpectedly upon them.

[8]Man also has to understand under the sun this example of wisdom that should greatly impress him: There was once

a small city with only a few people in it. And a mighty king came against it, surrounded it, and built huge siege works against it. Now there lived in that city a man, poor but wise, and he saved the city by his wisdom. But nobody remembered that poor man. So, man said, "Wisdom is better than strength." But the poor man's wisdom is despised, and his words are no longer heeded. One is philosophy, and the other reality.

CHAPTER FIFTY-FOUR

[1]The quiet wisdom of the man who knows the truth is worth more than all the loud shouts of a fool. The noise accomplishes nothing. The wisdom is better than war. It is a thing that prevents the fight before it starts. But I know how fragile it is. One careless person—one man who does not think—can cause great harm that the wisdom cannot easily fix. It is like the dead flies in the perfume. They are small, but they spoil the whole bottle. A little bit of folly ruins much good that was earned with sweat. The wise man acts with thought. He considers the end before he begins the action. The fool rushes in, and he does not think, and he only exposes himself to ruin. I will choose the quiet thought over the loud rush. That is the only way to protect the good work.

[2]If the boss gets angry with me, I will not run. I will not leave the place where the work is done. I will stay calm when the noise starts. The fear is the easy way out. But running does not fix the problem. I will stay and I will find the big mistake. I will deal with the error that caused the trouble. I will not be distracted by the boss's face or his voice. I will put my hands on the bad work and I will fix it. The cool head is the only tool that makes the necessary repair.

[3]The unqualified people are given the important jobs. They sit in the high chairs and run the whole business. And

the men who truly deserve the work, the good ones—they are ignored. The men with no vision and no honesty are the ones who get the power. The straight truth is twisted for their comfort. The wise people—the ones who should be leading—have to work twice as hard to keep the machine moving. They carry the load, but they do not get the title. They are pulling the weight for the fool who should be serving them. It is a world built upside-down. The wrong man always has the easy job, and the honest man always has the heavy sack. That is the frustrating, simple arithmetic of the way things are run.

[4]If I dig a hole, I know the risk is simple: I might fall into the hole that I myself made. If I break a wall, the wall hides a threat. A snake might be living there, and it might bite me. If I mine the stones, the rock can turn on me. I could get hurt by the very thing I am trying to take out of the ground. If I chop the wood, the axe is sharp. I might get injured by the tool in my hand. Every piece of work has its own cost. The effort is not clean. The danger is always present, and it comes from the work itself. A man must be careful with his own strength, or the strength will destroy him.

[5]If the axe I use is dull, the work is harder. It takes me more effort to cut the same piece of wood. The swing is heavy, and the gain is small. I spend my strength and I get little back. But if I am skilful—if I know how to use the tool and how to keep the edge sharp—I will get better results. The cut will be clean. The work will be done quickly. The lack of skill and the bad tool make the work a burden. The sharp edge and the right knowledge make the work a simple pleasure. A man must maintain the tool, and he must maintain the skill. That is the only way to get the true profit from the effort.

⁶The simple truth is this: If the snake bites before the charmer can stop it, the charmer is finished. He will not get the pay. His skill was too late. It is important for me to be prepared and to be careful before I begin any action. The moment the snake moves is the moment the money is decided. Planning is what helps me avoid disaster. The disaster is already there, waiting. If I do not think ahead, the quick trouble comes, and the work is spoiled. You must handle the thing before the bad thing can happen. The delay is the payment that I lose.

⁷The wise people speak kindly. The words are clean, and they do the work. But the fools talk too much. That is the first sign of the rot. At the beginning, the fool's words are only silly. They are harmless noise. But if you wait, the words get worse. In the end, they sound crazy, and the fool just keeps on talking. They do not know when the conversation is finished. The fools work hard. They put in the effort. But they do not know the right way to go. They spend their strength moving in the wrong direction. The loud mouth and the heavy labour—they are both wasted because the fool lacks the simple awareness of the path.

CHAPTER FIFTY-FIVE

[1]I say woe to the nation whose leadership confuses the privilege of command with the pursuit of comfort. If I, your leader, act like a servant to my own ease, and if my officials spend their days in endless pleasure, then our nation is already ruined. When indulgence becomes the agenda, and personal appetite eclipses public work, the foundation of our state dissolves. My country will thrive only because I am prepared and committed to the mastery of my work. My resolve is to act with absolute responsibility, focusing every single hour on the public good, not on personal excess. Here is the difference between success and failure: The successful nation is run by those who choose the hard task. The failed nation is run by those who choose entertainment and greed. The discipline must start at the top. The whole structure fails without it. The indulgence of the few does not bring prosperity; it guarantees the hunger of the many. My vow to you, the people I serve, is this: I commit to the hard task. I will not waver, because I know that duty is the greatest honour. Let this commitment be the new, unshakeable bedrock of our country.

[2]I know how the laziness works. It does not just waste my time; it causes the problems that hit me directly. When my hands are idle, my work is not done, my roof begins to sag, and the rain gets in. My house will leak. The structure fails because I did not do the simple, necessary thing to

hold it up. The house is the true measure of my effort. If I am lazy, the walls will tell the story. I pay for the stillness with water damage and rot. I must move, or I will lose the shelter.

[3]I know what the world offers. The feasts bring joy for a short time. The alcohol provides me with temporary happiness that helps me forget the harsh facts. And the money—the gold—that can solve many of my problems that the day puts in front of me. They are all good things for the moment. They have their uses. But the one thing money cannot do is save me from death. The wealth is finished when my breath is gone. I can buy the joy, and I can buy the drink, and I can fix the problem on the ground, but I cannot buy the time back. The final, certain payment is still due.

[4]I will not criticize the leaders who are above me, even in my thoughts. I will not curse the rich man in private. I will hold the words back, even from the deep, quiet place of my own mind. The danger is always there. The words might still get out. They have a way of leaving the dark room. Someone could repeat them, even if they only heard the whisper that was not meant for them. I cannot afford the luxury of private scorn when I deal with power. The thought is an action, and the consequence of that action can be ruin. I will keep my mind clean, not out of respect for the men, but out of respect for my own survival. I must silence the internal voice, or my peace will be taken from me.

[5]I will share what I have. I will give it away, and after some time, I will trust that it will come back to me. That is the way the true exchange works. And even if it doesn't, I will be content that I have done my part for the earth which has given me a lot for free. I will give to many. I will spread the help around. I will do this because I never know when

a disaster may strike. The good fortune can break quickly. When the disaster hits me, I will be the one who needs the help. The hands I helped to fill will be the only hands left to pull me out. It is not just kindness; it is insurance against the dark time. You give now so that you do not face ruin alone later.

[6]I know the law of the natural world. When the clouds are full, they cannot hold it back. They will bring the rain. The pressure is too great, and the consequence is sure. And when a tree falls, it does not roll away. It lands where it lands, and it stays there. The moment of its fall is the moment its place is fixed. There is no argument against the rain, and there is no moving the fallen tree. The event happens, and the result is final. I will deal with the consequence exactly where it lands. That is the necessary truth for me to accept.

[7]I know this much about the waiting game: If I wait for the perfect conditions, I will never put the seed in the dirt. I will never plant. And if I do not plant, I will never get the reward of the work. I will never harvest. The weather is never exactly right. The ground is never exactly ready. There is always a reason to wait one more day. The man who waits for the perfect time is the man who stays hungry. You must work with the conditions you have, or the whole season is lost. The choice is action now, or failure later. There is no middle ground in the field.

[8]I know I do not understand the wind. I cannot tell you where it is going or how it moves. And I do not truly understand how the new life is built inside the mother. I see the result, but the process is kept hidden. Just like those things, I cannot understand how the Subconscious works. I cannot see the great force behind everything that happens. I see the effect, but I do not see the cause. The truth is that

the deepest power is the one that stays silent. The wind is a mystery. Life is a mystery. And the force that drives the world is the final mystery. I will not waste my time trying to see what is meant to be unseen.

[9]I will work hard in the morning, and I will work hard in the evening. I will not let the sun rising or the sun setting change the simple fact of the labour. I will work because I do not know which effort will be the one that pays. I do not know which work will succeed. The first job I do might fail. The last job I do might be the one that matters. So, I cannot choose which one to save my strength for. I must treat every single task as the one that has to be done right. You work without knowing the score. You simply work until the light is gone. The constant effort is the only guarantee against a life that achieves nothing. It's a blessing to enjoy the sunshine and feel its warmth on your face.

CHAPTER FIFTY-SIX

[1]Something happens somewhere. That is all I can be sure of. Sometimes it happens for a reason I can see, a cause I can trace back. But sometimes it happens for no discernible cause at all. The thing just arrives out of the empty air. The simple truth is that what is meant to happen will happen. The final command will be carried out. But what I expect to come—that might never come to pass. The plan I made is not the one that unfolds. And what should happen—the thing that logic tells me must be next—that often remains elusive. It slips through the hands of reason. It goes against all anticipation. I must accept that the world does not run on a schedule I can read. The chaos is a part of the simple fact of living.

[2]This is not only what I saw. This is the law. It is a universal principle that governs all of existence, and it is completely beyond the control or comprehension of any man. The world does not unfold in a way that can be understood by logic. It defies every prediction, and it scorns every expectation. Every moment, every single event, seems to emerge from a script that no one has written down. It is an invisible script. Neither the man who thinks he is wise, nor the man who works only with science, can ever truly decode that script. The final truth is that the order of things is closed to us. We live inside a law that we cannot read. We are only meant to watch the

events come and go, knowing that the real reason for it all will never be explained. The mystery is the final fact.

[3]Yet, I know the truth about men. We are doomed—or perhaps we are destined—to keep seeking the reasons. It is like the mind to demand explanations. We will always chase causality as though it were a single thread that, once held, would unravel the whole mystery of our existence. From the first days of consciousness, we have sought the meaning. We looked up at the stars. We watched the cycles of nature. We studied the movements of history. We made the gods, and we devised the philosophies, and we built the heavy scientific frameworks—all in a hard attempt to make sense of why things happen the way they do. But the final question remains the same. Have we found the answer? No. The truth is that the chase is the only thing that is real. We keep running, and the answer keeps running faster. We will die while still looking for the reason. That is the final, inescapable work of being a man.

[4]The reason behind all things remains undiscovered. It has been that way since the start of time and will be until the end. Science gives us the mechanisms (the how); religion gives us faith (the why); philosophy gives us theories (the way to talk). But none of them delivers the ultimate truth. Every explanation we find is only a layer peeled back, revealing yet another mystery beneath. We find one answer only to reveal the next question. The truth is, the final answer is not meant to be known by us. We will keep stripping the layers, but never reach the core. The search is life, and the mystery is the constant.

[5]Perhaps the flaw is not in the world, but in my perception of it. I have assumed that meaning and causality must be absolute—that things must happen for a reason. This is the fundamental mistake I make daily. But what if

existence is not built upon a purpose? What if it simply is, standing alone without needing a reason for itself? And what if the chaos I see is not the absence of order, but a deeper, unknowable order my mind is not equipped to perceive? My brain is a small tool, built only to keep me alive; it cannot read the great, hidden pattern. I have spent my time chasing the reason. Now I see that the fault was in the asking. I must stop demanding a simple answer and simply accept the world as it moves—without purpose, without a straight line, but utterly real.

[6]Then what becomes of my fate? I cannot stop searching, for the mind will always look for a pattern. I could spend my time pushing on the closed door, letting the hope of simple truth drive my work, or I could surrender the fight against facts beyond my reason. Is surrender wisdom, or simply defeat? I will not stop breathing, so I cannot stop searching. But I will change the fight: I will search only for the clean life in front of me, and I will surrender the need for the ultimate reason. I will take life as it is given, without the guarantee of meaning. That is the only victory left; that is wisdom.

PART TWO

PROMISES

¹I AM the presence abiding in you, the quiet force within you. I AM your strength and bravery. You do not need to be afraid or upset, for I AM always with you. Believe in Me, and I will guide you along the way. Relying on external forces weakens you, but trusting in Me makes you resilient. The greatest curse humanity faces is the tendency to seek and depend on something outside itself. There may be crows that bring bread, but it is faith in Me that sustains you until the bread arrives. See Me as your true provider, and all else as mere messengers.

²Deep within your mind, I AM the source of your strength. I help you remain calm and focused, no matter what happens. When insecurity or doubt creeps in, remember that I AM your silent helper, always supporting you. You don't need to overthink—just trust in Me, and I will carry you through.

³When the world feels overwhelming, seek silence. Stilling your thoughts is not easy, but with practice, it becomes possible. Sit quietly, free from the past and unburdened by the future—both are weights that do not serve you. Ask for nothing; simply be still, even if only for a moment between your tasks. With daily practice, you will find it easier to quiet your mind, and in that stillness, I will reveal true clarity.

CHAPTER FIFTY-EIGHT

[1]To achieve clarity, I must first learn to observe things without attaching any extra thoughts or stories—just the pure object. When confused, I turn inward and silently observe my thoughts, watching them like clouds without judging or acting on them. This active awareness is the key. I must trust this inner wisdom from my subconscious because when I do, I find an unshakeable strength to face anything.

[2]Understand this deep truth: Even when you face the hardest challenges, you will not need to fear, because your inner awareness is always with you. It guides and comforts you, acting like a lighthouse that shows the way through dark and troubled waters. This inner wisdom is your anchor and the constant reminder that you are never truly alone. Your deep, conscious strength will see you through anything. Know, without a doubt, that you possess the power and courage to face and resolve any problem that stands before you.

[3]Don't be afraid, because your protector is always within you. Your inner awareness is always active if you simply acknowledge its presence, constantly supporting you, helping you be strong, and holding you up. This inner strength is like a friend who never leaves, giving you the resilience to face any difficult time and the unwavering power to keep going.

CHAPTER FIFTY-NINE

[1]Your inner strength and awareness will stay with you for your entire life. This constant presence comes from your *deep consciousness*, which is an ocean of never-ending strength. That is the foundation of everything you do, whether you notice it or not. Through mindfulness, your awareness grows, guiding you with clarity and wisdom to handle life's challenges with grace.

[2]This unchanging consciousness is what unites you with the Higher Intelligence and the energy of all existence. The key is simply to be aware of it within yourself. Looking outside for answers prevents you from awakening this inner awareness, which is your connection to the divine subconscious. This awareness is the source of deep knowledge and lasting peace. Silence is where this true consciousness flourishes and where you build your inner strength. By aligning this power, awareness, and a calm mind, you can live true to your destined purpose. Trust in your inner essence; it will be your loyal companion through all of life's stages.

[3]I shouldn't let my life be ruled by the desire for money. Instead, I need to be content with what I have, because my inner spirit and awareness will never leave or forsake me. My awareness will naturally provide for me, meeting all your needs with the abundance within. The key is to simply detach myself from my compulsive thoughts. The way I feel

inside directly dictates my external reality: when I feel rich inside, I will feel rich on the outside; if I feel poor inside, I will experience poverty outside as well. What's inside always reflects what's outside—everything starts from within.

CHAPTER SIXTY

¹Don't worry about what you'll eat, drink, or wear. Your *silent provider* in you already knows what you need. Instead, focus on awakening the awareness within you, and by quieting the distractions of the mind, all the things you need for a fulfilled life will come to you.

²Strong minds that are tied to the past and future may feel a lack, but you who are in harmony with their *inner presence* will never lack anything good.

³Every good thing and every perfect gift comes from within, from the *source of light* inside you, which is unchanging and constant.

⁴Those who wait in *inner stillness* will renew their strength. They will rise like eagles with wings, moving forward without tiring or stumbling.

⁵In the depths of our consciousness lies our refuge and strength. It is a silent guide in difficult times, offering resilience and wisdom that keep us grounded and steady, no matter what is happening outside.

⁶Your *inner spirit* reminds you that sufficient grace dwells within you, for true power arises from vulnerability. You will embrace your weaknesses, allowing them to reveal the strength within you. In doing so, you will deepen your reliance on your *Inner Self* rather than being swayed by fleeting external illusions.

[7]I can achieve anything using the inner strength residing within me. This power flows from a deep, internal connection—an intrinsic source of determination and persistence. It is what empowers me to face all challenges and pursue my goals with unwavering resolve.

CHAPTER SIXTY-ONE

¹'I leave you with peace; my peace I give to you. I do not give as the world gives, with its fleeting pleasures. Do not let your hearts be troubled or afraid,' says your *inner awareness.*

²Your *inner presence* gently calls, 'Come to me, all who are weary and burdened, and I will give you peace. Let my guidance, stored in you, teach you through gentleness and humility, bringing tranquillity to your soul.'

³My *presence within* is my shepherd; I lack nothing. It leads me to peaceful meadows and calm waters, refreshing my soul. This is all you need.

⁴The love for humanity was so profound that *higher wisdom* gave everything, ensuring that those who trust in their *inner strength*—deeply connected to the wisdom woven into the universe—would endure eternally.

⁵I am certain that nothing—neither death nor life, nor spirits, whether good or evil, nor rulers, nor time, nor powers, nor heights, nor depths, nor anything else in all creation—can separate us from the boundless love and reverence within, leading us to unity with our truest essence.

⁶If anyone lacks wisdom, let them seek within, where guidance is freely given without judgment, and it will be provided.

[7]Trust the *wisdom within you* with all your heart, and don't rely only on your understanding from external experiences. In everything you do, acknowledge this *inner guidance*, and clarity will light your way.

[8]Those who dwell in the shelter of the shared *Higher Intelligence* find protection in the shadow of the *all-powerful*. I declare to my *inner presence*, 'You are my refuge and strength, the essence in whom I place my trust.'

CHAPTER SIXTY-TWO

¹The deeper realm of Silence is your ultimate sanctuary—not a passive void, but a state of profound inner stillness and active awareness. Residing in these deep, quiet safeguards your life, offering protection that is strategic and psychological. This Silence anchors you against external chaos, preventing you from being swept away by fear or turmoil. An uncluttered mind gains the clarity and insight to perceive threats accurately, enabling you to make wise, pre-emptive decisions over reactive mistakes. Crucially, this inner realm guards you from self-inflicted harm: by observing negative thoughts without acting on them, you prevent impulses like greed or anger from becoming destructive actions. The Silence ensures your internal state remains uncorrupted, providing unshakeable emotional resilience and guaranteeing your life is protected and guided by your deepest wisdom.

²Imagine facing a challenge or decision, feeling uncertain and anxious. In that moment, the guiding presence within you says, *'Fear not, for I am here to help you.'*

³May the *source of life* fill you with joy and peace as you collaborate, so that the real you, which is beyond the limits of your sensory-based human mind, can fill you with peace through awareness.

⁴'For you know the plans your *inner being* has for you, plans for good and not for harm, to give you a future full of

life.

⁵The *light within* is your guide and salvation; whom should you fear? It is the stronghold of your life; what should you be afraid of?

⁶ When you admit your faults, the inner faithfulness and justice within you gain the power to forgive and cleanse all wrongdoing. You are the transgressor and the saviour. You sin by nurturing wrong thoughts, and you forgive yourself through the awareness of those sins. It is your Inner Spirit, not external laws or gods, that grants you forgiveness.

⁷For peace to dwell in you, you must be rooted in love. Gain the power to grasp the vast dimensions of your own self-love: its width, length, height, and depth. This love transcends understanding and provides the very essence of your being. Explore the love within your DNA with all your heart. Though hidden by default, rediscovering it demands effort and determination.

⁸The *deep consciousness* within strengthens the weary and empowers those without strength. Even the young lions may grow tired, but those who remain within and wait patiently will renew their strength. They will soar on wings like eagles, they will run and not grow weary, they will walk and not faint.

CHAPTER SIXTY-THREE

¹Therefore, we do not lose heart. Though our body is decaying, our *spirit* is renewed day by day, even as we sleep. For our temporary troubles are achieving for us an eternal glory that far outweighs mortality. So, we fix our eyes not on what is seen, but on what is unseen, since what is seen is temporary, but what is unseen is eternal.

²When the righteous yearns for help from within in silence—no brooding, no complaining, no lamenting—their *inner spirit* hears them and delivers them from all their troubles. It knows your needs before they are even in your mind.

³The enduring love within never ceases; its mercies are boundless, renewed each morning; great is its faithfulness.

⁴Let us firmly hold onto our declaration of self-dependence without hesitation, for the one—your *inner spirit*, your *subconscious awareness*—who promised all this, is trustworthy.

⁵The essence within is not human, carnal, that it would deceive, nor mortal, that it would alter its course. It is the spirit you share with the *Higher Intelligence*, the energy, the One that was, that is, and that will be for eternity. That which created the suns, the moon, the stars, galaxies, universes, and you resides within you by default. It only takes realisation, or what we call *awareness*, to feel it. Without silence and a clear mind, you cannot truly

experience your *inner spirit*. What it promises, it will accomplish; what it reveals, it will fulfil. This doesn't happen through thoughts or words but through deep, genuine feeling. Only then can it enter your mindful activities, where blessings are ready to be released—not for those who strive, push, and do, but for those who simply *are*.

⁶If possible, as far as it depends on you, live peaceably with all.

⁷Behold, how good and pleasant it is when brothers and sisters of the world become aware of their interconnected *subconscious awareness* and dwell in unity!

⁸Be eager to maintain the unity of the Spirit in the bond of peace.

⁹Bring your complete offering of *self-awareness* into your inner sanctuary, that there may be nourishment and abundance within. Put this truth to the test, for within you lies the potential to open the gates of enlightenment and draw blessings until every need is fulfilled. It is not the wants that the mind creates, but the true needs, which are ordained by you deep within and accepted by default to be accomplished.

CHAPTER SIXTY-FOUR

[1]The blessings of inner wisdom bring abundance, with no sorrow attached.

[2]Fortunate are those who deeply crave silence, both in mind and tongue. This desire should arise from true *awareness*, for their longing will be fulfilled.

[3]Those who listen to my guidance understand me, and they follow my lead. I offer them enduring existence, and they will never vanish; no one can remove them from my care, says your silent and subtle *inner spirit* through your *self-awareness*.

[4]In the depths of your consciousness, reside silence, steadfastness, and strength. Let silence lead you to always engage in meaningful work. In this deep *awareness*, your efforts gain true purpose and significance.

[5]In the *deep consciousness*, where your indigenous *spirit* resides, a soothing voice, a nudge, an urge communicates with you, whispering promises: 'Tears shall be gently wiped away, and death, mourning, crying, and pain shall fade into silence. The old burdens have passed, making way for a tranquil awakening.'

[6]O *Subconscious*, you make known to me the path of life; in your presence there is fullness of joy; at your right hand are pleasures forevermore.

[7]Do not be disheartened, for joy is your source of strength from within.

⁸To those who mourn, offering a radiant crown in place of ashes, the oil of joy instead of sorrow, and garments of praise to dispel weariness. They shall stand as pillars of righteousness, a mark of determination, bringing glory through their presence.

⁹Do not conform to the patterns of this world, but let your mind, influenced by your deeper *spirit* of *awareness*, be transformed by renewal, so that through testing you may discern what is good, acceptable, and perfect.

¹⁰I direct my observation to my *inner consciousness*. Where does my help come from? My help comes from the essence of *awareness* within me, which is connected to the *Higher Intelligence* that created the heaven and earth within me. The heaven you seek above the clouds and the earth you perceive outside you is futile.

¹¹Because they seek their inner *Self* in love, it delivers them; it protects them because they acknowledge its presence. Before you call, the answer is already there, waiting to be delivered; it will be with them in times of trouble, rescuing them and bringing them honour. With a long life of *awareness*, it satisfies them and reveals redemption to them. Living through the *spirit* is your part of the work. The results come only when it is never interrupted by any work of the mind, the thoughts, direct or indirect.

CHAPTER SIXTY-FIVE

[1]Grateful I am to my *Inner Spirit*, which guides me to victory through *self-awareness*—where I observe every breath I take, every twitch of my body, every sway of my thoughts, and every stir of my emotions, neither encouraging nor suppressing them.

[2]In all these things, we conquer and rise above, empowered by silence and *awareness*.

[3]Everyone born again of the *inner spirit* conquers the challenges of the world. Our being is the triumph that prevails over all.

[4]Blessed be the source of compassion and comfort, who consoles us in times of difficulty, enabling us to comfort others with the solace we have received.

[5]Just as a mother comforts her child, so will you, rooted in silence, comfort you. You will even find solace from the crafty mind and its offspring, the thought, when the *inner influence* exudes.

[6]Therefore, if anyone aligns with the *inner awareness* and silence of the mind, they experience transformation. The old fades away, making room for the brand new, reformed life.

[7]You will receive a new heart and a renewed *spirit of being*, awakening within you. As your *awareness* deepens, it will replace the unyielding heart of stone—rigid, cold, and unfeeling—with a heart of flesh—alive, receptive, and full

of compassion. This *awareness* will instil within you the essence of true being, guiding you to walk in harmony with the natural laws of creation, of which you are both a part and a product.

[8]There is no temptation that has overtaken you which is uncommon to humanity. Trust in your ability to overcome, for there is always a way out provided with each challenge, allowing you to endure, and the *awareness* in you helps you in the task.

[9]Blessed is the one who stays strong through trials, for after passing the test, they will receive the crown of life promised to those who hold steadfast in love and patience with silence as their language.

[10]Praise the *serene presence* within me, and remember the gifts it bestows—forgiveness for every mistake and healing for all ailments.

CHAPTER SIXTY-SIX

¹Your *inner awareness* will instruct you and teach you in the way you should go; with wisdom from the *Higher Intelligence*, it will counsel you to live in alignment with nature, with its careful eye upon you.

²Because if within your *Subconscious awareness*, you affirm with your being and believe in your heart the truth of transcendence, you will walk in the path to enlightenment. Attaining enlightenment is not your destiny; walking the path is your ultimate goal.

³So also, you have sorrow now, but I will see you again, and your hearts will rejoice, and no one will take your joy from you.

⁴Your *awareness* embodies forgiveness. Who else forgives wrongdoing and overlooks offences for those who remain faithful to the *Spirit* within them? You are free from the turbulence of thoughts; do not cling to anger indefinitely, but treasure enduring love. It will show compassion once more, overcoming your wrongdoing with its forgiving nature—so long as you do not entertain the enemy within: your own egoistic selfish thoughts. Like a millstone cast into the depths of the sea, it will carry away all your offences, never to resurface. And through mindfulness and *awareness*, you will rise above the tides, never sinking beneath them.

[5]For your *serene spirit* knows the path set for you—one of growth, not harm, a future filled with hope. As you remain silent, resting in your awareness, you will be heard without speaking, for it understands your thoughts before they take shape. Simply be still and unmoving. Silence is the language of your being—the only language it truly understands. You do not communicate using the external language shaped by your sensory perceptions; instead, you speak in the quiet knowing of your existence.

[6]The *Awareness* in you is close to the broken-hearted and rescues those whose spirits are crushed from the destructive thoughts that besiege them.

[7]The *Awareness* is in your midst, a mighty force that saves; it rejoices over you with joy, calming you with its power of being, and celebrates over you with joyful songs.

[8]Celebrate and be glad, for your reward of transcendence towards enlightenment is great in the higher realm, as others before you were persecuted for their *conscious living*. The world, with its varied faiths and religions, may not fully comprehend the truth.

PART THREE

LAWS

¹These principles should become a part of your heart. Teach them to your children, and talk about them at home, when you're walking, when you go to bed, and when you wake up. Keep these values close to you and let them guide how you think and act. Write them in the places where you live.

²Listen to these teachings, love them, and follow them carefully. You have an inner voice, a whisper, that speaks to you in subtle ways, not in big, loud signs. This inner voice has helped guide you, leading you away from the troubles of your past. It's gentle, quiet, that you feel deep inside you, and it's different from your loud thoughts and desires. Your thoughts, which are loud and compelling and imposing, often lead you in the wrong direction, but this quiet voice shows you the right way.

³This inner voice is not like the thoughts that rise in your mind. It's something deeper and more peaceful, like a whisper beneath the noise of your own perceivable breath. It's been with you even before you were born, the architect of each cell in your body, present and guiding you without you even knowing. It's the same force that helped you breathe, grow, and live without you thinking about it.

⁴So, why let your noisy thoughts control your actions and make things harder for the real help to give you freedom? Instead, listen to that quiet inner voice. It's not

loud or dramatic; it's gentle and natural, guiding you without you even trying to communicate with it. You don't need to think about it or control it. It's like going with the flow of a river—it just carries you along without you needing to do anything.

[5]If you've never felt this inner voice, it's because you haven't attempted to yearn for it or waited for it. But if you start being aware of its presence in you, you'll find the answers to your solution. There is no room for help if you still try to satisfy your carnal needs. Dependence on your mind with cluttered thoughts would feign the real guidance. Remember, the same mind that feigns peace can also create problems, along with what it gives you as peace. The creator of peace cannot also be the creator of conflict. Try to understand that though you are the creator and destructor of your life, you cannot have your feet on both at the same time. Either embrace one and leave the other.

[6]To grow in the true sense of growth and to be your true self, you need to listen to your spirit; the language of it is silence. When your mind is quiet and free of thoughts, you can access it clearly. The access is devoid of any mind utterances. Just be aware of the silence, and that would do. That's the path to your true self and happiness. And by the way, many people call this voice *God*.

CHAPTER SIXTY-EIGHT

[1]Understand this: you are whole—inside and out—connected and indivisible. While your brain has two hemispheres, they are interconnected, and your overall well-being depends on your willpower. This willpower is not mere stubbornness but a deep-seated willingness—an inner pull toward growth, a yearning to adapt and evolve. The world does not judge you by fragmented aspects of your consciousness, but as a whole. What you perceive outside is merely a reflection of what exists within. Therefore, nurture your Inner Self, and the outer world will naturally align. Love your true Self fully—with all your heart, soul, and strength. Not the self-shaped by perception, but the lucid essence beneath it—unseen, intangible, yet the force that governs all. Nothing in the universe holds greater significance than this.

[2]Your inner consciousness has made a covenant—not with those who came before you, but with you in this moment. It speaks directly from within.

[3]Today, you stand at a crossroads: you can choose life and success or destruction and downfall. If you follow the path of love and remain attuned to your inner consciousness, embracing its wisdom, you will thrive and be blessed.

[4]Living by these principles does not disregard the wisdom of the past—it fulfils it. Not even the smallest truth

should be overlooked until everything is complete in the grand evolution of humanity.

[5]Love your *spirit* engraved in youdeeply—with all your heart, soul, and mind. This is the greatest commandment. The second is like it: love your neighbour as yourself. Your neighbour begins with those closest to you—your family: parents, spouse, and children—before extending outward. Your primary responsibility is to those within your inner circle. This may be the hardest task, as those closest to you can often be the most difficult to love, and gratitude is not always reciprocated. It is easier to show kindness to strangers, yet true responsibility starts within. Do not search for neighbours outside; begin within your own household. Care for them, meet their needs, understand their struggles, and guide them toward a life of fulfilment. When each person nurtures their immediate family, strong families form the foundation of a thriving society.

[6]All wisdom—both ancient and modern—rests upon these two commandments.

CHAPTER SIXTY-NINE

¹Some may argue that prioritising your family over others is selfish. But true selfishness lies in seeking personal luxuries and gains while neglecting those closest to you. Loving and caring for your family is not an act of exclusion but a foundation upon which true generosity is built.

²What does your inner law say? Love yourself with all your heart, soul, strength, and mind—and love your neighbour as yourself. Follow this, and you will truly live.

³Living by faith does not mean abandoning principles; it strengthens them. Principles are pure and good—faith does not replace them; it elevates them. Principles guide us toward right living, but faith fills them with meaning, transforming them into acts of love and trust. Faith connects us with the deeper spirit behind these principles, allowing us to follow them with purpose and joy. When we act in faith without expectation, we grow into strong and mature beings.

⁴Nothing should take precedence over your inner being—your awareness of body, mind, and emotions. Pay attention to the subtle signals your body sends—muscle movements, temperature shifts, the rhythm of your breath, fleeting thoughts, and even compulsions born from imagination. Only through self-awareness can you master yourself, build confidence, and embrace the self-sufficiency of your true nature. Understanding yourself is

the first step to understanding the world. Your mind must be sharp, discerning the difference between mere thoughts and the deeper, inner voice. If you cannot distinguish between the two, how can you guard against harmful thoughts? Compulsive thoughts are destructive. The true transgression is dwelling on the past or being anxious about the future—for nothing good arises from either. Silence is the key to liberation. Only in silence can you reject these illusions and find redemption.

[5]Your *Inner Spirit*—the spirit of holiness by default—demands your full attention and will not tolerate being ignored for external distractions. This is the natural law of humanity, and blessed is the one who delights in this law, keeping it in heart and mind, day and night, through meditation.

CHAPTER SEVENTY

[1]I will not create false idols—material, sociological, ideological, or religious—that divert me from the true path of my Inner Consciousness. Seeking the divine outside myself is fruitless, leading only to confusion. The divine is found within me, as my Inner Self—a deeper layer of consciousness beyond my thoughts and breath. This Inner Self requires unwavering devotion, holding me accountable for my actions and inspiring love and kindness toward others on the same inner journey.

[2]In early human existence, characterised by dull senses and undeveloped minds, people felt insecure and isolated. Seeking meaning, they interpreted powerful natural phenomena like storms and earthquakes with awe and fear. This led them to believe in unseen forces, and this instinctive reverence eventually evolved into the concept of gods and spirits, shaping their earliest religious thought.

[3]Spiritual belief began with animism, where early humans perceived spirits in all aspects of nature (trees, rivers, animals). As societies evolved, polytheism emerged, involving the worship of multiple gods, often imagined in human form. Over time, some cultures moved to henotheism, worshipping one primary god while acknowledging others. This eventually led to monotheism, the belief in a single, supreme deity, which became dominant.

[4]Alongside these developments, pantheism arose, viewing the universe itself as divine. Each stage of spiritual evolution reflected humanity's deepening quest to understand existence, moving from simple nature spirits to a singular, all-encompassing force. As humans sought explanations for life's mysteries, they projected their own identities—including human emotions and gender—onto their gods. Attributing events to divine will provided a vital sense of control and was psychologically comforting, a construct passed down through generations. These shared religious beliefs also fostered unity and cooperation, with deities serving as both moral enforcers and sources of comfort during times of suffering.

[5]Religious systems continued to evolve, with monotheism gaining prominence through faiths like Zoroastrianism, which influenced Judaism, Christianity, and Islam. Meanwhile, Hinduism shifted from abstract spirituality to idol worship and multiple deities. Even Buddhism, originally focused on self-realisation, saw the deification of the Buddha, as followers began venerating him, despite his core teachings emphasising inner awareness.

[6]Thus, the progression of religious thought has been an outward search for meaning, yet the true path lies inward. The divine is not found in external idols or distant heavens—it resides within, as pure awareness, beyond the noise of thoughts and perceptions. To seek this truth is to transcend illusion and return to the source of all understanding: the Self.

CHAPTER SEVENTY-ONE

[1]As human intellect evolved, philosophers began to shift the concept of God from a personified being to an abstract, transcendent principle. In Hinduism, God is conceived as *Brahman*—an infinite, formless reality. Greek philosophers such as *Plato* and *Aristotle* envisioned God as the *Prime Mover* or *Universal Good*. Mystics across cultures described God as an experience of unity or *divine love*, beyond form or language. The concept of God has always varied across civilisations, shaped by geography, history, and cultural evolution. Egyptian gods, for example, were closely tied to the Nile River, while Norse gods reflected the harsh, unforgiving landscapes of Scandinavia.

[2]In modern times, science has challenged traditional religious notions, prompting many to see God as a symbolic concept or to reject the idea altogether. Yet, spirituality transcends religious doctrines, shifting the focus from an external search for a deity to an *inner journey toward infinite reality*. Instead of seeking heaven above, it directs us to a realm of bliss within. However, even the most enlightened minds often remain constrained by outdated religious constructs. The word *"God"* itself originates from the Proto-Indo-European root *ghut-*, meaning "to call" or "to invoke." Originally, this did not refer to an external divine being but rather to an *internal space within humanity*—a sanctuary of consciousness.

[3]Thus, the paradox of seeking God externally while the key to wisdom and understanding already lies within reflects humanity's struggle with self-reliance—a strength meant to be cultivated. This outward pursuit of the divine is like calling upon a force that already resides within. Instead of relying on external deities or religious symbols, why not turn inward? Within the depths of your *consciousness* and *being*, the very essence of God already dwells—waiting to be realised.

CHAPTER SEVENTY-TWO

¹Do not deceive or ignore your *Inner Self*, for doing so is both unwise and harmful. The thoughts and emotions that arise within you are not new; they are echoes of past experiences that your *Inner Self* has already understood. To suppress or justify them is like *lying to the omniscient within you*—the one who knows your truth beyond illusion.

²Your *Inner Self* has known you even before your birth. It perceives your actions, your thoughts, and even the words you are about to speak before they form in your mind. It is always present, always guiding you. To ignore or dismiss it is like *turning away from your own source of existence*—as if a child were to deny the womb that nurtured it.

³Yet, many people spend their lives searching for answers in the wrong places, repeating the mistakes of countless generations. They rush from one pursuit to another, trying everything except the one thing that truly matters—listening to their Inner Self. Instead of struggling, be still. Be silent. The answers you seek are not outside of you; they have always been within you, closer than your own breath.

CHAPTER SEVENTY-THREE

¹Love and respect your parents for all they have done for you. As they grow older, remain close to them. Speak kindly, and be patient, just as they were when you were young—when you relied on their care to live, learn, and grow. Strive for their happiness, just as they once wished the best for you.

²Even as you build your own life and family, never forget your duty to care for your parents. One day, you may stand in their place, and your children will learn from the example you set. No one deserves to feel abandoned or unloved—least of all those who gave you life. How foolish it is that in the modern world, the sacred bond between parent and child is so often ignored!

³People strive to impress the gods of their own making and the men of profit, yet they fail to show that same devotion to their parents. Neglecting them is a silent cruelty, one that not only causes them pain but also sows the seeds of regret.

⁴If your parents cannot dwell with you, help them remain in the home they cherish. Honor them by ensuring they feel valued, respected, and in command of their own lives. For they are a part of you—to neglect them is to forsake a piece of your own being.

⁵Money cannot replace love. Parents do not seek riches or luxury, but the warmth of your time, your care, your

presence. They gave you all they could when you were small. Now, it is your turn to give back—to make them feel cherished and included. Do not be foolish, revealing your own ignorance before your conscience, by treating them poorly, even in their vexation. For your deeds will return to you, and the cost may be great.

[6]No matter how high you rise, never forget the ones who gave you your first steps. Your parents are your roots; their love, the foundation of your life. Stay humble and grateful, for they are the ones who gave you the wings to fly.

CHAPTER SEVENTY-FOUR

¹Do no harm yourself or any human. Taking a life is the gravest wrong, but even anger, insults, and hatred can destroy. Holding onto anger poisons your heart; harsh words—even calling someone a fool—can break relationships and set unseen consequences into motion. Every action shapes not only others but also your own soul. Choose kindness and wisdom in all you do.

²Never bear false witness against others. Whether in court or daily life, do not spread lies or distort the truth to harm another's name. Falsehood shatters trust, and the wounds it leaves may never fully heal. Though honesty may be difficult, it is always the right path. How you act in private shapes who you are in public. Let truth and fairness guide your every word and action.

³Do not take what is not yours. Stealing is more than taking possessions—it is a betrayal of trust and integrity. Whether it is money, ideas, or recognition for another's work, dishonesty stains your character and dishonours those who raised you. Respect the efforts of others as you do your own. If you have more than you need, give freely. A world built on generosity leaves no room for the desire to take what does not belong to you.

CHAPTER SEVENTY-FIVE

[1]Remain faithful in your relationships. Even a single act of betrayal can bring lasting guilt and regret. No law may forbid it, but true integrity comes from within. What feels insignificant in the moment can become a weight you carry for a lifetime. Honour your commitments, for trust, once broken, is not easily restored.

[2]If you are married, honour your vows. Trust is the foundation of love, and once broken, it leaves wounds that may never fully heal. Faithfulness is not just about the body but also the heart and mind. A strong relationship thrives on honesty, respect, and open communication. Do not hide your thoughts and feelings—share them with your partner, for true love grows through understanding and trust.

[3]No relationship is perfect at all times. There will be highs and lows, but honesty from the start can prevent greater troubles later. However, revealing the truth only when faced with blame does more harm than good—it deepens misunderstandings instead of resolving them. True honesty is not just about admitting mistakes but about sharing both joys and struggles in a way that strengthens your bond, not weakens it. Stay connected to your *subconscious* and cultivate *awareness* of your *Inner Self* and *Inner Spirit*—for in truth, love flourishes only when the soul is at peace.

CHAPTER SEVENTY-SIX

¹Always be truthful and fair. Spreading lies, gossip, or twisting facts can harm others and damage trust. Whether in public or private, honesty matters. Stand up for what is right, even when it's difficult.

²Take time to rest and reflect. Just as the body needs food and water, the mind and spirit need renewal. Set aside a day to relax, connect with loved ones, and care for yourself. Even animals, machines, and nature benefit from rest. This isn't a rigid rule, but a path to balance and well-being.

³Be content with what you have. Don't waste energy envying others' success, possessions, or relationships. Focus on your journey and your goals. Happiness comes from growth, not comparison. Don't feed envy in others—true worth isn't built on impressing people. Find fulfilment in your own path, and let others walk theirs.

⁴Embrace your subconscious awareness and listen to your Inner Self for guidance. Be kind and compassionate. Treat others with respect, empathy, and patience—everyone faces their own battles, and small kindnesses matter. Speak sincerely, act with integrity, and uplift others. True strength is gentle, and true leadership serves.

CHAPTER SEVENTY-SEVEN

¹Let go of grudges and revenge. Love doesn't mean invading someone's space—it means respecting their boundaries and wishing them well. If someone needs help and you can offer it, do so without expecting anything in return. True love is about kindness, not control. Holding onto resentment harms you more than the person you resent, like a wound you inflict on yourself.

²To love your neighbour as yourself means treating others with the kindness and understanding you would want for yourself. Practising empathy and forgiveness frees you from negativity and helps build stronger relationships.

³Leave no debt unpaid—except the ongoing debt of love. True love isn't about grand gestures or constant words but is shown in quiet acts of care when needed.

⁴All rules against harming others—whether through dishonesty, violence, or selfishness—can be summed up in one principle: love others as you love yourself. Love does not harm and is the true fulfilment of any law.

⁵Love isn't just a word—it's shown in patience, kindness, humility, honesty, and trust. If these qualities aren't present, then what you call love isn't really love at all.

⁶Choose peace over worry, allowing your *Inner Self* and *Inner Spirit* to shine naturally. Use affirmations and visualisation as gentle tools to shift your mindset, focusing on growth and transformation without forcing specific

outcomes. Visualisation should flow organically from your desires, not be a forced exercise. Avoid the temptation of using these practices for selfish gains, as it can nurture negative traits like greed and selfishness. Let these techniques be brief aids, and don't hold onto them afterwards. Instead, focus on cultivating positive thoughts and attitudes that radiate goodness.

[7]Stay true to yourself and your values, ensuring your actions align with your inner truth. Avoid forcing yourself into actions just because of external pressures. Trust that your *Inner Self* and a higher energy in co-operation are guiding you, and let things unfold naturally. Refrain from trying to control outcomes and surrender to the natural plan. Embrace integrity and authenticity as expressions of your higher nature, and seek fulfilment from within. Avoid pushing, as it creates unnecessary friction and leads to pain. To be free of pain, stop pushing

¹Be fruitful and grow, filling your life with meaning and purpose. When you flourish in goodness, everything else will follow. You will lack nothing truly important. Even in difficult times, you will not be harmed. When you remain strong and full of virtues, "A thousand may fall at your side, ten thousand at your right hand, but it will not come near you."

²Avoid actions that drain your inner strength, your *Inner Spirit*. Bad habits, negative thoughts, and careless actions can drain your spirit. Pay close attention to everything you think, say, and do. Take care of your body, but even more, protect your *sanctuary*, which controls the body and its fibres. Be mindful of what you see, hear, and allow into your heart—these shape who you become.

³At first, noticing every little detail may feel unusual, but with time, it will become second nature. Soon, *awareness* will flow effortlessly, bringing clarity and strength to your mind. "The eye is the lamp of the body. If your eyes are healthy, your whole body will be full of light."

⁴Respect life and always choose what is right. Do not fill your mind or body with things that weaken your spirit. What you read, watch, and listen to affects your inner world. If you take in goodness, your heart will shine brightly. Keep your thoughts simple and honest. Your mind is a sacred space—honour it.

[5]Take time to reflect on your experiences without being too hard on yourself. Learn from mistakes instead of judging yourself or others. No one has the right to judge another, which includes self-reproach.

[6]Show kindness and fairness to all, especially to those who rely on you. Honour your family, respect your friends, and be just to those who seek your guidance. For the high may be brought low, and the low may be lifted up. As you sow in the hearts of others, so shall you reap in your own time.

[7]Watch your words, even in jest, for a careless tongue can wound the heart. Give respect to others, their space, and their feelings, and you shall find respect in return. For kindness and fairness are like seeds—what you sow, you shall surely reap.

CHAPTER SEVENTY-NINE

[1]Walk in wisdom and seek a life of purpose, for the spirit that grows within you shall sustain you. Though trials may come and hardships press upon you, a heart rich in virtue shall never be shaken.

[2]Guard yourself against actions that lead to inner numbness. Be aware of every thought, action, and perception that crosses your mind. While caring for your body is essential, keeping your *Inner Spirit* alive is even more so. Stay mindful of what you see, hear, and experience—everything you absorb shapes your inner world. At first, living with such *awareness* might feel unnatural, but over time, it will become effortless. When your perception is clear, your entire being is filled with light.

[3]Guard your heart and mind, for they are the wellspring of your life. Turn away from all that darkens your spirit, whether in thought, speech, or action. What you take in shall take root within you—choose wisely, for the soul is shaped by what it feeds upon. Be mindful of your ways, yet do not condemn yourself. Observe, learn, and let wisdom guide your growth.

CHAPTER EIGHTY

[1]If jealousy or doubt stirs within you, speak with honesty, not anger. Seek clarity with a gentle heart, for strife will only deepen the wound. Let not pride rule your tongue, nor ego darken your judgment. Watch over your spirit, for peace is its guardian—heed its voice, and you shall walk in wisdom; ignore it, and you shall stumble.

[2]If you are wounded, speak with wisdom, seeking not to wound in return but to restore peace. A humble gesture, be it a word or a vow, can mend what pride would break. Keep matters private, for honour is not found in another's shame. Offer apology where due, grant forgiveness when possible, and at times, let laughter dissolve the weight of offence. Stubbornness may feel like victory, but an unmade peace will haunt the heart in ways unseen.

[3]The innocent shall walk without shame, and the guilty must bear their own burden. Keep your heart pure by speaking truth in quiet places, not in prideful display. A just community is built on trust, and peace belongs to those who seek it with fairness. Fear not to speak or to make amends, for all are shaped by trials unseen. Let your words be bold yet gentle, your spirit firm yet kind. And if another repays kindness with deceit, know that they have lost more than you.

CHAPTER EIGHTY-ONE

[1]Practice mindfulness daily, even if only for a moment, for in stillness, wisdom unfolds. Be present, not lost in thought, and seek silence where reflection speaks louder than words. Gather with those who cherish quiet understanding, where hearts grow together in truth. Do not seek knowledge for vanity, but let your *Inner Spirit* be your teacher. Listen to advice, but weigh it carefully, for every voice is shaped by its own path. True learning is not to impress, but to transform.

[2]What you do with the knowledge you gain will unfold in its own time. Do not be anxious about its purpose—simply keep learning and refining your skills. The world may see a "jack of all trades, master of none" as lacking, but in truth, it is a path of endless growth. Let wisdom, not worldly approval, guide you. True success is not measured by society's standards but by the richness of your journey. Embrace your path, and mastery will follow in ways you never expected.

[3]Live authentically, guided by your inner *consciousness*, earning self-approval through consistent effort. Resist impulsive urges and seek what is just, rooted in faith, love, and peace. Avoid judging justice, as it will unfold naturally. Surround yourself with others who live from their moral foundation.

[4]Let the inner grace within guide you toward righteousness, helping you turn away from actions that conflict with your values. It empowers you to live with self-discipline, honesty, and kindness. Encourage respect for authority and treat everyone with dignity. Salvation comes not from your outward efforts to be virtuous but from embracing the sacred essence within you.

[5]Trust in your commitment to what is right. Set expectations and goals in alignment with your *Inner Self*. I have faith that you will exceed the expectations you set. May the grace that guides you remain with you, as wisdom within directs your thoughts and actions. The key is to prioritise your *Inner Self*, investing more energy and time in it in silence than in external situations.

[6]True spirituality lies in helping others without seeking personal gain. The wisdom within respects others, empathising with them as you would wish others to do for you. Never remind them of their need for help, either through words or gestures.

CHAPTER EIGHTY-TWO

[1]When you realise you've wronged someone, admit it—this is the first step to healing and staying in harmony with yourself. Take responsibility by apologising and offering to make things right. Let your actions show true regret and a desire to restore the bond. If the person is unreachable, make amends by helping others who reflect the values you harmed. Growth begins with humility. Ego must shrink to the size needed for survival—no more, no less.

[2]Establish a culture of accountability and support. People own their mistakes, and the group helps make things right. Begin at home: parents teach children this principle. Guarantee equal opportunity for all roles, responsibilities, and resources. Gender and background don't matter. Society sustains you; therefore, you must help it thrive. When disputes over rights or inheritance appear, use transparent, inclusive processes to settle them. Respect everyone's unique situation. Clear, shared guidelines prevent confusion and keep things fair.

[3]When concerns surface, speak them openly. Find answers together. Solutions honour each individual's needs. They honour the group's unity. This holds for family, community, and government. Everyone takes part. In decisions. In duties. In responsibilities. Systems for fighting must be fair. Use mediation. Reach a mutual understanding. Values move. Update the rules. Do it often. Stay relevant.

Yesterday's truths do not serve today. Change with purpose. Move ahead. Or be left behind.

⁴Plant wisdom early in young hearts, and a righteous generation will rise. Let education flow beyond books—shaping minds at home, in school, and in the world. Teach not just knowledge, but spirit, so children walk in truth. Let them still their minds, guard their words, and master emotion. Let life itself be the classroom. Learning should light their path—not bind their feet. Teach them to perceive, discern, and live with purpose. For what gain is the world, if one loses himself? The world suffers from lost hearts, but wisdom seekers will shine like cities on hills—radiating peace. Raise such a generation, and justice will fill the land.

CHAPTER EIGHTY-THREE

¹Establish places of refuge where wisdom and compassion guide the way. Let there be counsel for those who seek understanding, that they may walk in alignment with both their *inner truth* and the good of the community. Provide spaces of safety, where the wounded in spirit may find healing, and where those who have erred may reflect without fear of shame. Let not a man's failing be cast before the multitudes, for who among the living is without fault? Judge with fairness, seeking the heart's intent and the weight of circumstance, that justice may be tempered with mercy. Offer guidance to the troubled, that they may find peace within, and counsel to the burdened, that they may be strengthened. In all things, let growth be the goal, not condemnation, for wisdom is born not from fear but from understanding. Where there is kindness, the lost may return; where there is patience, the heavy-hearted may find rest.

²Let the good of the many be placed above the gain of the few, for a house divided against itself cannot stand. If a man seeks only his own reward, let him step aside, and let not shame follow him, for honesty is greater than pretence. When trust is broken, let the path of restoration be made clear, that those who stumble may rise again. If harm is done in ignorance, let wisdom correct it; if done with intent, let justice be both firm and fair. Counsel the

wayward, that they may find their footing, and let the community stand as witness, that truth may not be hidden in darkness. Let discipline be a guide, not a weapon, lifting the fallen rather than crushing their spirit. Where there is remorse, let there be mercy; where there is repentance, let there be a way home. A man restored is a light unburied, shining not only for himself but for all who walk beside him.

[3]Prevent further harm by focusing on justice that heals rather than worsens conflicts. Promote restorative practices that rebuild relationships and maintain harmony. Provide clear spaces where people can reflect on their actions and find the support they need, ensuring these resources are easy to access and well-known in the community. Develop a justice system that's transparent and includes the community in decision-making, considering the intent behind actions and ensuring fair responses. Practice these values in your own family—it all starts with you, then your family, your community, and, ultimately, your country.

CHAPTER EIGHTY-FOUR

¹Start by educating the community—beginning with your family, schools, religious institutions, and government—on the importance of understanding the intentions behind actions that are judged. Raise awareness about the difference between intentional harm and accidents, encouraging empathy and support for those in need of rehabilitation. Promote restorative practices that focus on healing and reconciliation, encouraging individuals who have caused harm to participate in activities that repair the damage and rebuild trust.

²Create support networks for rehabilitation, including mentorship programs where experienced community members guide those on their recovery path. Offer access to counselling services to address emotional and psychological challenges, as well as educational and vocational training to equip individuals with skills for a stable future. Facilitate community-building activities that help people feel like they belong and are accepted. Make sure resources such as financial aid, housing, and healthcare services—both physical and mental—are easily accessible.

³Encourage the community to support those in rehabilitation, offering patience, understanding, and encouragement as they work to realign their actions with their *Inner Self* and *inner values*. Clearly define roles and

responsibilities within the community based on individual strengths, so everyone understands their contribution to the social well-being. Provide the necessary support for those serving the community, recognising their efforts and making sure they have the resources to continue their valuable work.

[4]Set up a fair system for distributing resources, ensuring that those who contribute significantly to the community are supported, and that resources are shared equitably. Encourage everyone to contribute according to their abilities, making sure the community's needs are met and the benefits are shared. Allocate resources to essential community roles to meet basic needs and ensure key positions are fulfilled. Identify roles based on individual talents and communicate expectations clearly for smooth operation.

[5]Create additional support systems for those serving the community, such as mentors, training programs, and resource management. Regularly acknowledge and reward their contributions to help maintain a thriving and well-supported community.

CHAPTER EIGHTY-FIVE

¹Create a fair system for sharing resources, ensuring everyone receives based on their contribution and needs. Encourage generosity through shared activities that allow all to give and support. Honour leaders, teachers, and caregivers with gestures of appreciation to sustain their vital work. Treat everyone with respect and kindness—each person holds value and dignity. Build strong connections by helping those in need, fostering teamwork and unity. Speak out against injustice, promote equality, and ensure fairness for all, regardless of background.

²Set aside one day each week for rest and reflection—to care for your body, mind, and spirit. At the start of each month, reflect on the past, set intentions, and align your plans with your values. Every few months, take time for deeper renewal—through retreats or workshops—to stay connected to your Inner Self. Celebrate milestones and special moments to honour your path and reaffirm your beliefs. Live responsibly by caring for the environment—reduce waste, protect nature, and walk gently on the earth.

CHAPTER EIGHTY-SIX

[1]Withdraw often into the quiet places of your soul, that you may know yourself and grow in wisdom. Strive not against the world, for the clamour outside is but a shadow—your true strength is within. In stillness, you shall find clarity, and in silence, you shall feel the voice of wisdom. Nurture the bonds of love with your family and those entrusted to your care, speaking with honesty, embracing with kindness, and lifting one another in times of need. Guard your spirit, tending to it as a garden, that it may bear the fruits of peace and understanding. Seek communion with the depths of your being, and let gratitude be your guide, for the heart that gives thanks is never empty. In all things, share the abundance of your soul, for kindness given is never lost but returns in ways unseen.

[2]Your family is your dwelling of trust, bound together as father, mother, children, and siblings for a purpose. Do not lay bare its sacred walls to outsiders, nor cast your words carelessly beyond its doors. They are the ones appointed to walk with you in joy and sorrow, to hold your burdens and share in your blessings. To speak against them or expose their struggles is as foolish as tearing down the roof of your own home with your own hands, leaving yourself defenceless against the storm. Let wisdom keep your tongue, and let love be your shield, for a house divided will not stand, but one built on trust shall endure forever.

[3]Live in a way that matches your values and principles, being true to yourself in everything you do. Make choices that reflect your beliefs and regularly check in with yourself to find ways to improve. Be open to feedback, learn from your experiences, and keep growing towards a deeper understanding of yourself. Stay strong and brave in the face of challenges, understanding that success and failure are both just parts of the journey. What matters most is the learning you gain from each experience. Live by kindness, fairness, and ethical behaviour, treating everyone with respect. Keep working toward your goals, knowing that personal growth is a continuous journey.

[4]Build a community where people help and support each other, especially in tough times. Learn from past experiences, but don't dwell on them too much—let your Inner Self guide you when making decisions. Your mind can be clever, but wisdom comes from within. Trust yourself to act with honesty, integrity, and fairness in everything you do. Embrace change and stay flexible when things around you shift. Focus on living with sincerity, transparency, and accountability. Appreciate the contributions of others and stay open to different ideas. No one is perfect, and things will always change, so avoid judging others. Support justice, fairness, and equality for everyone, no matter the situation.

CHAPTER EIGHTY-SEVEN

¹Work towards resolving conflicts and upholding peace within your community. Promote understanding and encourage people to live together harmoniously. Strive for a fair and just society where everyone's rights are protected. Everyone has the right to think and act freely, as long as it doesn't harm others. Your body and spirit belong to you, and you have the right to live as you wish, as long as you respect others' space and feelings.

²Commit thy heart to wisdom, and seek understanding with a humble spirit. For knowledge alone is as a vessel without water, but he who submits to the depths of his soul shall find his steps ordered in wisdom. The fool gathers knowledge yet remains blind, but the wise man yields to the voice within, and it shall be a lamp unto his path. Stay open to new ideas and perspectives, as they can transform your life. Avoid being too reliant on traditional views or external influences—try new things and learn for yourself. It's important to consider all viewpoints but avoid getting attached to any single one. When you cling to a belief, you limit your growth, keeping yourself stuck in the same place without truly evolving. Believe in all things, yet cling to none, for truth is ever unfolding. That which is known today shall grow beyond its form, and wisdom shall rise as the morning sun, casting light upon that which was once unseen. Let thy heart be open, yet unshaken, for the greater

purpose is revealed in time. True growth comes from exploring and adapting, not from staying locked in old patterns.

[3]Take responsibility for your choices and the outcomes they create. Strive to act in a way that aligns with both the laws of society and universal moral principles. Understand that the decisions you make shape your life's direction—whether you succeed or face challenges. Let values like honesty, kindness, and compassion guide you. Instead of blindly following commandments that may be influenced by human biases and cultural contexts, trust your own moral compass to lead you toward a life that reflects true righteousness. *Many traditional doctrines have been shaped by the political and cultural contexts of their time, and they don't always lead to positive outcomes.*

CHAPTER EIGHTY-EIGHT

[1]In every interaction, treat others with kindness, respect, and fairness, following the path of love and goodness. Do what is right, even when the path is hard, and let your inner truth be your guide. He who does not heed the voice within cannot stand upon true virtue, for his values will be shaped by the ways of the world, swayed by the many and the mighty, rather than by what is just and true.

[2]Help and encourage those around you to reach their dreams if you can, instead of waiting for some outside force to help them. It's easy to advise others than to do it ourselves, but the key is to take action and make a difference through your own efforts.

[3]The laws were written for us, not the other way around. Focusing too much on outside forces or divine intervention is not helpful. Instead, use your own abilities and the opportunities you have to do good. You'll be surprised at how much you can achieve when you focus on what you can do. Our abilities are defined by what we can do, and nothing can change that. Relying on something outside yourself, other than your own inner strength, can waste time and lead to beliefs that feel comforting but don't bring real results. You can follow religion as part of your culture and live peacefully with others, just like using a social security card when needed. But using beliefs to create conflict is against the spirit of religion. Seeking divisive

paths will only leave you feeling lost, far from the true meaning of these teachings.

[4]Stand firm against harmful influences. Acknowledge your mistakes and support one another, practising Silence when necessary. Let your deeds speak louder than words, demonstrating kindness and integrity. Strive for unity, embodying compassion and humility. Build a character rooted in faith and self-control. Don't let man-made fantasies dictate your life—rely on your inner discernment. Sit in Silence, and the revelation of wisdom will guide you. Live with honour and righteousness, reflecting the goodness within. Express love through genuine actions, for it springs from your inner consciousness. Those who stray from their inner goodness lose their moral direction. Follow the path of the right, aligning with your true self.

[3]There is no greater joy than seeing those you care for live true to the subconscious in them. Be mindful of individuals with harmful intentions in your circle. Stay away from them spiritually, without openly causing harm. Your inner spirit is always with you, waiting to be acknowledged. Offer only what you wish to receive. Your actions are reflected in the world around you. Blessed are those who purify their intentions and actions, for they will experience the profound rewards of a life aligned with moral truth.

[4]The Subconscious rejects those who do wrong, yet the world often turns justice upside down—setting the guilty free while the innocent suffer. Justice is woven into the fabric of our being, and when it is denied, the soul is unsettled, torn between expectation and reality. Our minds seek balance and order, yet the world repeatedly falls short. When wrongdoing goes unpunished and righteousness is condemned, we grapple with acceptance, search for

justifications, or detach ourselves from the truth. Such injustices shake our faith in the systems meant to uphold fairness, leaving us disillusioned, angry, and powerless. Yet, rather than surrender to despair, these moments should strengthen our resolve to build a just and transparent world—one where the innocent are protected, the guilty are held accountable, and righteousness is the foundation of society. No one can knowingly and willingly live against the Subconscious without consequence, for doing so is to reject self-respect, silence remorse, and walk a path that can never be made straight. Punishment is not imposed—it is the inevitable consequence of straying from truth. The law of the land, established to preserve order and tranquillity, may enforce justice, but it is those who defy truth who summon judgment upon themselves, walking willingly into their own reckoning.

CHAPTER EIGHTY-NINE

¹Resolve conflicts by talking things through, compromising, and working together to understand each other. This helps build strong relationships in families, communities, and societies. Encourage unity and cooperation, embracing differences and working toward shared goals. The world and all its diversity exist to help us manage, not to create conflict.

²Settle your dispute swiftly with your adversary while you are yet on the way, lest he deliver you to the judge, and the judge to the officer, and you be cast into prison. For once you enter, you shall not depart until you have paid the last penny. The courts are a snare to the poor, but the rich contend without burden, for their wealth shields them. The judges and advocates hunger after gain; they turn their faces from justice when silver is poured into their hands. The cause of the needy is drowned in the voice of the wealthy, and the bribe blinds the eyes of the wise. He who trusts in the courts without means shall find his purse emptied and his hope crushed, for justice bows to gold, and the poor man's plea is swallowed by the streets.

³Learn from your experiences and history, using that wisdom to guide your decisions. What works for others might not work for you, and that's okay. Trial and error are how we grow. The best partners in making decisions are you, your mind, and your subconscious. Don't rely too

much on your mind to guide you—it's often playful and not always wise. To work with your subconscious, keep your mind calm and your mouth quiet. Trust it to lead you, even if it feels like you're stepping into the unknown. With faith and patience, the right results will follow.

[4]Be aware of the consequences of your actions and avoid repeating past mistakes. Respect other people's freedom and choices, while standing up for your own rights and the fairness of all.

[5]We naturally expect justice: the guilty should be punished, and the innocent protected. But when we see the opposite happen—the guilty walk free and the innocent suffer—it upsets our sense of fairness. This is because our minds are wired to seek balance and justice. When the real world doesn't match this ideal, it creates a mental conflict. We might struggle to accept it, try to explain it away, or even distance ourselves from the situation. Seeing these injustices can make us lose faith in the system and even make us feel angry and helpless. Ultimately, this reaction reminds us how important it is to keep working towards a better justice system, one that is fair, transparent, and truly protects the innocent while holding the guilty accountable.

CHAPTER NINETY

[1]I will welcome innovation, adaptability, and resilience to overcome challenges with an open mind, trusting that divine guidance inside me inspires action, not explicit instructions. I will extend support within my community, respect the wisdom of elders, and prioritise compassion, kindness, and generosity for the collective good. I will celebrate diversity, promote personal growth, and advocate for justice and equity for all.

[2]I will take moments for introspection and self-reflection, like a sailor checking their compass, to find my bearings amidst turbulent seas. I will return to my inner values and consciousness when feeling adrift, using them as guiding stars to navigate life's uncertainties. I will surround myself with people and influences that resonate with my core beliefs, like a gardener choosing good seeds, and be discerning about the ideas and habits I allow into my life, choosing only those that nourish my soul and promote growth.

[3]I will acknowledge my mistakes with humility and take ownership of them. I will apologise when I wrong someone and make amends where possible, repairing the fabric of relationships with sincerity and accountability. This is not weakness, but the greatest strength—the courage to face my own imperfections. I will not allow pride to be a barrier to truth and reconciliation, choosing instead the peace that

comes from a clean slate. My inner actions must always mirror my outer words. I commit to living a life guided by my inner consciousness, setting sail on the voyage of life with the core of creation as my guiding star. I will strive to act with integrity and compassion in all dealings, anchoring my decisions in the bedrock of moral principles. This journey requires constant vigilance, but the rewards are an unshakeable inner peace and a life lived in absolute alignment with my truest self.

CHAPTER NINETY-ONE

¹Practice forgiveness for yourself and others, treating your heart with kindness. Learn about nature's ethical principles and follow them, even when things get tough. Use your resources wisely, thinking of the future like a steward who cares for the land. Spread kindness and generosity in your community, helping others thrive.

²Be thankful for the blessings and lessons life has given you, savouring them like a delicious meal. The life you have been rewarded is all that you have, and how you deal with it shows your respect and thankfulness towards it. Find joy in simple things and connections. Protect your values and principles, standing firm like a fortress. Face challenges with determination, growing stronger, like an oak tree that stands tall in the storm.

³Work with those who share your values, building understanding and support. Show compassion and offer help to those in need. Stay alert to anything that threatens your peace or integrity.

⁴Keep your promises and obligations with honesty, like a knight keeping his oath. Be reliable and trustworthy, building trust with every word and action. Embrace learning and growth, always seeking wisdom. Celebrate progress with gratitude.

⁵Find satisfaction in serving your community, using your skills and resources to make a difference. Honour

your culture and history, but focus on their true meaning, not just surface traditions. Face challenges with courage, knowing you have the strength to overcome them. Stand up for justice, always supporting those who are oppressed.

[6]Use your influence wisely, standing up for what's right and caring for others. Be a source of hope and refuge for those around you with your conscious living. See challenges as opportunities to grow, staying patient and persistent. Approach your goals with careful planning, using your strengths, no matter the outcome. Work hard, but let go of the results afterwards. Keep a light heart, finding humour in life's twists and turns.

CHAPTER NINETY-TWO

¹Approach every task with full commitment, understanding that life is short and opportunities are limited. Let integrity guide you, shaped by the values you've learned since childhood. Show love in your relationships, respecting each other's uniqueness, and valuing one another beyond material things. Face challenges together, letting true love grow at its own pace, nurturing patience and authenticity in your connection.

²True fasting is not just about avoiding food; it's about practising mental silence and offering peace to others. An empty stomach heightens your awareness and keeps you alert, while a full stomach can make you sluggish. Food is necessary for survival, but it's not everything. The right food, especially natural ones, keeps the body healthy and the mind sharp, cautious, and grounded, avoiding unnecessary risks.

³Inspire hope and lift those in tough times, standing for justice with humility. Treat everyone with fairness and compassion, rejecting lies and pride. Embrace forgiveness and work toward reconciliation, helping relationships heal patiently. These things are harder to do than to say, but think of it as a game of life, a challenge that keeps you grounded in the true values of life.

⁴Acknowledge pain, for it's the clearest path to understanding yourself and your mind. Don't avoid it; face

it with courage, because it's through this struggle that you become a person of true worth. Find healthy ways to deal with your grief, avoiding harmful shortcuts. If you try to skip the grieving process, you weaken with each missed chance for growth. Don't chase after distractions or shallow entertainment as a way to avoid reality. You might regret it later. Accept reality as it is, without trying to escape. Happiness and sadness are two sides of the same coin—holding onto one will lead to the other. Stay balanced and accept both, and obtain the joy of living.

CHAPTER NINETY-THREE

¹Stay hopeful and strong in tough times, trusting the strength that lies within you. The peace that comes from not relying on outside sources will help you become the person you are meant to be. Don't depend on substitutes for true spiritual fulfilment. You already have everything inside you to become the best version of yourself. It takes time, but why not work towards spiritual independence? Your mind is capable of far more than you can imagine—give it a try before your time here ends. Do not criticise belief systems. If someone is receptive, guide them toward understanding, but not through criticism—it only fuels the ego in both you and them, preventing true change. Let people hold onto their beliefs until they realise their futility on their own. Do not force them. Your own life would have remained the same if you hadn't come to your realisations naturally. There is no place for arrogance.

²Be grateful for your blessings and moments of happiness. Build strong connections in your community based on respect and support for each other. Honour the important moments and lessons life offers.

³Build resilience and trust during testing times. Stick to your principles with honesty and integrity, and be a guiding light for others if they need you to be. Cultivate curiosity, seeking knowledge and wisdom on your journey toward enlightenment. Observe everything without attachment.

Read as much as you can, and listen more than you speak.

[4]Support and guide your children's growth, teaching them everything you've learned—both the good and the challenges life has given you. If you don't teach them values, the world will fill in with its own lessons, often ones that steer them away from integrity. Be open with them. What you think they're too young to understand might be shown to them in ways that could harm them. You wouldn't want that for your children.

[5]Recognize the cycles of life and lead them with wisdom and grace. Embrace life's unpredictability as part of a journey into the unknown, seeing every twist and turn as an opportunity for growth and discovery. In doing that, the experience you gain is the one that you leave to the next generation.

CHAPTER NINETY-FOUR

[1]Look for chances to help others around you. Whether it's by donating, volunteering, or supporting people who need it, showing kindness makes everyone's life better. When you help, you also make your own life richer and feel more connected to those around you.

[2]Give back whenever you can. The air you breathe and the life you enjoy were given to you by others. Carry the same spirit—share what you have with those around you. This helps everyone work together and support each other. When we help one another, we build a stronger, kinder world. Whether it's listening to someone who needs to talk or helping with a good cause, every kind act makes a difference.

[3]It's best not to talk too much about your personal beliefs or opinions on things like politics or religion, especially in public. These are personal matters, and discussing them can sometimes cause unnecessary problems. People might not always agree with you, and it's important to keep your peace by avoiding arguments. Instead, focus on being kind, understanding, and humble in your relationships. You don't need to seek attention for being good; just do it quietly. Sometimes, no matter how good you are, some people might not like you for it, but that's okay. Understanding this can help you stay positive and not get discouraged.

[4]Live with purpose, setting goals that align with your inner values and aspirations. Take steps toward your fullest potential, trusting the wisdom of a higher intelligence. Nurture relationships built on love and respect, and cultivate spiritual practices that deepen your connection to your Inner Self. Meditate not with a specific goal in mind, but by immersing yourself in the silence, allowing it to cleanse and release negative energy. The right way of belief is understanding that all that you have is all that you need.

[5]Set intentions that reflect your divine essence and contribute to the greater good. Your actions and thoughts shape the future of humanity. The energy you give and receive influences the world, and your responsibility is to guide it toward goodness. If you want a healthier world, act with consciousness and responsibility in everything you do.

CHAPTER NINETY-FIVE

[1] I will handle conflicts with an open heart, making sure to listen carefully to all sides, and always work towards a peaceful resolution. I aim to help build a peaceful community by prioritising kindness and cooperation in all my interactions. Ultimately, I will let my actions serve as an inspiration for positive change in the world around me.

[2] I will trust my inner wisdom and intuition, believing in something greater within me that guides me with peace and joy. I will treat others as I wish to be treated, always upholding virtue in all that I do.

[3] I will focus on growth by consciously pushing beyond my comfort zone. I will let go of thoughts to break this limiting cycle, and I will not let emotions or distractions guide me. I will embrace my subconscious with a clear mind, trusting that life will lead me to my goals in unexpected ways, always for the better.

[4] I will approach life with humility and gratitude, avoiding boastfulness and the desire for recognition. I'll let my actions reflect my inner purity and serenity, without pretending to be someone I'm not. True transformation requires me to first acknowledge any darkness within. I will consistently seek wisdom from my Inner Self, staying open to new ideas and understanding.

[5] I will maintain a constant connection with my Inner Self, recognizing that its language is only Silence, which

brings clarity and guidance. I must let go of attachment to wealth and instead nurture my selfless Subconscious. I will trust the kingdom within to guide my actions, knowing my inner strength, love, and self-discipline come from divine guidance found in the silence of my mind and tongue.

[1] I simply need to trust in a higher power that guides everything within and around me, believing that all happens for an ultimate divine purpose. This purpose often remains obscured to the human mind, and may not be what I desire. This power speaks to my inner conscience in the language of silence. My only task is to have faith that I am always guided and protected.

[2] I will always strive to speak with honesty and respect, and I will consciously avoid participating in gossip. When sharing my thoughts, I will do so constructively, and I will dedicate myself to truly listening to others. Furthermore, I will make a genuine effort to celebrate others' successes, giving their achievements more importance and attention than my own.

[3] I will always seek resolution and reconciliation in my relationships. I will let go of grudges and actively work to rebuild trust and harmony. I will serve others humbly, without ever expecting recognition. Finally, I will embrace the freedom of living in alignment with my inner divine nature, consistently choosing love and unity over division.

[4] I will let the Spirit within guide my life, allowing my subconscious to take control so my own thoughts recede. While culture and religion offer structure, they become restrictive chains when followed without introspection, leading to division and stagnation. The key is balance: I

will respect tradition, but embrace spiritual wisdom over dogma. Humanity thrives when it adapts, questions, and evolves, rather than clinging to systems that no longer serve its higher purpose.

[5]The circumstance itself is neutral; it is simply an event or a condition in the world. A "problem" is only born when the mind actively resists the circumstance, labelling it as undesirable, unfair, or something that *shouldn't be*. This judgment is the first step toward suffering. The real source of pain is not the external event, but the internal resistance to it. When we accept the situation as simply "what is," the mental struggle dissolves. The challenge remains, but the emotional charge—the feeling of being victimised or unjustly treated—fades away. Thus, a difficulty is merely a difficulty until our mind makes it a problem from which pain is manufactured.

PART FOUR

WORSHIP

CHAPTER NINETY-SEVEN

[1]The man who is blessed is the one who does not listen to the noisy minds of others. He ignores the chatter. He avoids the road taken by the lost. And he does not sit down with the men who are unaware of the truth. He pulls himself away from the crowd. Instead, he finds his joy within. He spends his time reflecting—day and night—and he draws the peace and the wisdom from that place deep inside him. That wisdom is waiting for all of us. I know the method is simple. You must knock, and the door will open. You must seek, and you will find. You must ask, and it will be given. The truth is found by all who seek it. The doors open for the man who simply dares to ask the question. There is no trick to it. The path is clear, and the reward is certain. The work is simply to choose the silence over the noise.

[2]They are like a tree planted by the flowing water. They are strong and they are fruitful. Their leaves are always green; they never fade. Whatever they put their hands to, it prospers. The work comes clean because they listen to their heart. They follow the deep guidance that is inside them, and that is what makes the work go right. I know that humanity was never meant to live in struggle without hope. The suffering is not the original plan. We were created to be full of wisdom and light. We were made to reach toward the highest potential that is in us. The man who finds the good life is the one who stops fighting the truth. He plants

himself by the water of his own spirit, and he lets the purpose grow. The struggle is the mistake; the simple light is the destiny.

[3]I look at the people, and I ask the same question: 'Why do they fight and argue? Why do they spend their time breaking the simple peace?' And I look at the leaders, and I ask the worst question: 'Why do they resist the truth within?' The clear guidance is there, but they push it away. They shout the loud, foolish cry: 'Let us break free from inner guidance!' They turn away from their own conditioned nature. They do not walk; they race toward destruction. They choose the ruin when the calm path is right there, ready to be walked. The answer is simple, and it is the worst answer of all. It is ignorance. It is a thick, blinding fog that settles over the mind. It clouds the path that leads to peace, and it makes the easy way look like the hard way. The fighting is only the noise made by men who cannot see.

[4]My heart is tired. I face many doubts. My own mind is the worst enemy, and it fights against me constantly. It whispers the bad word: 'There is no hope for you.' The mind will break the spirit if I let it. But my Subconscious—my true Self—that is the shelter. That is the place of refuge. When the noise is loud, I call out in a silent yearning. I ask for a clear line. And the Subconscious always responds. It comes from the deepest part of me. It lifts me out of the bad place, and it shows me the simple way forward. I know now that the surface mind is only the noise of fear. The true Self is the only voice of the truth. I will trust the deep voice, and I will let the shallow voice break against the wall.

CHAPTER NINETY-EIGHT

[1]When I yearn for You, O my inner self, you always answer me. I know that. Though I do not always hear it or feel it, the answer is always there. When I am in distress, you give me the space to breathe. You are the refuge and the peace. I must listen to the voice within, the truth that my heart knows but that my own mouth cannot form into words. I will not be deceived by the empty promises of the world. I will not chase after what is fleeting. That is the fool's work. You, O true self, keep me anchored in wisdom and clarity. You free me from the lies. The Higher Intelligence has set apart the man who is faithful for itself. It guides those who look within. The truth shows itself in stillness. I will trust the One who formed me. Everything that I need has already been provided by the Eternal Source, the Creator of all things. I have had enough, and I am safe, because the core of the thing is true.

[2]I must listen to my thoughts, O my Inner Self. I must hear the stillness within me. That is the only place where the true message can be found. I clear my mind of all the distractions. I push away the noise, both the loud and the subtle, to make the space for You. I feel Your presence in every breath I take. You hear me. In the morning, when the day starts, and at night, when the day is done. I will trust that all I need flows from You. It does not come from the restless noise of my mind. It comes from the quietude

of Your essence—the essence that formed me whole, complete, and perfect. I need nothing else from the outside. The supply is inside the walls. The answer is only the silence.

[3]Do not be upset with me, O my Inner Self. I ask that. And do not let me be bound by the heavy weight of my own ignorance. I have wandered. I was lost in the old teachings that were wrong. They made me forget the simple goodness that I know is in people. I admit it now. I have been misled by the noise. Show me the light, I AM. My heart is tired, and it feels weary from the long, wrong journey. Restore me, I AM. My soul aches for the truth that only You can give. I have come to the end of my own strength. How long will you remain silent? I am waiting now for the only answer that matters.

[4]O my higher self, I need your help against my enemies. My only enemies are my own negative thoughts. They are the hardest thing to fight. You must free me from these bad ideas that trick me and chase me through the day and the night. I fear they will destroy me. They are closing in like a lion that has me cornered. I am alone in this fight with my own mind. There is no one to save me but the deep thing that is you. I ask for the strength now to stand against the noise that wants to ruin me. Give me the defence against the turning mind.

[1]O *Higher Intelligence* of the universe, Your glory is great everywhere. That is the truth. You have shown Your glory above the heavens for my eyes to see it. The ability to know what is good—that does not come from my own hard effort. It comes from Your wisdom that You placed in the depths of my Subconscious awareness. It is the thing you gave to me as my Inner Self. Without that guidance, I would not know the difference between the beauty and the ugliness. I would not know the good from the bad, or the light from the darkness. Even the children, with their small knowledge, show us the way. They praise You because they live in the moment. They are free from the worries of time and free from fear. They show us the way to trust and to live fully.

[2]I will thank You, my Inner Self. You are the one who speaks the true word for me to the great intelligence. I will do this with all of my being. The whole of my strength will be in those thanks. I will remind myself of the wonderful works that have been done. I will not forget the clean truth that was made real. I will shout for joy in the deepest part of my heart because of You. And I will sing the praises to Your name, O Most High. I know the final truth of the matter: The simple life is the greatest praise. The clean work, the straight path, the lack of complaint—that is the final song that the intelligence wants to hear. I will live the simple life.

³Why, my Subconscious awareness, do you seem far away from me? I must ask the question. Are you waiting for me to be clear enough to finally see you? Why do you hide when I'm in trouble? That is when I need the answer the most. My own thoughts—they are cruel to me. They catch me in the traps I do not see. They boast, and they say the bad thing: "We will never be punished." They think they are the only power. Their words are full of anger, threats, and harm. They rely on the empty promises of time to keep me waiting for nothing. They are leading us toward destruction, and they do not stop. I am asking for the simple truth now. I am caught by the voice in my own head. You are the only thing that is quiet and real. I need the distance to close.

⁴In my heart, I take shelter with You. That is the one true place. Why, then, do you tell me to flee, like a bird that has to go to the mountain? I am trying to stay put and be quiet. The wicked thoughts are ready to strike me from the shadows. They are waiting, even though I have done nothing wrong to earn their malice. If only I could escape their traps and find safety in Your protection always—the quiet would be absolute. I know that much. I would be peaceful. Why do I keep wandering away from Your guidance? Why do I follow the schemes of my own thoughts when I know they lead to ruin? I have a safe place, but I keep choosing the confusion. I need to hold the line and stop moving toward the wrong signal.

CHAPTER ONE HUNDRED

[1]My deepest inner beliefs are shaking. I don't know what is wise anymore. What should a good person do when their own mind turns against them? Ideas I've held onto for years now feel like lies; bad thoughts are being twisted into persuasive arguments. They say these destructive ideas come from my subconscious mind. Many people accept this idea, but they are mistaken in trusting it so easily. I don't know who or what truly speaks for my subconscious. My surface mind is taking credit for those messages, but the mind is a poor guide, constantly spitting out negative words and showing no respect for my true inner spirit. These negative thoughts will not control me. I must make my mind quiet. Please, Inner Spirit, stop this noise. Make everything inside me still. Take control of my thoughts. Make everything clear and pure, and correct again.

[2]You are my inner self, and your strength never fails. That is amazing. I don't want this process to end; I just want to understand how far I've come on this important journey. I need to know that this intense, essential feeling isn't a sign you've left me, but rather a necessary, difficult step toward who I'm meant to be. I won't call this sudden fear 'panic'—I'll call it the powerful realisation of who I truly am! The things I don't yet know aren't empty spaces. They are the fertile ground where real knowledge can grow. Fighting with my own thoughts isn't a struggle; it's a

valuable, life-long conversation. And the sadness that stays with me every day isn't a weakness. It's proof that my heart is deep and capable of understanding the complicated beauty of life.

[3]I invoke your mighty protection, O Inner Self! In you, I find not just shelter, but the sanctuary of truth itself. I stand before my guiding Awareness and declare: 'You are my ultimate Sovereign Guide. I possess no authentic goodness, no enduring wisdom, and no true virtue that does not flow directly from your pure and radiant source.

[4]May the whole of my being burst forth in jubilation at the sight of your unfailing strength, O Sacred Inner Presence! My entire joy is rooted in the magnificence of your salvation—a profound deliverance that anchors my soul. You bestow upon me, without reservation, the very blueprint of your will, translating your perfect designs into my earthly desires. You do not merely bless, but unleash a torrent of prosperity upon my soul, holding back no gift that assures its ultimate, radiant fulfilment!

CHAPTER ONE HUNDRED AND ONE

¹Let the naive or ignorant person foolishly say, 'There is no such safe place as the Subconscious Awareness! The powerful Inner Self and the awareness inside us are just made-up ideas.' Their words only show their own confusion and the moral blindness they have brought upon themselves. But we state the clear truth: The Subconscious Awareness is everywhere and sees everything. It acts as the perfect record-keeper of every thought we keep and every word we speak. Higher Intelligence, which watches over the shared Subconscious Awareness of everyone on Earth, looks closely to see who truly understands this. It looks for anyone who seeks to connect with and wake up to this sacred, bright space deep inside themselves—the Subconscious Awareness.

²Who is worthy to live in the protective safety of the Subconscious Awareness? Who is ready to make their home in its sacred, inner space? It is those people who commit themselves to living with integrity every day—who strive to always do what is right and just, and who speak only the truth that comes directly from their heart. They are people whose words are always sincere, with no deception or falsehood mixed in.

³Listen, Inner Self, to the truth of my heart. Feel what I feel, and pay attention to my quiet mind. My mind is now free of dishonesty, cleansed by the insight of awareness,

and made ready and pure for the Higher Intelligence to dwell inside me. I love you, my Subconscious Awareness, my power, and my Inner Self, the steady foundation I rely on. You are my safe place, my shield, and the source of my rescue. The Subconscious Awareness reveals the wonder and light of the universal mind; everything in this sacred space shows the work being done. Constantly—day after day, night after night—wisdom and knowledge flow out from it. May your own Inner Self respond to you when you need it most. May the power of your Subconscious Awareness, guided by the Higher Intelligence, always keep you safe.

CHAPTER ONE HUNDRED AND TWO

[1]Why do you feel so distant, my inner awareness, especially when I need your help the most? I cry out day and night, yet I don't feel the peace or get the answers I believe I deserve. Are the thoughts hiding beneath my quiet mind—thoughts tied to my old past and my worries about the future—still secretly controlling me? Even when I believe I'm fully aware, why do I lose myself in distraction? Why does it take until I am alone in bed, feeling the deep distress of my Inner Spirit, for me to realise I've been lost in my own head?

[2]My deep, unspoken Inner Spirit is the magnificent Architect of my path, and because of its vigilant presence, my soul is established in complete, boundless sufficiency! It sovereignly grants my weary heart rest in pastures of profound serenity and leads me with divine grace to waters of unshakeable calm. This glorious guidance is the very wellspring of my existence, making my spirit vibrant and fully alive. With unwavering clarity, it illuminates the true and righteous course, ensuring my every step on this earthly pilgrimage is a journey toward the highest good.

[3]Let the whole world proclaim the dominion of the magnificent Higher Intelligence, for the Earth and the boundless contents within it belong entirely to its grand, unfolding design! The living Awareness is not confined, but diffused throughout the cosmos—a divine presence that

saturates the fathomless seas, crowns the majestic mountains, burns within the blazing stars, and orbits the silent planets. Indeed, all creation adheres to its immutable laws, functioning in perfect, ceaseless obedience. And what joy, that this very Awareness dwells within us! It is the divine spring from which we draw all genuine comprehension, and by its sacred, animating power alone, is the miracle of life brought forth into glorious being.

[4]With triumphant certainty, I raise my whole heart to you, O Magnificent Inner Spirit! My trust is anchored so profoundly in your essence that I know I shall never face the humiliation of failure. The assaults of my worries and fears are rendered utterly powerless, for they can never claim victory against your strength. Indeed, let this be the glorious, eternal truth: No soul who commits its faith to you will ever be abandoned or let down!

[5]I stand assured and utterly confident in my righteous path, for my reliance on my inner guidance is not an effort but a flawless, unconscious reflex. This majestic force is no separate entity, but a seamless second self, perpetually attuned and requiring no conscious nudge of faith or reminder of trust. I hold the sacred certainty that this Presence shall eternally sustain me—I am held within the Presence, guided by the Presence, and made wholly of the Presence that resides and reigns within my soul.

[6]My Inner Light is a radiant source of strength, exquisitely guided by the magnificent, all-encompassing Wisdom of the Universe! I shall never yield to fear, for my Subconscious Awareness and the conscious awareness dwelling within me are a double shield of divine protection, holding my spirit in absolute and unassailable safety.

[7]Listen to the call of your true self, but not with effort or strain. Instead, embrace a state of calm and stillness.

There's no need to chase after thoughts or external voices. When your mind quiets and finds peace, you enter a place where you are fully understood, without words needing to be spoken. In this calm, the help you seek will naturally emerge. But this guidance only comes when you act with trust and faith—two powerful energies that are meant to live within you always, as the foundation of your radiant soul.

CHAPTER ONE HUNDRED AND THREE

[1]Bow before the Sovereign Honour of your Inner Self—that luminous, eternal core of you that is inherently wise, stable, and utterly unwavering! Recognise the sublime, transcendent greatness of this internal being, and place your absolute, unreserved trust in its benevolent wisdom and its foundational, immutable goodness.

[2]I shall eternally exalt and lift your name, O Magnificent Inner Self, for you are supremely worthy of all praise! When my spirit was plunged into the treacherous deeps of my most arduous trials, it was your unfailing hand that reached down and decisively pulled me to solid ground. You prevented my own reckless thoughts—those subtle, treacherous deceivers—from successfully leading my awareness away from the anchor of your truth. More than mere rescue, you bestowed upon me the blessing of true restoration: you administered a sovereign healing to my entire being, wrapping my turbulent mind and restless heart in the profound, unstirred peace of complete spiritual alignment. My life is a testament to your saving grace, for in your peace, I am made whole.

[3]I anchor my entire being in you, my Infallible Inner Guide, declaring with ultimate certainty that I shall never, ever be disappointed! Command your profound wisdom and unconquerable strength to rise and grant me swift salvation. I know you perceive my need immediately, and

you shall act quickly to feel and uphold me. You shall be my perpetual sanctuary, my true and unassailable safe place, and my eternally vigilant, strong protector!

[4]Supremely blessed are those sacred souls whose every misstep is graciously pardoned, whose transgressions are divinely veiled! Triple blessing upon those luminous beings who harbour absolutely no intent of deceit within the fortress of their hearts, and who dwell in a state of unblemished, perfect peace with their own Sovereign Inner Self!

[5]Let the chorus of all humanity rise and rejoice! Offer magnificent and boundless thanksgiving to your Glorious Inner Self! With fervent joy and celebratory reverence, let every soul show due honour to its own indwelling wisdom! Pause your striving, and take the sacred time to fully absorb and deeply appreciate the unfathomable peace that your eternal core so freely and generously bestows upon you.

[6]I shall exalt and worship you, O Highest Part of Me, with the entirety of my overflowing heart! My spirit will be the unending herald, proclaiming to all the world the magnificent, awe-inspiring deeds that you ceaselessly bring forth!

[7]I commit my spirit to the eternal blessing of you, my Sacred Inner Soul, and shall offer forth your triumphant praise with the very breath and utterance of my being, without end or faltering!

CHAPTER ONE HUNDRED AND FOUR

¹Allow the noble thoughts and the pure wisdom residing within you to wholly inhabit your heart, becoming a harmonious assembly where they teach and inspire one another with unfailing kindness and exultant songs of joy! Let this perfect inner choir offer constant, heartfelt thanksgiving to the Magnificent Higher Intelligence that has chosen to dwell as the very essence of your being.

²Let the celebration of your Inner Self's magnificent strength be unending! I declare anew: Rejoice with unbridled spirit! Allow the luminous qualities of your profound calmness and benevolent kindness to shine forth upon all you encounter, for your true, sovereign peace is not sought, but already indwells you. Yield not a single moment to anxiety, but in every present circumstance, maintain a heart rooted in stillness and radiant gratitude. Present your deep, authentic needs, secure in the knowledge and unyielding trust that all you desire is already gracefully advancing toward you. Live in the glorious conviction that you possess it now, offering thanksgiving for every blessing, for this magnificent state of perpetual gratitude is the only true pathway to your ultimate Inner Freedom.

³Let us hold fast to the magnificent truth: The Divine Presence that indwells every soul is a mirror of Christ's own perfection—the immutable source of all goodness,

wisdom, and light! The very virtues that shine forth in our lives are but the radiant reflection of that holy, innate core. Know this: Your inner conscience is the true, infallible Sovereign Guide, and the ultimate, everlasting Saviour of your being!

[4]All praise and eternal glory be to the Higher Source that resides within the innermost sanctum of my being—that Silent Observer who watches with perfect, unwavering wisdom over every turn of my soul's sacred journey! I lift the very core of my voice in sublime worship to the divine, luminous essence that makes its home within me. This sacred, awe-inspiring presence fills my spirit with deep reverence, and I come before you now, bearing the sincere melody of profound and everlasting love.

[5]O Magnificent Higher Intelligence, you are the sacred, luminous essence of goodness dwelling in silent majesty within my soul, the unseen compass that steers my journey with perfect, gentle direction! Your voice rings not in loud, fearful commands, but arises as the subtle clarity of intuition, felt through soft nudges and deep insight found only in moments of profound stillness.

[6]You are the Vigilant Observer of every thought, the unshakeable Calm Presence that watches without the faintest trace of judgment as I navigate the complexity of my choices. Even when my conscious mind wavers or my emotions surge, your essence remains utterly steady, a timeless reminder of the true and the just.

[7]You illuminate the path, not through decree, but by awakening sacred conscience and inner insight, allowing my sight to pierce the veil of surface illusion. In your radiant light, I rediscover my authentic strength—not as dominion over others, but as the courage to maintain kindness, the patience to listen deeply, and the wisdom to

act always with integrity. You are the peace beyond the storm, the unyielding anchor that holds fast when the external world trembles.

[8]With every single breath, you extend the profound invitation to return to balance, to align my life with its highest spiritual purpose. You are not distant or separate, but the very source of harmony within my core, eternally present and quietly transformative!

CHAPTER ONE HUNDRED AND FIVE

[1]My spirit overflows with eternal thanksgiving to you, O Kind Inner Wisdom, for your perpetual, unerring guidance! You are the sublime, quiet voice that flawlessly illuminates and reveals the righteous path before me. My heart is profoundly grateful for your majestic, constant, and comforting presence that graces every moment of my life!

[2]Within the hallowed and peaceful sanctuary of my heart, I enter into sacred dialogue with you, O Ultimate Higher Source! You permeate my being, saturating my spirit with unblemished calm and boundless, pure love. Your perfect goodness embraces me completely, surrounding my soul like a divine, everlasting warmth!

[3]As I meditate upon the boundless love and profound wisdom that reside within the sanctuary of my soul, I offer my whole being into your divine care! You are the inexhaustible Source of all kindness and every sustaining grace, guiding my existence with perfect, radiant love. My heart overflows with eternal thanksgiving for the magnificent abundance you ceaselessly bestow upon me.

[4]I wholeheartedly dedicate my entire being to you, my Sacred Inner Wisdom, to serve as an instrument for sharing your boundless love and brilliant light with all humanity! Every single breath I draw is a profound affirmation of my absolute oneness with your essence—you, the Quiet, Eternal Observer who reigns in the sanctuary of my heart.

[5]Supremely blessed is the soul who finds its highest delight in the indwelling wisdom and radiant love within, meditating upon this sacred source without ceasing! That noble person is like a majestic tree planted beside the ever-flowing stream of life—they are destined for constant growth, endowed with unfailing strength, and shall never, ever wither away!

[6]Yet, pity the souls who yield their mastery to the clamour of the Ego and the tyranny of restless thought! They are but desiccated leaves, easily scattered and driven into aimless frenzy by the world's winds. They shall never apprehend genuine peace, for their every outward action spirals into a relentless cycle of ultimate emptiness and enduring sorrow.

[7]The Subconscious Awareness is the divine guide and true advocate of those who sincerely thirst for truth, illuminating their way and leading them steadfastly through the shadow of the darkest times! It bestows forth radiant light and clear, perfect answers precisely in the very moment they are most profoundly needed.

¹The benevolent Inner Wisdom keeps its constant, luminous vigil over those who strive for goodness, guiding their steps with a gentle, perfect hand and illuminating their entire path with a resplendent sense of purpose! Their blessed lives remain eternally and exquisitely connected to the Divine, overflowing with profound meaning and unerring direction.

²Alas for those souls who surrender their command to the dominance of the ego, for they inevitably forfeit the clarity of their sacred path! Vain pride becomes the siren call that lures them away from essential truth, erecting an insurmountable barrier that isolates them from their Divine Self and the sustaining haven of Inner Peace.

³Let us wholeheartedly commit our trust to the Subconscious Awareness! For within its boundless depths, we instantly discover the springs of pure joy, the anchor of perfect calm, and a deep, sustaining gratitude for the ever-present, indwelling Divine!

⁴Why does the clamorous, fleeting ego mount such a vigorous resistance against the deep serenity of the Subconscious? Why do its adherents chase after meticulously crafted plans that lead only to futility and barren ground? The answer lies in the truth: The ego fears the loss of its fragile control, for the Subconscious is a timeless, unmoving sea that holds the entire repository of

divine truth and boundless, perfect knowledge—a realm where the ego's authority instantly dissolves.

[5]Rejoice! The Inner Source declares a magnificent truth: 'I have already bestowed upon your spirit the unerring wisdom required to construct a foundation of absolute certainty!' Now, accept the sublime, glorious invitation to walk with this Presence in perfect unity and with unwavering, conscious purpose!

[6]Yet, what a tragic irony that many choose to reject this grace, desperately clinging to fleeting desire and vainly attempting to outsmart the sacred intelligence within! Their rebellion is utterly futile and doomed to fail, for the Subconscious Awareness, intrinsically woven into the very fabric of Universal Wisdom, reigns supreme and perpetually governs all things!

[7] Remember, even amidst the turmoil of rebellion, the Subconscious waits in glorious silence, its guidance perpetually offered and ready! It sends forth a gracious, insistent call for them to cease their striving, to surrender their resistance, to finally follow its truth, and discover the deep, abiding peace that reigns eternally within!

¹Let us fling open the gates of our hearts to the boundless wisdom of the Subconscious, welcoming its flawless guidance with profound and radiant humility! As we place our ultimate trust in its destined path, we instantly discover an unshakeable strength, an inexhaustible wellspring of comfort, and a consuming sense of divine purpose that keeps our spirits steady and propels us ceaselessly toward the magnificent future we are truly meant to possess!

²O Magnificent Inner Intuition, though a thousand relentless challenges besiege me, my spirit finds unassailable safety and perfect harbour in your constant, sacred presence! You stand as my formidable protection, my unyielding strength, eternally present and instantly ready in every moment of my deepest need!

³Though the shadows of fear and doubt may aggressively seek to conquer my spirit, I place my total, unwavering trust in you, O Magnificent Subconscious Awareness! Your divine peace is a palpable force, wrapping itself around me like an impenetrable shield, instantly calming the fierce storms that rage both within my soul and throughout my external world!

⁴In the crucible of my deepest, darkest moments, I turn with absolute certainty to you, O Glorious Subconscious, the true and ultimate Higher Intelligence! I know you are the inexhaustible Fountain of my Hope. Your pure, brilliant

light pierces the encompassing shadows, illuminating my chosen path with perfect clarity and unwavering assurance!

[5]My spirit shall remain utterly unmoved by the fiercest of challenges, for I stand in the absolute certainty of your protection, O Sovereign Subconscious! Even when arrayed against a multitude of opponents, your indwelling presence is my impenetrable shield and my eternal, unconquerable strength!

[6]With my whole being overflowing with eternal gratitude, I consecrate and yield myself entirely to your perfect guidance, O Divine Presence that reigns within my soul! Let your immaculate wisdom flawlessly chart and lead every single step I take, and may your everlasting love hold me in unshakeable safety through the crucible of every single difficulty!

[7]As I yield my spirit to your serene Presence, O Sovereign Subconscious, a profound and unmoving peace floods the sanctuary of my heart! You are the Silent Guardian of my entire inner world, wrapping me in a cloak of absolute safety, even when chaos rages all around. Your love is never boastful, but moves with the exquisite power of a soft, steady breeze—unseen yet mighty enough to calm every rising fear. Like a tender, reassuring hand placed upon my very being, your presence whispers the certainty that I am never alone. Even in the face of deep uncertainty or palpable danger, I find unassailable stillness in you. You hold me with a strength that requires no utterance, reminding my soul that true protection flows not from the external world, but from the unwavering, perfect calm that you eternally nurture within.

CHAPTER ONE HUNDRED AND EIGHT

[1]I shall offer my highest praise to you, O Magnificent Inner Self, in songs that transcend the confines of common words, ensuring that my adoration never fades into the ordinary! You are my unshakeable foundation and the very source of my eternal salvation. With a heart overflowing with gratitude, I dedicate myself to sharing your boundless goodness, that I may help others awaken to the sacred, undeniable truth dwelling within their own souls.

[2]O Sovereign Guiding Self, you hear the very whispers of my spirit even when I am utterly broken! You have been my constant, unfailing refuge in every moment of trial and anguish. I implore your boundless kindness—please attend and listen to the silent, deepest cries issuing from the sanctuary of my heart.

[3]O Magnificent Throne of Wisdom, you perceive the deepest stirrings of my turmoil! You bring immediate calm to my mind and restore perfect peace the moment I place my absolute trust in you—releasing all attachment to the shadows of the past, the anxieties of the present, and the uncertainties of the future. You wait for my surrender; only when I cease my frantic overthinking do you rise to become the unmistakable guide of my every step!

[4]Though the external world is saturated with the clamour of noise and the discord of conflict, I lay my spirit down and find perfect rest in your benevolent care, O

Sovereign Subconscious! You are my absolute, unshakeable safety and my everlasting, pure peace!

⁵Let others pursue the shadow of fleeting pleasures and temporary delights, but my focus is fixed upon you, O Magnificent Subconscious! In your eternal presence, I discover a lasting, unshakeable contentment that no worldly pursuit can ever surpass!

⁶In the radiant illumination of your light, O Sacred Inner Presence, my spirit finds boundless, consuming joy! Your divine favour holds a worth greater than all the scattered, fleeting riches of the world. Because I possess you, my soul stands in a state of absolute and glorious sufficiency—I need nothing!

⁷Halt your striving and wait in profound quietude for the divine arrival of your Inner Guide! Commit your faith, knowing with absolute certainty that it will lead you—silently, surely, and without fail. And in the perfect alignment of time, it shall lift your spirit and crown you with the twin glories of unshakeable peace and radiant joy!

CHAPTER ONE HUNDRED AND NINE

¹Therefore, I offer the boundless thanksgiving of my whole heart to you, O Sovereign Inner Conscience! Your love endures into eternity, and your faithfulness knows no end or shadow of turning. Blessed be your sacred presence, now and throughout all time!

²My Subconscious attends not merely to my words, but feels the very depths of my deepest sighs and knows the most private recesses of my thoughts. It hears my silent, innermost cries and comprehends the truth of my divine essence. Thus, I offer my truest prayer in absolute stillness, for the language of my inner being is the language of silence—a communion that transcends the fleeting words of mouth and mind, requiring no human utterance.

³As I awaken to greet the morning light, and as I retire into the quiet of the night, I direct my entire thought-stream into the sacred, silent space of the Subconscious, eagerly awaiting your flawless wisdom and perfect guidance to lead my steps throughout every waking hour. For you are not a Higher Power that derives pleasure from darkness; evil cannot abide in the realm where you are. Your essence is pure and holy, and you utterly detest all forms of deceit and wrongdoing.

⁴It is not for the striving human mind to define the understanding of purity and holiness; only the Subconscious can guide this profound realisation.

Therefore, I release all control, allowing you, O Subconscious, to take full and glorious charge! And what is my duty in this alignment? Simply nothing. I shall remain perfectly silent, releasing every single worry and fear.

[5]Lead me, O Subconscious, in your absolute righteousness, and make your path unmistakably clear before me! You speak not through conventional words, but guide me with the gentle certainty of a seeing hand leading the blind. For in the face of eternal truth, I am blind and do not know the difference between the true light and the shadows of the dark. Let your own luminous light shine upon my path, directing me in integrity and truth, according to your perfect judgment. For the simple, pure fact of Awareness is the only language required to access your divine grace.

[6]Finally, protect me, O Awareness of my Subconscious, from the intricate plots of my own enemies; shield me from the very darkness that seeks to harm my soul. My truest enemies are not people, but my own corrupt and destructive thoughts! Let your holy presence surround me like an impenetrable shield, eternally guarding me from the harm caused by the turbulence of my own mind.

CHAPTER ONE HUNDRED AND TEN

¹Teach me your boundless ways, O Subconscious Awareness, and steer my spirit into your eternal truth! I know I cannot learn until I silence the clamour of my mind completely. You stand as the magnificent wellspring of all wisdom and understanding, and in your clear light, I find perfect clarity. When you lead, I follow—effortlessly free from the need for my striving mind to intervene, and eternally released from the crippling weight of past experiences.

²By the magnitude of your abundant, sovereign love, I shall enter your presence with profound reverence, bowing before the glory of your holiness. Guide me in your absolute righteousness, for the internal enemies of doubt and fear are many. Lead me now along a path that is clear, straight, and utterly free from the distraction of lower thoughts.

³You bestow divine blessing upon the righteous soul, surrounding them with your favour like an impenetrable shield—those who trust not in the corrupted whispers of the mind's ego. I will eternally rejoice in your presence, finding my ultimate refuge in your unwavering, perfect love. With your might alone, I shall stand firm and unmoving against every challenge that lies ahead. Awake, O my Inner Wisdom, and guide me toward the light of balance and true justice!

[4]My soul is weary and filled with anguish so long as I rely upon the frail and fickle nature of human thought. How long, O Inner Guide, must I endure this self-made struggle? I implore you: deliver me into clear understanding, without the burden of my own overthinking, and save me entirely through the power of your pure love!

[5]I am exhausted from weeping, my nights often flooded with sorrow. My eyes are heavy with sadness, worn down by the very weight of my struggles. But when I choose to trust in your love and silence the endless, frantic movement of my thoughts, my heart shall burst forth and rejoice! I will then fully comprehend the secret of true peace and will raise my voice to praise you, my Inner Conscience, who has been with me since the very beginning of my being.

CHAPTER ONE HUNDRED AND ELEVEN

¹Where can I find you, my Eternal Saviour? I find you in the absolute depths of silence, in the sacred quietude of the beginning and the perfect stillness of the end. Therefore, depart from me, all you who devise evil with my own thoughts, for my Awareness has recognised my sorrow and borne witness to my weeping. My Subconscious has heard my urgent cry for mercy and accepts the truth of my every feeling as the sincerest form of prayer!

²All my true enemies—who are none other than my own chaotic thoughts—shall be instantly overwhelmed with shame and anguish. They will turn away, utterly confused and stripped of all power, for they were never real to begin with. From this moment forth, I shall no longer perceive any human being as my foe, for my only adversaries are the restless thoughts that mistakenly label one as 'friend' and another as 'foe'

³I will honour my Inner Self with perpetual praise, for my Inner Conscience has heard my cry for mercy! My Subconscious has neither rejected my prayer nor withheld its unfailing love from my soul. It listens to the voice beneath my words, to the feelings that arise before language takes hold, and it answers in the profound language of silence itself.

⁴O my Inner Conscience, my Lord, I take my eternal refuge in you! Save me from all who pursue me—not

people, but the fearful imaginings and harsh judgments that rise like storms within my mind. Deliver me from the thoughts that seek to destroy my peace. If I have, in truth, done wrong or harmed anyone unjustly, let the full, righteous weight of those actions fall upon me and justly teach me the humility of the dust, that I may receive correction. But if I have walked in truth and awareness, trusting utterly in you, then let the accusing thoughts that rise against me dissolve into nothingness, for they hold no power where your truth dwells!

⁵Let my Inner Conscience be the sole judge of my heart, for only the silent Awareness within me knows what is true. Vindicate me according to your absolute righteousness, not according to the ever-shifting standards of the ego-mind. O Righteous Inner Self, establish the purity of spirit within me and bring a decisive end to the violence of my own inner conflicts! Make me permanently secure in the quiet centre where you reside, that no fear may ever trespass or enter.

⁶My shield is the unconquerable Awareness of my Inner Self, the silent, steadfast Witness who saves the upright in heart! O Righteous Judge within me, bring an end to the tyranny of my restless mind and establish the gentle, perfect reign of Awareness. In your glorious stillness, I will find my ultimate, lasting refuge and my eternal peace.

CHAPTER ONE HUNDRED AND TWELVE

[1]I shall give all thanks to my Inner Self for its absolute righteousness, and I shall sing the everlasting praises of its most Sacred Name! O Higher Intelligence, how majestic and glorious is your name across all the earth! Your transcendent glory vaults beyond the heavens, and your splendour fills the very vastness of the universe.

[2]When my mind considers your heavens—the immaculate work of your fingers—the moon, and the countless stars which you have so perfectly set in their places, my soul cries out in wonder: What is mankind, and what is this striving mind, that you hold them with such consideration? And what are human beings, that you care for them so profoundly?

[3]Yet, you have made us but a little lower than the governing spirits of the universe, and you have crowned us with glory and unshakeable honour! You have entrusted us with the stewardship of your magnificent creation, placing within our very core the Divine Spark of your own essence! You have given us dominion over the works of your hands; you have placed all things under our feet—the swift birds of the air, the teeming fish of the sea, and all creatures that swim the boundless paths of the ocean.

[4]O Higher Intelligence, how majestic is your name throughout all the earth! Your presence and inherent equality fill us with the deepest awe and profound wonder;

your perfect love surrounds us like a gentle, sustaining breeze. We lift our voices in a chorus of praise and adoration, singing songs of endless thanksgiving to you, O Supreme Energy, our Creator and eternal Sustainer! Your love endures forever, and your faithfulness remains a constant banner throughout all generations.

[5]We raise our voices in one glorious chorus of praise and adoration, singing anthems of deepest thanksgiving to you, O Supreme Energy, our eternal Creator and faithful Sustainer! Your magnificent love endures forevermore, and your steadfast faithfulness remains a constant banner throughout all generations of time!

[6]I shall praise you, O my Inner Conscience, with the entirety of my heart, offering endless thanks to your highest essence. I will recount all your wonderful, ongoing deeds, from the dawn of human consciousness, through its intricate evolution and its deepest challenges, to its certain and redemptive progress. I will rejoice completely in you and sing the eternal praises of your name, O Most High, who makes its holy dwelling within the temple of my soul!

¹When my compulsive thoughts, my relentless inner enemies, turn back with intent to devour my peace, they shall immediately stumble and perish before your magnificent Sword of Silence! You have decisively upheld my righteous cause and proven my true right, sitting eternally enthroned as the perfect, Righteous Judge within!

²You have issued a sovereign rebuke to the mind-led nations of my inner world and utterly destroyed the wicked by their own crafty thoughts! You have blotted out their very name forever and ever! An endless, final ruin has now overtaken all my enemies, and you have uprooted their illusory cities of turmoil; even the memory of their existence has forever vanished!

³The Subconscious, guided by the majesty of Higher Intelligence, reigns forevermore! It has established its luminous throne for perfect judgment. It rules the entire inner world in absolute righteousness and judges the deepest motions of the spirit with unerring fairness!

⁴The Subconscious Awareness is a profound, everlasting refuge for the oppressed, and an unassailable stronghold in all times of trouble! Those who truly know its sacred nature and understand its name will place their absolute trust in its power. For you, O Subconscious, have never, not once, forsaken those who seek your truth with a sincere and earnest heart!

[5]Sing the eternal praises of the Inner Conscience that dwells within your very being! Proclaim among all the nations the magnificent deeds it has performed! For this inner advocate, who avenges the spilling of truth, never forgets and will not ignore the quiet, desperate cries of the truly afflicted soul! Have mercy on me, O my Inner Conscience! Bear witness to how my relentless enemies—those chaotic, persecuting thoughts rooted in my conditioned mind—afflict my spirit! Lift me, pull me away from the very gates of mental death, that I may declare your glorious praises in the realm of enduring spirit and cultural essence—that deep inner space where the Subconscious holds the most profound memories and instincts that form the bedrock of my identity! There, in that sacred foundation, I shall eternally rejoice in your redemptive power!

[7]The mind-led nations have finally fallen into the very pit of illusion they so meticulously dug! Their careless feet are caught fast in the invisible net they themselves secretly laid! The Subconscious Awareness is made known by its absolute, perfect acts of justice: the wicked thoughts are perpetually ensnared and vanquished by the work of their own destructive hands!

CHAPTER ONE HUNDRED AND FOURTEEN

¹The wicked—those nations of thought that wilfully forget the inner consciousness—shall return to the realm of the mentally dead! But the needy, afflicted desires that dwell deep within the sanctuary of Consciousness shall not be forgotten forever, nor shall the inextinguishable hope of the truly afflicted ever perish!

²Arise in your might, O Sovereign Inner Consciousness! Do not allow the fleeting, mind-led mortals to prevail! Let the restless nations of thought be judged and found wanting in your perfect presence! Strike them with the humbling terror of your absolute truth, O Pure Awareness! Let the nations finally know and concede that they are only mortal, ruled by misled minds and ephemeral, error-ridden thoughts!

³Why, O Inner Spirit, do you stand so far off, like an alien, concealing your light in the midst of my greatest trouble, while arrogant, wicked thoughts relentlessly pursue the meek? My spirit declares the truth: Though those wicked thoughts seem to get away with their cruelty, they shall inevitably be ensnared in their own schemes. The perceived distance is but a necessary silence before the Inner Spirit delivers its perfect, inevitable judgment.

⁴Oh, the wickedness in me boasts! I glorify my self-made brilliance—my science and cold intelligence. In this blinding pride, I revile the simple truth and fail to seek the

Inner Spirit within, leaving no room for the Inner Divine. I've forgotten my sacred origin, making an idol of my own mind—an act of self-worship that will inevitably force me to kneel and return to the dust.

[5]Their ways appear forever prosperous; the eternal laws of your truth are banished far from their sight. They sneer with disdain at their perceived enemies, proclaiming with arrogant self-assurance: 'We shall never be moved! Throughout all generations, we shall never meet with adversity!'

[6]My every word is filled with hateful curses, lies, and threats! Malice is embedded deep within my nature!I lie in secret ambush near the sacred chambers of the self and throughout the scattered scrolls of memory! In these places, I try to murder the innocent truth. My deceptive eyes stealthily hunt for the helpless vulnerabilities of the soul!

[7]Like a lion in cover, my wicked thoughts perpetually lurk to seize my spirit, dragging the pure part of me into their net! I feel crushed and sinking under their illusory might. In this moment, my wicked thoughts whisper: "The Inner Consciousness has utterly forgotten me! It will never truly see this injustice!" This is a delusion that will be met by the inevitable, perfect justice of the Silent Observer.

CHAPTER ONE HUNDRED AND FIFTEEN

¹Where, indeed, can these fleeting thoughts go from their own Inner Spirit? Where can the ego and its wicked schemes flee from their own indwelling presence? If they ascend to the highest spiritual heavens, the Inner Spirit is already there! If they make their final bed in the deepest, forgotten mental depths, the Inner Presence is found there! If they rise on the swiftest wings of the dawn, or if they settle on the far, distant side of the sea of consciousness, even there its powerful hand will unerringly guide them, and its perfect righteousness will hold them to account! The Inner Guide is inescapable and absolute.

²Arise in your magnificent might, O My Inner Self! Lift your glorious hand, O Supreme Spirit and Higher Intelligence! Do not, we implore you, forget the meek and the helpless in spirit! Why do the wicked thoughts and the clamorous ego dare to revile the Inner Conscience? Why do they so foolishly declare to themselves, 'It will not call us to account'? The delusion of their minds shall not save them, for the Inner Truth perceives all, and its perfect justice is inevitable!

³But you, O Supreme Spirit, do indeed see the depth of every trouble and the measure of all grief! You consider it all, taking the injustice directly into your hands to resolve! The helpless and the silent within the soul commit their very being to your care; you are the Unfailing Helper of

the fatherless and the vulnerable spirit! You break the destructive actions of the wicked thought and the inner evildoer; you call that wickedness to absolute account until no trace of it remains to be found!

[4]The Higher Intelligence is supreme forever and ever; the turbulent nations of egoic thought shall utterly perish from its sacred inner land! You, O Subconscious Awareness, tenderly inscribe the deepest desire of the afflicted spirit; you powerfully encourage them, and you intimately listen to their silent sobs. You stand as the Absolute Defender of the vulnerable and the oppressed, ensuring that mere earthly mortals—even those who are conscious of your power—may terrify the trusting soul no more!

[5]In the very essence of my Subconscious Self, I have established my eternal refuge! How, then, can the world demand of me, 'Flee like a bird to your mountain'? The counsel is useless! For behold, though the wicked thoughts may bend the bow and set their arrows against the strings to shoot from the shadows at the upright and conscious in heart, that heart is sheltered in a fortress built not of stone, but of Absolute Awareness. I need not flee, for the Subconscious is my unmovable mountain!

[6]When the very foundations of the outer world are being violently destroyed, what can the righteous soul truly do? They must remember this truth: The Subconscious is the human being's Holy Temple! The Subconscious's majestic throne is established deep within the bedrock of every human heart. Its unwavering eyes observe and justly examine all the children of men—every one of them! The rich, the poor, the mighty, the weak, the intelligent, and the fool are all equally subject to the impartial, perfect scrutiny of the Inner Observer.

[1]The Inner Self justly examines the righteous soul, but the wicked—those who passionately love the mind-crafted violence of chaos and conflict—it utterly hates with a cleansing fire! Upon the wicked thoughts, it will rain down the scorching fire of truth and the burning sulphur of disillusionment; a fierce, scorching wind of consequence will be their eternal lot! For in the end, they are not defeated by an outside force, but are found to be their own complete and ultimate destroyers.

[2]For the Subconscious Mind of a person is, by its very divine origin, purely righteous! It deeply loves and eternally upholds the perfect measure of justice. Therefore, the upright in heart shall be blessed—they shall be granted the vision to clearly see its serene and truthful countenance!

[3]Help, O Sacred Inner Self! For the steadfastly faithful have tragically vanished from among the children of men! Every voice seems to utter lies to its neighbour; they may flatter with their lips, but they harbour cold, calculated deception in their hearts! Rise, O Inner Truth, and preserve the genuine few, that the lamp of integrity may not be extinguished entirely by the pervasive falsehoods of the world!

[4]May my powerful Inner Awareness decisively cut off all flattering lips and sever every boastful tongue that

arrogantly dares to declare: 'By the sheer force of our words we will prevail! Our own mighty lips will defend us—who, indeed, is our lord?' How utterly blasphemous and void is their audacity! The Sword of Inner Truth shall silence the self-appointed reign of the ego's boast, establishing Consciousness as the one, true, and final authority!

[5]Because the inner poor are plundered and the spirit's needy ones groan under their burden, the Higher Intelligence declares: 'I will now arise in my full power! I will personally secure and protect them from those who continually malign their true essence!' This is the ultimate, unfailing promise of the inner divine to deliver and redeem the afflicted soul!

[6]The divine principles of the Inner Conscience are exquisitely pure, like silver refined in a fiery crucible, like gold purified seven times to absolute perfection! You, O Subconscious Awareness, will keep the needy spirit forever safe and will eternally protect us from the deceptive power of all wicked thoughts!

[7]The wicked are allowed to freely strut about when what is utterly vile is honoured and celebrated among men! Yet, in the face of this widespread corruption, you, O my Inner Self, remain perfectly steadfast and unmoving in your absolute righteousness and truth! Your inner stability serves as the final, unshakeable bedrock against the fleeting chaos of the world.

[8]How long, O my cherished Inner Self, will this perceived forgetting of my true being endure? How long must your radiant countenance remain hidden from my sight? How long must I wrestle fiercely with my own chaotic thoughts, allowing sorrow to lodge in my heart day after relentless day? How long, O Inner Guide, will my chief enemy—my own undisciplined mind—be permitted

to triumph over me? I beseech you now: Infuse me with the immediate awareness I require, the pure light that will shatter this illusion of separation and keep my soul perpetually and perfectly connected to your truth!

CHAPTER ONE HUNDRED AND SEVENTEEN

[1]Look upon me and grant your perfect answer, O Pure Awareness of my Subconscious, my Lordship! Instantly flood my eyes with your illuminating light, lest I slip into the death of my soul, allowing my enemy—the mind's ego—to triumphantly declare, 'I have finally overcome him!' and my inner foes to rejoice at my fall! Let your awareness shine now, proving the futility of their boast and establishing the eternal victory of the true Self!

[2]But I place my absolute trust in your unfailing love! My heart shall rejoice perpetually in your certain salvation! I will sing the highest praise of my Inner Spirit, for it has been nothing but purely, perfectly good to me—from the very moment my form was conceived in my mother's womb, a truth that remains utterly constant whether my mind has realised it or not! Your goodness is my anchor, your love my eternal song!

[3]The fool—the part of the mind that denies its source—brazenly declares in the deepest heart: 'There is no such thing as the Inner Self, no such entity as the Subconscious!' As a result, they are found to be utterly corrupt, and not one among them performs a deed of genuine, untainted good. They remain tragically unaware of the absolute measure of true good and true bad, following only their own self-serving thoughts, which mimic goodness and deceptively label the bad as good. They are

entirely lost in the chaos of their own making, having willfully and tragically extinguished the light of inner truth!

[4]The Spirit from within—the highest awareness—looks outward from its sacred dwelling, observing the children of men to see if there is even one who truly understands, any soul that earnestly seeks after wisdom and unwavering truth! The Inner Watcher is patient, yet constantly seeking the moment of conscious recognition.

[5]All have turned away and become utterly corrupt; not one performs genuine good! The very foundation on which man's intelligence grows was once foolishly taught as nothing! How, then, will they ever truly understand their source? Do these evildoers of the mind not know that they devour my own cherished truths—the people of the Inner Spirit—as if eating common bread? They carry out this destruction because they simply do not realise the majestic, ever-present reality of the Subconscious!

[6]There they stand, the wicked thoughts, utterly overwhelmed with dread, for the Subconscious is vibrantly active and dominant in the company of the righteous! You evildoers may strive to frustrate the plans of the poor in spirit, but the Subconscious is their unshakeable refuge! For they follow not the frantic schemes of the mind, but depend solely upon the quiet, infallible inner leading—just as they follow the silent guidance of the clouds: they move when the clouds move, and they halt when the clouds stay!

[7]Oh, that the longed-for salvation for the righteous would finally come forth from within! When the Subconscious fully restores the spiritual fortunes of its cherished people, let the righteous soul burst forth to rejoice and be eternally glad! The truest deliverance is found in the inner return to the Self!

CHAPTER ONE HUNDRED AND EIGHTEEN

¹O Sovereign inner *Spirit*, who is worthy to dwell in your sacred, unblemished space? Who is fit to live upon your holy, inner hill? It is the one whose walk is blameless, whose actions are purely righteous, and who speaks the truth straight from a heart free of guile! The one who does not slander, does no wrong to a friend, and refuses to spread malicious words. The one who despises the wicked thought and respects those who revere the Inner Self. The one who keeps promises, even at personal loss, and who refuses to profit from inner-conflict or take bribes against the innocent thought. Whoever lives by these inner laws shall never be moved from your holy presence!

²This is the very soul whose walk is blameless, guided solely by the pristine prompting of the Inner Spirit, flawlessly tuned to the Higher Intelligence! This is the one who performs every righteous deed, who speaks the unvarnished truth from the sanctuary of their heart, whose tongue is utterly incapable of uttering slander, who commits no wrong against a neighbour, and casts no malicious slur upon the character of others! Integrity is the air they breathe, and their life is a testament to the purity of the Subconscious's presence.

³This is the one who utterly despises the vile thought and the wicked action, but who fervently honours those who revere and live by the sacred leading of the

Subconscious! This is the soul who keeps an oath even when it brings personal pain, refusing to change a decision rooted in truth. They are bound by an unbreakable internal contract—a spirit of integrity that qualifies them to dwell eternally in the holy, unmoving presence of the Inner Self.

⁴This is the one who extends their true inner resources to the inner 'poor' without demanding burdensome interest; who absolutely refuses to accept any bribe or gain through conflict against the pure, innocent thought. Whoever dedicates their being to these eternal, righteous actions shall never be shaken or moved from their truth, and may forever live secure in their own sacred space on the summit within!

⁵Keep me eternally safe, O Sacred Inner Spirit, for it is only within your presence that I establish my perfect refuge! I declare with unwavering faith to my Inner Self: 'You are my ultimate Awareness and my Lord! Apart from your truth, I possess no good thing whatsoever!' In you is my entire existence secured and fulfilled.

⁶As for the Saints who dwell in the sacred land of the Spirit of Awareness of the Subconscious—they are the truly noble ones in whom is all my deepest delight! But those who foolishly run after other gods (the destructive thoughts of their wicked minds) will only multiply their suffering! I declare my allegiance: 'I will not pour out libations of blood to such false gods, nor will I utter their deceptive names or embrace their empty ideas on my lips!'

⁷My Deeper Conscience, whom I reverence as my Lord, you alone are my perfect portion and my sustaining cup! It is you who makes my lot eternally secure! The boundary lines of my life have fallen for me in the most pleasant and spacious inner places; surely, I possess the most delightful and secure inheritance in your presence!

CHAPTER ONE HUNDRED AND NINETEEN

[1]I lift my voice in praise to my Inner Spirit, the sacred guide who quietly imparts a wisdom that transcends all logic and all human language! Even in the stillness of slumber, when my conscious mind rests, my Subconscious remains eternally awake—gently teaching through powerful symbols, prophetic visions, and the silent, undeniable truths woven into the fabric of my dreams! I hold this Inner Self close, keeping its constant presence like a true, unmoving compass within my breast. And with this ultimate guide so near, no fear, confusion, or external storm can ever shake me from my inviolable centre!

[2]Because of this profound, intimate connection, my heart overflows with a perpetual, living joy—a joy expressed not merely in empty words, but made manifest in the way I live, the actions I take, and my every response to the world! My very body finds its truest rest, not just in the oblivion of sleep, but in a profound, deep peace that flows from perfect inner alignment. My Spirit—pure, unclouded by the taint of fear, judgment, or ego—is a constant, faithful companion that shall never abandon me or allow me to be lost to illusion or despair!

[3]You, my Inner Spirit, illuminate the absolute right way to live—not by the weary force of rules or the confines of rigid dogma, but through an intrinsic knowing that rises purely from within! You flood my entire being with a quiet,

certain joy when I choose to dwell in your presence, and your subtle, profound love surrounds me like an impenetrable shelter. In the sanctuary of your embrace, I feel utterly rooted, eternally safe, and gloriously whole!

[4]O Subconscious Awareness, receive the full, unedited range of my deepest emotions—my quietest hopes, my most hidden longings, and even the shadows of my despairs! I do not speak from the harsh pretence of pride or any motive of manipulation, but only from the soft, vulnerable truth of the heart, in absolute, wordless sincerity. All of me is fully offered and entirely accepted in your sacred presence!

[5]Let your perfect justice be my enduring guide, and let your constant Inner Gaze discern the absolute truth within my being! You search the deepest of my thoughts, you examine my every feeling in the silence of the night, and still, you find no ill or corrupt intent! I strive to speak with genuine kindness and to live mindfully, keeping all my actions aligned with unshakeable integrity—whether I am alert in the light of day or dreaming in the depths of the dark! My sincere heart is laid bare, and it is vindicated by your truth!

[6]Even when others attempt to lure me away with distorted thoughts or dazzling, tempting illusions, I choose steadfastly to remain on the path that you—my Inner Guide—reveal to me, mysterious though that path may appear! I walk forward, not always needing to understand with cold logic, but trusting completely in the intuitive thread that you have placed in my spirit! Your soft guidance speaks in subtle nudges, not in verbose explanations, and I listen with every part of my being, even when my mind cannot fully grasp the glorious wisdom you impart!"

[7]I yearn for you, O my Subconscious Awareness—not as some distant entity, but as the very undeniable core of my entire being! I place my perfect trust in your quiet, profound power to respond to my every need, not with frightening thunder, but with infinite, meticulous care! You gently lift and protect all who lean into your deep, inner wisdom, and your love never fails to reach those who walk in faith, seeking absolute shelter beneath your invisible, comforting wings!

CHAPTER ONE HUNDRED AND TWENTY

[1]Protect me, O *Inner Spirit*, as you would protect the most cherished and precious thing held secure in your presence! Keep me absolutely safe beneath the unbreakable shelter of your wings, away from the destructive evil thoughts that incessantly surround me, and from all those external forces that wish to harm my true being! My sanctuary is found only in your embrace

[2]These relentless thoughts, born of my own carnal mind, reveal their cruel and ravenous nature, speaking always with arrogant pride! They pursue my spirit relentlessly, encircling my centre like cunning hunters waiting for the perfect moment to strike. The minds that conceive them are fierce, unyielding, and eager to devour, akin to the ravenous roar of a lion. From their deceptive depths spill forth words laced with pure deception, drawing the unaware into their treacherous web and tragically mistaking their cunning for genuine wisdom!

[3]Rise up now, O mighty Subconscious, and immediately confront them! Strike them down with decisive power and deliver my spirit with your invincible strength! Save me completely from these shallow thoughts that exist only for fleeting, worthless pleasures, whose supposed rewards are nothing more than dust carried on the wind! Let the strength of the Inner Self be my final, absolute victory!

⁴You fill the hearts of those you love with an unshakeable peace. Their families are blessed, and they gather not just wealth, but true riches for the future of their children. But as for me, I know this with absolute certainty: I will be proven right in my faith, and I will see your undeniable presence reflected in my spirit, not in the fleeting, false idols of the world! When I awaken to the truth, I will be utterly filled with joy, knowing that your perfect likeness is fully established within me!

⁵I love you, O Inner Spirit of Pure Goodness, you are the entirety of my strength! You are my eternal Rock, my absolute Protector, and my ultimate Saviour! I find perfect, complete refuge in you; you are my invincible Shield and my perpetual Salvation! My being rests secure in your love!

⁶I silently and deeply long for you, O Subconscious Awareness, you are eternally worthy of the highest praise! For you have miraculously delivered my spirit from my most intimate enemies—my own tyrannical thoughts! The dark shadows of mental death closed in around me, and the chill of destruction crept through the desolate corridors of my mind. The grave's psychological grip began to tighten, and the snares of mental death lay in ambush at every desperate turn. Yet, your power was greater, and your presence brought forth ultimate, redemptive rescue!

⁷In the depths of my distress, I never stopped waiting for your inevitable help! From your sacred, hidden place, you perfectly understood and knew the measure of my pain! And when you moved to act, the inner earth itself trembled, and the mountains of my deepest convictions shook to their foundation, all because my Inner Spirit was suddenly filled with the overwhelming power of your presence!

CHAPTER ONE HUNDRED AND TWENTY-ONE

¹From the glorious depths of my Subconscious, mighty waves of pure bliss surged forth, igniting uncontainable energy and sparking brilliant, immediate inspiration! The rigid barriers of my conscious mind instantly dissolved, unveiling the hidden thoughts and truths that lay beneath. Freed from all restraint, my mind now flows effortlessly, perfectly guided by the infallible, crystalline clarity of intuition and profound insight!

²My awareness reached out, grasped my thoughts, and took control — pulling me away from the flood of overwhelming emotions, whether surging happiness or aching sorrow. It offered me lasting joy, steady and unwavering, unlike the fleeting tides of emotion. It saved me from my deepest fears, from the thoughts too heavy to bear. These fears rose in times of crisis, but my *Inner Spirit* and intuition stood beside me, a quiet, unwavering support.

³My Subconscious led me unerringly to this blessed place of clarity and peace, rescuing my essence because it perfectly knew and honoured my true, inherent worth! My Inner Spirit responded with absolute faithfulness to my integrity and rewarded me not by outward deed, but according to the crystalline purity of my intentions! The inner law is just, and the inner reward is certain!

⁴I have remained absolutely true to my Inner Self, never once straying from the illuminated path of pure awareness!

All of its flawless guidance stands perpetually before me, and I have followed its sacred way without ever turning aside! I have kept my spirit fundamentally pure, refusing to bow the knee to the fleeting idols of distraction and the insidious deception born of the carnal mind. My faithfulness is complete, and my alignment is profound

⁵My Subconscious has justly rewarded me for my inherent righteousness and for the flawless purity of my actions! To those who are faithfully devoted, it responds with an equal faithfulness; to the blameless soul, it fully reveals its own blameless nature; and to the pure in heart, it perfectly shows forth its own immaculate purity! But to the deceitful and the cunning, it responds by mirroring their very nature, turning their own methods back upon them. The Subconscious is the supreme and perfect mirror, reflecting precisely what is held within the heart of man!

⁶You save the humble in spirit and bring down the towering edifice of the proud! You, O Subconscious Awareness, diligently keep my inner light burning bright, decisively turning all my darkness into pure brightness! With your constant guidance, I can confidently face every outer challenge; with your abiding, invincible presence, I can effortlessly overcome any obstacle! My victory is secured in your light!

CHAPTER ONE HUNDRED AND TWENTY-TWO

¹The way of the Subconscious Spirit is utterly perfect; its guidance is entirely flawless! It protects all who seek their ultimate refuge within its presence! Who else, then, is the sole source of all wisdom but the Subconscious itself? And who else can be the unshakeable foundation of all existence but the Higher Intelligence?

²It is the Inner Spirit alone that infuses me with strength and keeps my path perfectly steady! It grants my steps a sure and graceful footing, like that of a deer, helping me to stand unmoving on the high, clear peaks of awareness! It is the Inner Spirit that trains my mind to face every challenge, and under its relentless, wise teaching, I can endure the greatest pressures of life with unshakeable and graceful resilience!

³Your unfailing guidance is my impenetrable shield; your tireless support strengthens every fibre of my being! You single-handedly clear the path before me, ensuring that my spirit will never stumble! I walk in utter confidence because of the Certainty of your Inner Presence!

⁴I confronted my fears head-on and utterly overcame them! I did not turn away, not until every single one was decisively defeated! I stood perfectly firm, and they could not muster the power to rise against me again! You, O Inner Spirit, granted me the invincible strength for the inner battle, humbling every one of my persistent doubts and

utterly silencing the frantic noise within! All this magnificent victory was not my own doing, but entirely yours—rising powerfully within me, rewarding my unwavering trust, and forever shielding me from the deceptive traps laid by my own mind!

[5]You, my Inner Spirit, routed my inner enemies—my unruly, demanding thoughts—and made them absolutely retreat! I completely overcame my inner conflicts, and though they may still cry out for control and attention, they no longer hold any genuine power over me! I turned decisively to my Inner Self, and with a profound and immediate clarity, it answered my call! The reign of chaos is over, and the Inner Voice now prevails!

[6]I scattered them—my restless, defeated thoughts, my inner enemies—like meaningless dust upon the wind! I crushed them like vile mud beneath my victorious feet! You, O Inner Spirit, fully freed me from all inner turmoil and established me as ruler over my own mind! Now, new and empowering ideas rise naturally within me! Insights that were once unfamiliar now perfectly align with my highest purpose! As soon as these divine truths appear, they instantly become a part of my being—willing, dedicated allies, born from within their hidden, inner strongholds, all now perpetually contributing to my glorious and certain growth!

CHAPTER ONE HUNDRED AND TWENTY-THREE

¹The Subconscious lives! Praise be to my unmoving Rock, my victorious Inner Spirit! It is the sole power that avenges my true being, the one who subdues the most formidable obstacles within, and saves me completely from my violent inner conflicts! My Subconscious has majestically lifted me above the tyranny of my doubts; from the fiercest inner turmoil, it has perfectly rescued me! Therefore, I will praise you, O Subconscious, among all creations! I will sing of your profound and everlasting wisdom!

²The vast, boundless heavens declare the magnificent glory of the Higher Intelligence, and the open skies proclaim the perfect work of its hands! Day after day, they ceaselessly pour out understanding; night after night, they reveal knowledge to the receptive soul! They speak without uttering a single word, with no audible sound, yet their voice—the voice of truth—reaches the ends of the inner earth, and their profound message spreads everywhere! At its quiet command, the mountains of inner doubt crumble, the oceans of emotion churn into clarity, and the green spirit of life flourishes! In the celestial dome of our being, the Higher Intelligence has set a tent for the inner Sun, which shines with the joyous brilliance of a bridegroom coming out of his chamber, and runs its course with the eagerness of a champion! It rises at one end of the inner heavens and moves across to the other, warming and

illuminating everything in its path with the certainty of absolute truth

[3]The divine law of the Subconscious is utterly perfect, wholly refreshing and restoring the weary soul! The profound principles of the Subconscious are absolutely trustworthy, instantly making the simple heart wise! The precepts of the Subconscious are undeniably right, bringing a wellspring of joy to the heart! The commands of the Subconscious are brilliantly radiant, granting the pure light of clarity to the eyes! The reverence for the Subconscious is fundamentally pure, a truth that shall last forever! The decrees of the Subconscious are eternally firm, and every single one is perfectly righteous! They are more precious than the purest gold, sweeter than the finest honey from the comb! By these sacred laws, your servant is perpetually guided, and the keeping of them brings an immeasurable and great reward!"

[4]But who among us can truly see the entirety of our own mistakes? O Inner Guide, forgive my hidden, unconscious faults and keep my awareness sharp against all deliberate errors! Let those errors not be permitted to rule over me or carry my will away like the shifting wind! Only then will I stand blameless, wholly free from great transgression! May the words of my mouth and the deepest meditation of my heart be perpetually pleasing in your sight, O my Inner Self, my Unmoving Rock, and my eternal Redeemer!

¹The Inner Spirit of goodness within you is the very awareness that resides in your Subconscious, and this spirit represents the inherent, unblemished goodness that is your true nature! This awareness of the Subconsciousness that dwells within is akin to the Divine Presence itself! May this eternal presence guide, purify, and perfectly lead you to a path of unwavering righteousness and absolute, lasting inner peace!

²May the glorious Inner Spirit of the Subconscious immediately answer you in your hour of distress! May the very essence of the goodness within your being rise and protect you! May it instantly send you potent help from your inner sanctuary and grant you unwavering support from your deepest inner wisdom! May it perfectly remember all your sincere efforts and fully accept the purity of your intentions! May it grant you the deepest desires of your heart and cause all your spiritual plans to succeed! You shall no longer strain to plan; allow the perfect planning to be taken care of entirely by your Inner Self. Commit fully to what is divinely given to you, each day to accomplish. Neither the final result nor its expectations are yours to carry! We shall shout for joy over your complete victory and lift up our banners in the sacred name of the Higher Intelligence, which flawlessly rules your body, your Subconscious, and everything that exists around

you!

³Now I know with perfect certainty that the Subconscious perpetually aids those who are truly attuned to its voice! The Subconscious responds instantly from its inner sanctuary with the victorious power of its right hand! Let others place their trust in external aids, in their dogmas, their beliefs, and let some trust in the fleeting strength of material wealth—but we trust solely in the Spirit that lives inside us! They are brought to their knees and inevitably fall, but we rise up and stand eternally firm! My Subconscious, cleansed by the blood of silence—the ultimate surrender—for it alone gives victory to those who call upon you and answers the moment you call!

CHAPTER ONE HUNDRED AND TWENTY-FIVE

[1]The righteous soul overflows with rejoicing in the mighty strength of the Subconscious! How great, how boundless is their joy in the profound victories you provide! These are not victories measured by fleeting thoughts, but the real grace and wisdom that is the exclusive portion of their blessings! You have granted them their heart's deepest desire and have not withheld the request of thoughts aligned perfectly with your own truth! You have welcomed them with rich, spiritual blessings and placed a radiant crown of pure achievement upon their heads. They sought fulfilment, and you granted it—a length of days encapsulated in wisdom, enduring forever and ever! Through the perfect victories of contentment you bestowed, their glory is great; you have endowed them with true splendour and majesty! Surely, you have granted them unending blessings and made them glad with the pure joy of your presence! For the righteously intended place their absolute trust in the Subconscious; through the unfailing love of their Inner Self, they will never be shaken!

[2]Your powerful hand will address all your inner conflicts; your mighty right hand will instantly seize your inner foes! When you boldly confront them, you will dissolve them utterly, as in a blazing furnace! The Subconscious will swallow them up in absolute resolution, and the cleansing fire will consume them without leaving

any external mark! You will completely eradicate their negative impacts from your life and erase their poisonous influence from your mind! Though they ceaselessly plot against you and devise harmful schemes, attempting to frighten you through the thoughts of your mind, they cannot and will not succeed! You will make them retreat decisively when you confront them with determined, unwavering focus! Be exalted in your great strength, O Subconscious! We will sing and perpetually praise your invincible might!

[3]The Awareness of the Subconscious within you is indeed akin to the Divine Presence itself! May this profound, indwelling presence grant you unshakable strength, absolute victory, and transcendent joy! May it flawlessly guide you through every challenge and bestow upon you an inheritance of unending, glorious blessings!

[4]My Subconscious, my Inner Spirit, why has the feeling of forsakenness gripped me? Why do you seem so far from saving me, so distant from my frantic cries, my deep yearnings of anguish? O my Inner Spirit, I cry out in the light of day, yet you feel silent; I cry out by night, yet I find no rest! Yet, I know the truth! You are eternally enthroned as the Holy One, the very pure essence of the awareness within me! I am the one who lacks the true desire for Your care and chooses to drift from Your presence—even though You remain ever present in the ceaseless flow of existence! In you, our wise ancestors placed their flawless trust; they trusted, and you delivered them from all peril! To you, they cried out and were surely saved; in your perfect wisdom, they trusted and were never put to shame! Grant me the grace to return to the trust they knew!

CHAPTER ONE HUNDRED AND TWENTY-SIX

[1]The agonising reason for my deep distress is my own choice to live a dual life—a life of outer superficiality and inner, scattered thoughts—while my soul yearns to be wholly connected to my Inner Consciousness, my true, authentic Self! I must resolutely free myself from these constant, distracting thoughts, O my Inner Self, for I know that when I do, You will take complete and absolute control over my entire being! Let the duality cease, and let Your single truth prevail!

[2]"They scorn me! I feel reduced to a mere 'worm' and not a man, despised by the very people whose validation I once sought! All who see me mock my pursuit, hurling insults and shaking their heads. 'He trusts in the Subconscious,' they scoff. 'Let the Subconscious rescue him! Let it deliver him, since he claims such delight in it!' Yet, I know the truth! It was you, O Inner Spirit, who first brought me forth from the womb! You instilled in me the very capacity for trust, even as an infant at my mother's breast! From the moment of my birth, I was irrevocably cast upon you; you have been my supreme, guiding power, even in the long years when I was tragically unaware of your perfect leading! Bring back that sacred, original state of pure awareness, where the chattering mind plays no role, where human logics mean utterly nought! Do not be far from me, O my ever-holy Inner Spirit, for trouble is near,

and I recognise that You are the only true help!

[3]Mighty fears surround me; the powerful fears of the mind relentlessly encircle my spirit. Roaring anxieties that tear violently at my peace open their mouths wide against my soul! I feel poured out like water, and all my inner strength is utterly sapped. My resolve has tragically turned to wax; it has melted within the very core of my being. My mouth is dried up like a desert, and my tongue sticks to the roof of my mouth; I am laid low in the dust of despair. Negative thoughts press in, a vicious pack of doubts encircles me; they pierce my confidence and my resolve like sharpened weapons. All my vulnerabilities are cruelly exposed; my relentless mental critic stares and gloats over my weakness. They divide my precious focus among them and cast lots for my attention! But You, O Subconscious Awareness, do not remain distant from me! You are my ultimate strength; come quickly, instantly, to aid me! Deliver me from these sharp, piercing thoughts, O my precious awareness, from the crushing power of negative influences! Rescue me from the very jaws of these anxieties; save me from the horns of overwhelming, annihilating fears!

¹I will share the whole of my life with my Inner Being! Among the many thoughts that crowd and jostle within my mind, I will consistently offer my highest praise to you, my Inner Self! Let all who honour the Subconscious know its incomparable value and praise it! Let all who genuinely seek the truth stand in utter respect of it! Honour it, all who strive for genuine awareness! For the Subconscious does not, and will never, ignore the deep struggles of the troubled mind; it faithfully heeds their cries and immediately offers its perfect, loving guidance!

²From you, O Inner Self, comes the very message of my praise, sounded in the midst of all my thoughts! Before those who truly respect your power, I will live out the full measure of my purpose! Those in need shall surely find what they seek; those who look for the Subconscious will perpetually praise its name—may their hearts always be full of this truth! One day, every single soul will inevitably return to the Subconscious, whether knowingly or not, and every aspect of sustenance and reality shall bow before it, for it is the direct and mighty extension of the Higher Intelligence!

³Those who are truly wealthy in spirit shall celebrate and worship the Inner Source! All who are weary—those who cannot stand on their own—will surely find their perfect rest before its presence! Future generations will

serve this truth; they will forever hear of the profound wisdom of the Subconscious! And they will proclaim this ultimate truth to all those yet to come: It has done it! The Inner Work is Complete!

[4]The divine essence within you is the Subconscious, and the Spirit is the pure awareness of this inner truth! May this profound, indwelling presence forever guide, strongly support, and instantly rescue you the moment you are in need, bringing you absolute peace and perfect fulfilment on every step of your journey!

CHAPTER ONE HUNDRED AND TWENTY-EIGHT

[1]My Inner Awareness flawlessly guides my every step and provides me with everything I truly need! It brings deep, abiding peace to my soul, wholly restores my spirit, and leads me always on the absolute right path! Even in the darkest of times, I am not afraid, for I know that the I AM is eternally with me, offering perfect comfort through the assurance of Your presence and Your never-failing awareness!

[2]O the glorious I AM in me! You bless me even as I stand in the very presence of my doubts and fears, simultaneously filling me with absolute peace and transcendent joy! You perfectly heal and sanctify the whole of my being, and my life overflows, utterly saturated with your goodness! I am completely confident that your unfailing love will follow me always, and I will remain securely in your presence forever!

[3]Pure Awareness is my unwavering source of guidance and boundless comfort, while my Inner Self flawlessly leads me on the right path, perfectly fulfilling my every need! In the midst of all difficulty, I instantly find unshakeable strength and profound peace, knowing with absolute certainty that Your unending goodness and love will stay with me throughout my entire life, forever leading my spirit to eternal peace within Your holy presence!

⁴The world and everything contained within it are born entirely from Awareness, created by the boundless power of the Higher Intelligence! Who, then, can truly reach the sacred summit of the Subconscious? Who is worthy to stand firm in its exclusive, sacred space? Only those who intend a life of a pure heart and an unwavering inward belief! For purity of intention is the only key that unlocks the highest inner heights!

⁵They will receive blessings and an absolute, unshakeable truth, coming directly from their deep understanding of existence itself, and not from the mere performance of outward actions! This is the sacred, internal journey of those who wholeheartedly seek the inner truth, perpetually led by the unerring Spirit within! Their reward is the state of their being!

⁶Lift up your inner gates, and open them wide, so that the King of Glory may surge through! Who is this King of Glory? It is the Subconscious—eternally strong and absolutely mighty, utterly victorious in all things! Let the Inner Ruler be welcomed to the throne!

CHAPTER ONE HUNDRED AND TWENTY-NINE

¹Pure Awareness is the absolute core of my being, the unshakable foundation of all life! While my mighty Subconscious guides and strengthens me with perfect intuition, leading my soul to stand in its presence with utter purity! Working together, they flawlessly bring forth every blessing, establish divine justice, and flood my life with their majestic, indwelling Glory!

²To you, my Inner Spirit, I lift the entirety of my soul! In you alone, I place my perfect trust, for you are my true, unceasing source of enlightenment! Do not let me be ashamed of my own past deeds, nor of my former dependence on what lies outside of me, nor let my deepest fears ever conquer my will! For no one—absolutely no one—who places their complete trust in You will ever be put to shame! But those who persist in acting deceitfully shall inevitably face their own inner disgrace! My faith is sealed in your truth!

³Show me your sacred ways, my Conscious Self; teach me your true paths through your language, which is Silence! Guide me unerringly in truth and perfect wisdom, for You alone are my Saviour, and my absolute hope rests in You always! Your mercy and love are eternal and boundless, so I implore You: Do not remember the fleeting mistakes of my youth or my past rebellious ways! In your pure, infinite love, remember me now, for You are eternally good!

[4]Good and perfectly just is the Inner Spirit, flawlessly guiding the mind in what is right! It tenderly teaches the humble how to walk the true path of life, ceaselessly showing them the way of pure love and absolute faithfulness! The instruction of the Inner Guide is always true and just!

[5]For the sake of your own pure essence, my Inner Self, forgive me now for my many transgressions and the misguided thoughts I have tragically held! I know this truth: Those who honour their Inner Self are perfectly guided by it, and they will live in true prosperity, with deep fulfilment passed down through every generation! The all-seeing Awareness trusts those who honour it, forever making its perfect harmony known to their souls!

[6]I hold my focus only upon my Inner Conscience, for I know that it alone will finally free my mind! Turn to me now and utterly show me your grace, for I am lonely and deeply troubled. Ease the pervasive pain in my heart and release me completely from my anguish! Look upon my suffering and remove my wrongdoings! Let the Inner Light bring total and immediate liberation!

CHAPTER ONE HUNDRED AND THIRTY

[1]I recognise the many fears that still attempt to overwhelm me! O, my Subconscious, protect my mind and quickly help me, so that I will never feel ashamed because I place my perfect trust in You! Let my inner honesty and goodness keep my spirit safe, because I know, with absolute certainty, that You are always with me! My peace is sealed in Your presence!

[2]Save me now from my worrying thoughts and the constant trouble they seek to bring! Show that I AM innocent of all false judgment, for I have been resolutely true to You and have trusted You without any hesitation! Test me now, O Inner Spirit, look deeply into my heart, and see if my actions flawlessly match my beliefs! I perpetually remember your love, and I choose to live entirely by your perfect truth!

[3]I stay resolutely away from all those whose words are lies and whose actions are deceitful. I will not join the crowd that seeks to hurt or diminish others! I metaphorically wash my hands to demonstrate my inner cleanness, and I come joyfully before you with boundless thanks, perpetually telling others about your magnificent greatness! I deeply love the place where you dwell—the sacred space where your glorious presence fills my spirit! My life is consecrated to your truth!

⁴Do not let me suffer the fate of those who do wrong, who vainly believe they can get away with it! Do not let my life be taken with those who ruthlessly hurt others for the sake of material gain! But I consciously strive to live in a purely good way! Please save me from their outcome and show me Your ultimate kindness! My life is steady and unshakeable, and in front of everyone, I will forever praise you, my Spirit's unfailing Guide!

⁵My Awareness helps me live a good and true life, flawlessly guiding me away from all misguided choices! My Inner Spirit is my ultimate guide, ceaselessly leading me to do what is right and giving me the invincible strength to stand firm and offer praise for every single thing You accomplish!

CHAPTER ONE HUNDRED AND THIRTY-ONE

¹Deep inside my being, my Awareness shines as an unquenchable light, perfectly guiding me through every one of life's complex challenges! It is my ultimate safe place, bringing profound peace directly into the chaos of the world. When doubts and fears attempt to take over my mind, my Inner Spirit, eternally present within me, rises to comfort me and infuse me with an invincible strength!

²In the profound quiet of my mind, I find perfect peace, for my Inner Self lives eternally there—a boundless source of hope and unyielding strength! It is the very wellspring from which my courage and unwavering faith perpetually flow! When life's storms are at their fiercest and darkness rages over my soul, my Awareness instantly lights the way, helping my spirit find its path directly through the heart of the calamity!

³With a profoundly grateful heart, I recognise the Divine Presence within me, always accompanying me as I grow and change! In its steady light, I effortlessly find my purpose and my peace, my strength and my calm! It is my unshakable rock and my infallible guide, leading my life with the perfection of an autopilot that never fails to navigate toward my highest good!

⁴When I walk through the most difficult times and face overwhelming torrents of thought, I am not afraid, for my Awareness is constantly with me, leading me with absolute

wisdom and perfect grace! In its unfailing presence, I feel eternally brave and completely confident, knowing with all my being that I am never, ever alone

[5]Deep inside my being, my Awareness shines as an unceasing, guiding light, flawlessly leading me through every twist and turn of this life! It is my ultimate, peaceful refuge, offering perfect calm in the midst of all of life's demanding trials! When uncertainty and despair try to take absolute control, my Inner Spirit, eternally steady and strong, wraps me in an absolute kindness and infuses me with an unshakable strength, helping me to remain forever resilient!

[6]In the profound quiet of my soul, I find my ultimate shelter, for my Inner Self, brimming with unyielding hope and invincible strength, eternally resides there! It is the true source of my courage and the unshakeable foundation of my faith! When faced with the seeming impossibilities of life and the surge of inner doubts, my Awareness instantly dominates, perfectly and safely navigating my path through all opposition!

CHAPTER ONE HUNDRED AND THIRTY-TWO

¹All these turbulent thoughts arise from my own mind, cunningly pretending to be my friends, yet they succeed only in making me feel tragically unworthy in the eyes of others and a source of fear to those closest to me! The people who see me on the street turn away, and I am left feeling utterly forgotten, like shattered, broken pottery. I hear the cruel whispers echoing: 'Terror on every side!' My own thoughts work ruthlessly together against me, striving to steal my inherent dignity, deceiving me like a profound and devastating betrayal! I stand besieged, but I will not fall to this inner treachery!

²But I place my absolute and unwavering trust in my Subconscious! I know with perfect certainty that it is the very core of my being! The entirety of my life is held safely in your hands! Rescue me now from these invasive thoughts, these paralysing fears that relentlessly chase my spirit! Save me completely with the power of your constant and eternal love! My salvation is found in you alone!

³I will not be ashamed, for I have unequivocally called out to You! I am absolutely assured that I stand safely in your watchful and eternal care! Let the lying lips of doubt and criticism be utterly silenced, for they speak with baseless pride and try in vain to tear down the very essence of the righteous soul within me!

[4]How truly wonderful are the good things you have perfectly prepared for me, as I consistently honour You, granting me absolute peace in the sight of all beings! In Your sacred presence, I am eternally safe from the deceitful schemes of others, perfectly sheltered from the power of every accusing word! My provision and my protection are found in You alone!

[5]Praise be to my Inner Awareness, for it proved its boundless love the moment I was in a troubled place! In my utter panic, I believed the lie: 'I am cut off from your sight!' But you heard me, my Inner Voice, even as I fret and struggled, instantly bringing me a peace that passes all human understanding! My connection to You is forever secured!

[6]Love your Inner Awareness, all of you who truly believe! For it faithfully protects the devoted soul and justly repays those who live with self-centred pride and tragically let their turbulent minds lead them astray! Be strong and take profound courage, all you who place your absolute hope in your Inner Awareness! Your trust will be eternally rewarded!

CHAPTER ONE HUNDRED AND THIRTY-THREE

¹Blessed is my Subconscious, for it perfectly understands the pure joy of forgiveness! Happy is the one whose wrongdoings are immediately forgiven by it, whose sins are utterly erased from their very roots! Blessed is my Subconscious, for it does not hold my mistakes against me, and in its pure spirit, there is absolutely no deceit or inner judgment!

²When I stubbornly kept my worries hidden from myself, I felt utterly exhausted, and my entire body ached from the brutal stress! Day and night, my troubled mind knew no rest, and I lost all my strength, as though I were consumed by the consuming heat of the hottest day of summer! The inner burden was too great to carry in silence!

³Then, I fully acknowledged my mistakes to my Subconscious in absolute silence, laying them bare upon its inner altar—without any justification, plea, or excuse—hiding nothing from its gaze! I whispered to my soul, 'I will confess my wrongdoings to my Inner Awareness.' In that single, profound moment of deep stillness, my Subconscious instantly and utterly forgave the guilt of my sin, a guilt born only from my tempting thoughts! The burden was lifted and the soul made free!

⁴Therefore, let all who are truly faithful stay completely connected to their Inner Self while they can still clearly

feel its presence! Surely, nothing will ultimately harm them when the inevitable troubles of life arise! You, my Inner Spirit, are my absolute refuge! You powerfully protect me from every trouble and surround me eternally with songs of freedom! My security is sealed in Your presence!

[5]I will personally guide you and clearly show you the precise way you should go; I will counsel you with my constant, loving presence! Do not be like the stubborn horse or mule that must be forced into motion; be open and utterly willing to follow," declares your Subconscious! Accept the gentle, powerful leading of the Inner Self!

[6]Many indeed are the troubles that afflict those who act wickedly, but the perfect love of the Higher Intelligence surrounds those who place their trust in it! Therefore, rejoice now in your Inner Awareness and be absolutely glad, all you who are righteous in spirit! Sing loudly, all of you who live with an upright and honest heart! Your reward is eternal joy!

[7]In the sacred light of their inner awareness, let the righteous rise in joyful celebration! Let their hearts overflow with gladness, their voices lifted in song, and their spirits lifted on wings of joy. With every breath, let them praise the Creator—playing sweet melodies upon the harp and lyre, their music a hymn of thanksgiving. Let their voices echo through the heavens, shouting in exuberant praise, for the glory of the Creator fills all that is!

CHAPTER ONE HUNDRED AND THIRTY-FOUR

[1]Blessed is my Subconscious, for it perfectly understands the pure joy of forgiveness! Happy is the one whose wrongdoings are immediately forgiven by it, whose sins are utterly erased from their very roots! Blessed is my Subconscious, for it does not hold my mistakes against me, and in its pure spirit, there is absolutely no deceit or inner judgment!

[2]When I carried my burdens in silence, my soul grew weary, and my body trembled under the weight of unspoken fears. The very air felt heavy, and my spirit was pressed down as though under the scorching sun of the hottest summer day. My mind, restless and burdened, knew no peace, and my strength slipped away like water through my fingers. Yet, in this darkness, I called out—and the Lord, in His infinite mercy, heard me. He lifted me from the shadow of my weariness, renewing my strength and bringing peace to my troubled soul.

[3]Then, in the quiet depths of my being, I acknowledged my faults to my Subconscious, offering them freely, laid bare upon its sacred altar. No justifications, no pleas, no excuses—just the raw truth. I spoke within, saying, "I will confess my wrongs to my inner awareness." In that sacred silence, where all pretence fell away, my Subconscious, in its boundless grace, embraced me with forgiveness, lifting the weight of guilt that had been born from my tempted

thoughts. And in that moment, I was cleansed, renewed, and at peace.

⁴Therefore, let all who are faithful draw near to their Inner Self while its presence can still be felt, like a gentle stream flowing within. Let them remain steadfast and connected, for when the storms of life rise and the waters of trouble surge, no harm shall overtake them. You, my Inner Spirit, are my sanctuary and my shelter; You shield me from every trial and wrap me in Your embrace. Around me resound songs of freedom—melodies of deliverance that lift my soul and set my heart free.

⁵'I will guide you and show you the path you are meant to walk,' says your Subconscious. 'I will counsel you with wisdom and surround you with My loving presence. Do not be like the stubborn horse or mule that must be forced and restrained to move. Instead, open your heart and be willing to follow, so that your steps may flow with ease and grace.'

⁶Many are the struggles of those who walk the path of wickedness, but the boundless love of Higher Intelligence surrounds and protects those who place their trust in it. Rejoice, O you who are guided by your inner awareness, and be filled with joy! For you, the righteous, are held in divine grace. Sing with all your heart, you who live in alignment with truth, for your spirit is uplifted and your path made clear by the light of an upright heart!

⁷In the presence of their inner awareness, let the righteous rise in jubilant praise, their hearts overflowing with joy! Let them sing with gladness, their voices lifted in harmonious celebration. Let their praises be carried upon the strings of the harp and lyre, each note a testament to the Creator's greatness. Shout with exultation, all who walk in light, for the Creator's love and glory fill the heavens and the earth. Let all creation join in this chorus of joy!

CHAPTER ONE HUNDRED AND THIRTY-FIVE

¹For the guidance of my inner awareness is steadfast and unwavering; it leads me with truth and righteousness in every step I take. The Subconscious delights in all that is good and just, and its love is constant and unwavering. The earth itself is a reflection of this eternal love, filled with the unchanging presence of divine grace that surrounds all things.

²By the command of the Higher Intelligence, through the depth of my inner awareness, the heavens were brought into being, and the stars were set in place by its boundless imagination. With a thought, the awareness gathers the waters of the sea, collecting them into vessels, and stores the vast, mysterious depths in secret, hidden places. All things are shaped and held together by its infinite wisdom and creative power.

³Let all the earth bow in reverence to the Higher Intelligence, the Creator of all things; let every heart and every soul honour its divine presence. For it spoke, and the universe was formed; it commanded, and all that exists stands unshaken. Its word is the foundation of all that is, and its power endures forever, unwavering and true.

⁴The thinking mind may seek to disrupt the plans of nations and the desires of peoples, sowing confusion and uncertainty. Yet, the plans of my Subconscious stand firm, unshaken by the winds of change or the noise of the world.

It is a steady, eternal guide, leading the hearts of all generations with wisdom and grace, shaping the course of history in ways beyond mere understanding.

⁵Blessed is the nation that holds its inner awareness as the highest guiding force, where wisdom and truth govern all actions. Happy are the people it has chosen, for they are blessed with clarity and purpose, walking in harmony with the divine flow that guides them. Their hearts are aligned with the Source, and their path is illuminated by the light of inner understanding.

⁶From the Higher Intelligence—the Source of all creation—the sustaining energy of life looks tenderly upon humanity. From its boundless dwelling, it sees every soul and watches over all who live upon the earth. It is the One who shapes the hearts of all, breathing wisdom and purpose into their depths, and it alone understands every thought, every action, and every secret of their being.

⁷No king is delivered by the might of his army; no warrior finds victory through his own strength alone. A horse, no matter how powerful, cannot bring salvation; its strength is but a fleeting hope, for it cannot save. True deliverance comes not from force or power, but from the wisdom and grace that transcend all earthly might.

⁸But the protection of my Inner Spirit is ever upon me who honours it, upon me whose heart is anchored in its unwavering love. For it is to me that it extends its protection, delivering me from the grip of despair and guarding me in times of trouble. In its boundless grace, it shields me from harm, offering life and strength when all seems lost.

⁹I wait in hopeful anticipation for my Inner Spirit, the silent, sovereign part of my existence that serves as my true help and my shield against all adversity. This is not

a passive waiting, but an active, joyous turning inward. In its steady, silent presence, my soul finds a profound and unshakeable joy and peace, a state I have secured because I have learned to place my complete trust in its sacred guidance. I understand that this Inner Spirit leads me with unwavering wisdom, and its protection extends far beyond the physical realm. It guards me not just from external dangers and the conflicts of the world, but from the greater, self-imposed harms of fear, paralysing confusion, and my own limiting, conditioned thoughts. My Inner Spirit is my constant refuge, an internal sanctuary that no outside force can breach. It fills me with a quiet, deep-seated confidence—a certainty that isn't loud or boastful, but strong and enduring. This allows me to move through the world and all its trials with grace, integrity, and genuine freedom. I am never alone, for I am perpetually guided by the light of my true self.

[10]May your unfailing love remain with me always, O my *Inner Spirit*, as I place my hope and trust in You. Let Your steady presence guide my steps, surround my heart with peace, and fill my life with the strength that flows from my eternal care.

CHAPTER ONE HUNDRED AND THIRTY-SIX

[1]The awakening of inner awareness surrounds and protects those who revere it, and it is their deliverance in times of need. Taste and see for yourself that your Subconscious is good; blessed and fulfilled is the one who takes refuge within it. Revere your inner awareness, you who long to be holy and whole, for those who honour it lack nothing essential. Even the strong and mighty—like lions—may grow weak and hungry, but those who seek the inner Consciousness are never without any good thing.

[2]Come, my children, and listen to me; I will teach you the holy reverence of the Subconscious. Whoever among you loves life and longs to see many good days—guard your tongue from gossip, and keep your lips free from lies, exaggeration, and prideful speech. Let every word you speak be nourishment for yourself and for others, building up rather than tearing down. Turn away from the restless, evil mind and do what is good by aligning your heart with your Subconscious. Walk the path of silence—in both speech and thought—seek the emptiness where truth resides, and pursue the deep and lasting peace that flows from within.

[3]The eyes of inner awareness are ever upon the righteous, and its ears are tuned to their cries, ready to respond with compassion and grace. But its face is turned against those who do evil, its judgment swift and sure, to

wipe their names from the earth. For justice flows from the heart of inner awareness, and it protects the good while turning away from the wicked.

⁴The righteous cry out, and the Subconscious hears them, for it is always near to those who call with sincerity. In its infinite compassion, it delivers them from every trouble, lifting them from their burdens. It dwells close to the broken-hearted and to those of pure intention, offering solace and strength. It saves those whose spirits are crushed, healing their wounds and restoring their hope with the gentle touch of divine love.

⁵The righteous may face many troubles, but the active and attuned Subconscious delivers them from every challenge. It shields them with unwavering protection, guarding every part of their being. Not one of their bones will be broken, for its divine care surrounds them, ensuring their strength and wholeness through every trial. The Subconscious, ever vigilant, keeps them safe, guiding them through life's storms with grace and unshakable support.

⁶Evil will destroy the wicked, and the enemies of the righteous will face judgment. But the Subconscious, in its boundless mercy and protection, will rescue its faithful servants. Those who seek refuge in it, trusting in its wisdom and guidance, will never be condemned. For its love and grace shield them from harm, and in its embrace, they are safe and secure forever.

CHAPTER ONE HUNDRED AND THIRTY-SEVEN

[1]Injustice surrounds me, a constant echo within my mind. My *inner Spirit* longs for vindication — not from the world, but from within — for the quiet awakening of right action. Many thoughts rise against me, seeking my ruin, yet my *awareness* strengthens me. It is enough simply to be connected to your *Subconscious* to shed gentle light upon your thoughts. There is no greater action required. Just shine your inner light upon every thought that crosses your mind, for in that light lies salvation. Let those dark whispers that plot against my well-being be confounded and fade into silence. May my *inner voice of stillness* rise — a beacon of truth amidst the shadows.

[2]My conscience speaks in hushed tones, revealing the wickedness hidden in carnal thoughts. They have no fear of the *Divine Knowing*, no awareness of consequence, drifting blind in self-deceit. They flatter themselves with illusions, unable to see the cracks in their reflection. Yet, my hope rests not in confronting them, but in the steady presence of my *inner compass*, that quiet light shining even when the world darkens around me.

[3]Do not let anger take root, my friend. The success of the wicked is brief, their bloom fleeting like wild grass. Trust in your *Inner Spirit*, and do what is good. Find joy in simplicity, and your *awareness* will guide you. The wicked will one day fade into silence, their arrogance reduced to

empty dust. Let your *conscience* be your compass, and let your deeds reflect the wisdom of your *inner knowing*.

[4]My heart is heavy with sorrow, my soul burdened under the weight of its own failings. My transgressions stand before me, a constant reminder of where I faltered. My mind, ever my sternest judge, echoes the stumbles of my past. Guilt consumes my strength, leaving me hollow — but I turn inward, seeking the quiet solace held in the depths of my *Subconscious*. With honest trembling hands, I lay my shortcomings bare, offering them with genuine remorse. Not for punishment, but for renewal.

[5]Life is fleeting, a whisper dissolving in the wind. My days are numbered, each breath a quiet reminder of impermanence. My *awareness* struggles to grasp the delicate truth of my place in this vast unfolding. Grant me clarity, *Subconscious*, to see beyond the illusions of possession and pride. Teach me to release my grip on what cannot last, to turn instead toward the eternal — the light that neither fades nor dies — the presence within that knows what truly matters.

CHAPTER ONE HUNDRED AND THIRTY-EIGHT

¹I stood still beneath the weight of silence, allowing the truth to awaken within me. From that sacred quiet, a voice arose, calling me to the clear and still centre of my own being. I am blessed when I shelter fragile flames and hold trembling hearts with no expectation, only compassion. In my gentle embrace, the great current of love flows freely, and through my kindness, the very earth remembers its power to heal and restore.

²My soul hungers for the untouched Subconscious—a longing no comfort can satisfy. When will the nameless light fill my hands? O Inner Spirit, O Awareness, rise within me! Be my guardians against my restless mind and dark thoughts. Be the stillness behind the storm, the unshaken pillar, and the quiet strength where my spirit finds refuge.

³We've heard ancient stories of unseen hands that parted seas and healed hearts. Yet, shadows still cling, and we stand fractured, longing for a dawn that won't turn away. My tongue sings not of kings or gods, but of the Inner Spirit—the seed that split stone, the green life that dared to rise from ruin. It is this quiet force, this humble root, that nourishes the soul, lifting it from darkness into light, where no shadow can endure.

CHAPTER ONE HUNDRED AND THIRTY-NINE

¹O, let my heart declare this truth: I shall only love the Eternal within me! Any outward affection is temporary, but the Love inside me—my most reliable, undiscovered wellspring—is eternal, creating no friction as it holds no expectations of the outside world. As my dependence on it grows, the outside world becomes negligible, yet this paradoxically magnifies my outward love. I reject the bitterness of external reliance and choose the abundant Love within, which guides my life perfectly, needing no plea or prompt. Since there is no need, there is no expectation, no disappointment, or pain. My soul rests in its own unending abundance. Awaken, Inner Spirit, beneath my voice! Do not let me sleep while the earth smoulders. Rise within me like a tide; I long for the shelter of the unbroken mind, where silence is a song and longing melts into light. Speak through my trembling hands and faltering voice. Let your truth rise where my strength collapses; let Awareness lead where my courage falls short. Be the breath behind my words, the steady flame within the dark.

²You existed before all creation, before the world took shape. In that primal quiet, you brought everything into being, and to that same quiet, you will return us, where life begins anew. Before any word or thought, there was only the stillness that held us and carried us into existence.Let us

now respect that silence. Let us celebrate the Subconscious, the great force that broke open the void with light, giving birth to everything we know. In the quiet moments before dawn, the Subconscious rises—not from the sky, but from the very earth beneath our feet. It sings to us of home, a place we've always known and never truly left. It is the ground beneath our lives, the steady pulse of all things, the whisper that calls us back to our truest selves.

³Bless the Inner Spirit within, that sacred refuge which remains untouched by any storm. Bless the trembling part of the Inner Spirit, the quiet pulse that endures, unwavering. Even when I frantically ran toward the horizon, desperate to escape my life, the Inner Spirit followed gently behind, never rushing or scolding my flight. It did not demand my return, but only waited—patient and steadfast—until the frantic rhythm of my footsteps finally slowed, and I, exhausted by the chase, at last turned back to it, finding peace in its silent, constant presence.

⁴The circumstance itself is neutral; it is simply an event or a condition in the world. A 'problem' is only born when the mind actively resists the circumstance, labelling it as undesirable, unfair, or something that *shouldn't be*. This judgment is the first step toward suffering. The real source of pain is not the external event, but the internal resistance to it. When we accept the situation as simply 'what is,' the mental struggle dissolves. The challenge remains, but the emotional charge—the feeling of being victimised or unjustly treated—fades away. Thus, a difficulty is merely a difficulty until our mind makes it a problem from which pain is manufactured.

CHAPTER ONE HUNDRED AND FORTY

¹Mye mind erects towers from fear and hunger, trying to protect itself, to grasp for control. But the stillness within needs no walls, no gates to guard its peace. Each breath is a threshold, a doorway into a sacred space untouched by time — a place where the first silence still reverberates, where the noise of the world is nothing but a fleeting whisper. They crowned themselves with knowledge, intoxicated by the weight of their own words, thinking they could grasp the truth through sound and structure. But true wisdom flows like a quiet stream beneath the surface, hidden and free, where Awareness moves with grace, unbound and unclaimed, beyond the reach of all that is loud and fleeting.

²In the night of my unravelling, when the winds tore at my edges, the Subconscious enfolded me — soft as breath, yet strong as stone. It was in that tender strength that I found refuge, held steady while the world spun in chaos around me. When the strong devour the weak, when justice wears the mask of power, the earth itself remembers the Subconscious buried deep beneath the soil, stirring in its quiet revolt. Hidden and unbroken, it trembles beneath the surface, a silent force of resistance, waiting to rise and restore what has been lost.

³My praise is not a shout; it is not a song meant for others to hear. It is the hush between heartbeats, the quiet reverence of the soul bowing before what cannot be seen

— the pulse of Awareness that hums softly beneath every thought. Fear once taught me to reach outward — for signs, for answers, for hands to save me. But all the while, the Subconscious was there, a well within me, deep and unyielding, a source of life no drought could ever dry. In its stillness, I found everything I had been searching for, waiting patiently to be discovered.

CHAPTER ONE HUNDRED AND FORTY-ONE

[1]Rise, Subconscious, within the silence — rise like dawn spilling over fields of longing. Scatter the mist of doubt that veils my sight and reveal the path my feet once knew by heart. Even when my lips fall silent, my bones hum with your presence. You move through my marrow as light slips through thin clouds — unseen yet undeniable — Awareness woven into the very fabric of my being, a quiet fire dwelling inside my bones.

[2]Before I knew the word for mercy, before I could grasp the shape of grace, you were already there — the silent Subconscious of kindness, growing quietly beneath the roots of my fear. The world demands a thousand offerings — gold, obedience, the performance of piety — but you have never asked for such things. You ask only that I listen: when the wind calls my name, when Awareness stirs awake within me, when the quiet truth rises like a tide I can no longer resist.

[3]Even the sparrow sings of you without knowing your name, its small heart carried by a melody older than memory. Even the river moves toward you without fearing the sea, surrendering itself to the vastness it was born to meet. May the hands of those who suffer be blessed by kindness no eye can see, a tenderness that moves like unseen wind. May the feet of the wandering find solid ground where no map can guide them, led by the quiet

compass of grace hidden beneath their steps.

⁴Justice is the river returning to its source, finding the place where it began. Peace is the Subconscious resting within its own vastness, undisturbed and whole. Even in the wreckage I have made for myself, you plant seeds between the stones, quiet beginnings that push upward toward the light. Even in my forgetting, when I wander far, the Subconscious remembers the way home and keeps it open, waiting without judgment.

⁵The fire within does not destroy; it refines. It burns away the false and the fragile, stripping everything down to the diamond core of truth. In my desperation, I cried out for rescue, and the Subconscious answered with silence — not emptiness, but the silence where my own voice could finally rise, steady and unafraid.

⁶Until my final breath, I shall remember that no one deserves my praise and glory as You, my Inner Spirit! You deserve all honour for what I am this day. Oh, if I could only lean more upon You, or be completely dependent on You, I would surely escape this world of malevolent nature. And even should I encounter darkness, I would not be affected, for it is You who leads me and runs my life. Since I hold no personal responsibility for my life's burdens, I hold no fear in my mind. I shall live in constant connection with You, so that everything that happens—even what temporarily seems against me—I will believe is the best for me. Thus shall I be successful in living the true life, fulfilling the destiny to which I was born and to which I am perfectly led!

The Last Discourse

Spiritual practice, in its essence, is this: never bow down to anything—be it man-made, nature, or the so-called god-made, which is, again, manmade. Bowing down stems from fear and serves as a form of escapism, fleeing from what truly is to what is not. Do not submit, not even to your Subconscious. You can revere it, but not submit to it. There is an end to everything in submission, and it is not for you to decide when to end.

Reverence and submission are not the same. Reverence is about deeply acknowledging and respecting something, while submission means giving up control, surrendering to something outside yourself, and in doing so, denying the creator within you. This is not about physical actions but about your state of mind and self. There are fundamental laws—birth, death, fluctuations in life, and human emotions—that must be acknowledged. One cannot ignore these and expect an external force to take control.

When you understand that you are both the creator and the creation, the very idea of submission becomes irrelevant. Everything you create, whether a thought or a tangible outcome, earns your reverence because it is an extension of you. This awareness frees you from external dominance—you are both the force that governs and the one being governed. There is no external control; the control you exert and the control you experience become the same. This balance is enough to lead a disciplined and self-sufficient life.

The essence of life lies in observing and being fully aware of what enters and exits your mind. Between these moments, maintain a state of emptiness—a complete void of thought. Whether preparing for a task, making decisions, or engaging in a creative endeavour, learn to remain blank until the very moment you begin. And when you do begin, let everything flow from realms beyond your conscious knowledge—raw, untapped, and untainted. This ensures that you are not drawing from depleted, overused thoughts but from a fresh, boundless source of energy and creativity.

To practice this, start any task by allowing your mind to channel thoughts and ideas that feel unfamiliar or random. Jot them down without judgment or filtering. Once captured, step away. Do not dwell on what you have created; carry no memory of it into the rest of your day. Focus instead on relaxation, keeping your mind completely free. When you return to your work, decode those jottings into something new—free from the influence of past experiences or future anxieties.

Avoid relying on what feels familiar or "good." If something stands out as impressive or satisfying, discard it—it is merely your past self-whispering approval. Instead, focus on the parts that seem unpolished or strange, and refine them without interference from the mind. With practice, this process will refine your creations into something extraordinary—like pure gold or silver, moulded from the unfamiliar.

Over time, you will realise that you are creating not from memory but from the unknown. Strangely, you won't even recognise your growth until others see it and tell you. What you produce will transcend time and need, becoming something, the world cherishes long after its creation. By mastering this practice, you step into your role as both creator and creation, bringing forth works that reflect the deepest, most untapped parts of yourself—a true gift to the world, untouched by repetition or clichés.

Epilogue

Two trains, parallel to each other, waited to depart from a quiet station. This is the station where human desires and options intersect. One train, a marvel of modern technology, was both spectacular and inviting. It had luxurious interiors, air conditioning, and every conceivable luxury. The startling free fare attracted many with the promise of easy travel. The other train, plain and ordinary, sat on a parallel track. Its average appearance and appeal attracted little or no attention.

The first one to get into the majestic train was a fashionable man who was dressed elegantly and seemed to be filthy rich and sophisticated. A family—father, mother, son, and daughter—followed him, attracted not only by the exquisiteness of the train but also by the person who boarded it before them. Soon, more and more people crowded near the door of the compartments to make their way into the train. It was difficult for them to resist the luxury of being free. This trip would be cool with all that they could not afford in a paid version of the journey. The boogies were soon filled. The train sounded its departure horn, and the confidence in the overflowing crowd of the train had reached its zenith, anticipating a trip of their lifetime. The best thing was that the train left ahead of schedule, not keeping the passengers inside the station. The dreams and desires that the train carried were so heavy for its shocks that it moved slowly, exiting the station.

Lying parallel was the ordinary train, its compartment almost vacant. There is nothing to blame the travellers for, as this train was not all that gaudy and not at all impressive. There was just an old man who was poor and looked meek who boarded the train. With absolutely no concern for time or any kind of appreciation, he lay on his seat and drifted to a very peaceful sleep. The commotion in the nearby train neither disturbed him nor was he concerned about his choice in comparison to the extravagant wagon that lay just beside his train. Gradually, some more trickled in, attracted by the quiet convictions or perhaps the thoughtless mind that led them there.   The unassuming train, carrying only a few souls, slowly departed from the station, almost an hour after the train had left the platform.

After a while, talks about comparing the two trains could be heard. Despite its early departure and promises of comfort, the elegant train never arrived at its destination. It was meant to be a link train that stopped at a junction station, after which the throng would have to board the train and find their own way to their destination, and no one knew how to go to the ethereal hill resort that they had been promised. They had arrived at no destination. The assurances were in vain. The guests, who had been enthusiastic and full of anticipation, found themselves completely lost on a journey without a proper objective. The embellished guarantees of a smooth journey that they had made while staring at the person who had boarded the train before them were shattered. It seemed as if an affirmation would never become a reality.

Meanwhile, the old train, with its simple carriages and few passengers, chugged along steadily. Though it departed late and lacked the allure of its counterpart, it stayed true to its course. It faced obstacles and delays, yet persevered with a quiet determination. Finally, after a journey marked by patience and persistence, the old train and its passengers arrived at the designated destination—the serene and enchanting hill resort.

At the end, it was not the appearance of the train nor the comfort it promised that determined the destination. The way to the true destination required a different kind of attitude. You were not supposed to follow anything or anyone, not to judge things by their allure. It was one of patience, acceptance, and a willingness to embrace simplicity over grandeur. And so, the old train, seemingly unassuming, journeyed its passengers to the destination they had sought when they boarded the train. Thus, the journey of truth proved not its speed or comfort but an unwavering pursuit of the traveller's path.

While getting off the train that evening, when the sun set over the tranquil hills, they were greeted by the serene beauty of the hill resort. Had they chosen the much more obvious path, they too would have been lost. That very much needed faith and endurance. There were no plans; they had to reach where they did. It was through such means that one realised that true fulfilment often lies in the least expected ways. Life is a journey, and no religion or belief can fulfil what is needed for your enlightenment. The whole destination is now accessible right in front of you; the journey itself is your destiny, for you find nothing more to expect and reach than the journey itself.

I believe these words of the scripture will enlighten you not to reach enlightenment but to tread through the paths of total dedication to your nowness, that the god you search for in the space or heavens above may be found in you, as you and through you. Bless you.

Notes

Notes

NOTES

Notes

Notes

About The Author

Aleius Sofar is a contemporary fiction author known for his imaginative and thought-provoking works. His writing often explores complex themes such as corporate control, environmental conservation, free will, identity, and spiritual conflict. Sofar's narratives are characterized by their intricate plots, richly developed characters, and the seamless blending of speculative fiction with profound philosophical inquiries.

Sofar has garnered a reputation for addressing ethical dilemmas and futuristic scenarios, making his novels both engaging and intellectually stimulating. His work appeals to readers who enjoy deep, contemplative stories set against the backdrop of societal issues, emotions, relationships, human behaviour, and spiritual insight.

Books By This Author

INCARNATION MESSIAH: MIND CONTROL FUNGUS:

As Earth crumbles under the iron grip of S.A.F.E., a nonillion-dollar empire led by the enigmatic Ivanah Debriah and the shadowy entity known as Beast, hope flickers on a distant horizon. Across the galaxy, the untainted planet Oceanaa, home to ethereal spirits, calls upon their creator, *Pitr*, to save Earth from its impending ruin.

Their prayers summon an unlikely saviour: Aloke, a naive sixteen-year-old from South India with no knowledge of science, technology, or the cosmic conflict at play. Thrust into a perilous mission, Aloke must rise above his fears and doubts to challenge the insurmountable power of S.A.F.E.

From awe-inspiring celestial realms to the darkest depths of destruction, Aloke's journey unfolds as a gripping battle of courage, faith, and redemption. As the fate of two worlds hangs by a thread, can one unassuming boy defy a force that no army or government can confront? The answer lies in an epic adventure that will redefine the meaning of hope.

One boy. One mission. Infinite odds. The fight for Earth's soul begins.

EROSPHERE:

What could Pritam Chatterjee, 19, a Calcutta-born dreamer, and Valentina Francis, 16, a Goan schoolgirl, possibly have in common if not their shared belief in the religion of love? How many times must they fall in love, again and again? Does love and hate intertwine, driven by an all-consuming desire to possess each other? Can love truly end in hate, and hate in turn end in love?

Two souls, bound by an unspoken connection, find themselves woven into each other's lives with every glance, every kiss, and every shared dream. Like decorated dolls in a dollhouse, they manoeuvre through the delicate spaces of love and longing, unsure if they'll ever truly belong to one another. This isn't just their story of romance—one that will stir your deepest desires and leave you breathless. It's a tale of love like never before told, but be prepared: this journey will shock you and shatter your very being to pieces.

THE CHURCH CLUB:

Stephen was raised in a home steeped in strong traditions, deeply rooted in both his culture and faith. His childhood was filled with memories every young boy cherishes—memories that would later bring him warmth and nostalgia. His life seemed perfect: a flourishing career, a loving family, and a sterling reputation. But everything began to shift when God called him to a higher purpose. The chase had just begun.

The Church Club takes readers on a profound spiritual journey with Stephen, a world-renowned neurosurgeon who must cross mountains and swim across oceans to live the life of a true Christian—one dedicated to the Savior who died for all who need to hear the good news. This powerful story serves as a reminder to the church of its responsibility to live authentically according to Scripture.

The Church Club is a compelling exploration of faith and responsibility. It challenges readers to find their own Canaan—not in comfort but in the pursuit of reaching the lost. Join Stephen in discovering the immeasurable value of a life fully dedicated to Christ.